About Jonathan Lebed—a teenager who made money day trading on the Internet but ran afoul of Federal regulations—Arthur Levitt, former Chairman of the Securities and Exchange Commission, is said to have commented, "Put it this way, he'd buy, lie, and sell high."[1]

Buy, Lie, and Sell High:
How Investors Lost Out on
Enron and the Internet Bubble

ISBN 0-13-009113-8

9 780130 091130

Buy, Lie, and Sell High: How Investors Lost Out on Enron and the Internet Bubble

D. Quinn Mills

An Imprint of PEARSON EDUCATION

Upper Saddle River, NJ • New York • London • San Francisco • Toronto
Sydney • Tokyo • Singapore • Hong Kong • Cape Town
Madrid • Paris • Milan • Munich • Amsterdam
www.ft-ph.com

Library of Congress Cataloging-in-Publication Data
A catalog record for this book can be obtained from the Library of Congress.

Editorial/Production Supervision: *Carol Wheelan*
Composition: *Ronnie K. Bucci*
Cover design director: *Jerry Votta*
Cover design: *Talar Boorujy*
Art director: *Gail Cocker-Bogusz*
Interior design: *Meg VanArsdale*
Manufacturing buyer: *Maura Zaldivar*
Executive editor: *Jim Boyd*
Editorial assistant: *Allyson Kloss*
Marketing manager: *Bryan Gambrel*

FINANCIAL TIMES
Prentice Hall

©2002 Pearson Education, Inc.
Publishing as Financial Times Prentice Hall
Upper Saddle River, New Jersey 07458

Financial Times Prentice Hall books are widely used by corporations and
government agencies for training, marketing, and resale.

For information regarding corporate and government bulk discounts please
contact: Corporate and Government Sales (800) 382-3419 or
corpsales@pearsontechgroup.com

Printed in the United States of America

10   9   8   7   6   5   4   3   2   1

ISBN: 0-13-009113-8

Pearson Education LTD.
Pearson Education Australia PTY, Limited
Pearson Education Singapore, Pte. Ltd.
Pearson Education North Asia Ltd.
Pearson Education Canada, Ltd.
Pearson Educación de Mexico, S.A. de C.V.
Pearson Education—Japan
Pearson Education Malaysia, Pte. Ltd.

FINANCIAL TIMES PRENTICE HALL BOOKS

For more information, please go to www.ft-ph.com

Dr. Judith M. Bardwick
  Seeking the Calm in the Storm: Managing Chaos in Your Business Life

Thomas L. Barton, William G. Shenkir, and Paul L. Walker
  Making Enterprise Risk Management Pay Off:
  How Leading Companies Implement Risk Management

Michael Basch
  CustomerCulture: How FedEx and Other Great Companies Put the
  Customer First Every Day

J. Stewart Black and Hal B. Gregersen
  Leading Strategic Change: Breaking Through the Brain Barrier

Deirdre Breakenridge
  Cyberbranding: Brand Building in the Digital Economy

William C. Byham, Audrey B. Smith, and Matthew J. Paese
  Grow Your Own Leaders: How to Identify, Develop, and Retain
  Leadership Talent

Jonathan Cagan and Craig M. Vogel
  Creating Breakthrough Products: Innovation from Product Planning
  to Program Approval

Subir Chowdhury
  The Talent Era: Achieving a High Return on Talent

Sherry Cooper
  Ride the Wave: Taking Control in a Turbulent Financial Age

James W. Cortada
  21st Century Business: Managing and Working
  in the New Digital Economy

James W. Cortada
  Making the Information Society: Experience, Consequences,
  and Possibilities

Aswath Damodaran
  The Dark Side of Valuation: Valuing Old Tech, New Tech,
  and New Economy Companies

Henry A. Davis and William W. Sihler
  Financial Turnarounds: Preserving Enterprise Value

Sarv Devaraj and Rajiv Kohli
*The IT Payoff: Measuring the Business Value
of Information Technology Investments*

Nicholas D. Evans
*Business Agility: Strategies for Gaining Competitive Advantage
through Mobile Business Solutions*

Kenneth R. Ferris and Barbara S. Pécherot Petitt
Valuation: Avoiding the Winner's Curse

David Gladstone and Laura Gladstone
*Venture Capital Handbook: An Entrepreneur's Guide
to Raising Venture Capital, Revised and Updated*

David R. Henderson
The Joy of Freedom: An Economist's Odyssey

Philip Jenks and Stephen Eckett, Editors
*The Global-Investor Book of Investing Rules: Invaluable Advice
from 150 Master Investors*

Thomas Kern, Mary Cecelia Lacity, and Leslie P. Willcocks
*Netsourcing: Renting Business Applications and Services
Over a Network*

Al Lieberman, with Patricia Esgate
*The Entertainment Marketing Revolution: Bringing the Moguls, the
Media, and the Magic to the World*

Frederick C. Militello, Jr., and Michael D. Schwalberg
Leverage Competencies: What Financial Executives Need to Lead

D. Quinn Mills
*Buy, Lie, and Sell High: How Investors Lost Out on Enron and the
Internet Bubble*

Dale Neef
E-procurement: From Strategy to Implementation

John R. Nofsinger
*Investment Blunders (of the Rich and Famous)…And What You Can
Learn From Them*

John R. Nofsinger
*Investment Madness: How Psychology Affects Your Investing…
And What to Do About It*

Tom Osenton
   Customer Share Marketing: How the World's Great Marketers Unlock Profits from Customer Loyalty

W. Alan Randolph and Barry Z. Posner
   Checkered Flag Projects: 10 Rules for Creating and Managing Projects that Win, Second Edition

Stephen P. Robbins
   The Truth About Managing People...And Nothing but the Truth

Fernando Robles, Françoise Simon, and Jerry Haar
   Winning Strategies for the New Latin Markets

Jeff Saperstein and Daniel Rouach
   Creating Regional Wealth in the Innovation Economy: Models, Perspectives, and Best Practices

Eric G. Stephan and Wayne R. Pace
   Powerful Leadership: How to Unleash the Potential in Others and Simplify Your Own Life

Jonathan Wight
   Saving Adam Smith: A Tale of Wealth, Transformation, and Virtue

Yoram J. Wind and Vijay Mahajan, with Robert Gunther
   Convergence Marketing: Strategies for Reaching the New Hybrid Consumer

To Betsy and Shirley

Contents

Acknowledgments   *xix*

Part I   **The Bubble and Capital Markets**   *1*

chapter 1   How to Use This Book   *3*

Why This Book Has Been Written   *3*
How This Book Was Written   *4*
An Unusual Feature of This Book: Contributions from Others   *5*
The Message of This Book: How to Avoid Another
    Bubble and How to Protect Yourself If It Occurs   *5*
Talking Points   *5*

chapter 2   Destroyed by the Bubble   *7*

The Capital Markets as an Engine of Progress   *12*
The Social and Economic Utility of Capital Markets   *12*
The Internet, Capital Markets, and Innovation   *13*
The Early-Stage Financing of the Internet   *14*

The System Hits a Glitch 15

Talking Points 16

Part II **How the Bubble Happened** 17

chapter 3 **Causing the Bubble** 19

The Technology Bull Market 19

The Bubble 20

Why Did the Bubble Form? 22

Day Trading and the Source of the Bubble 23

Other Bubbles in History 24

The Software Cycle 25

The Transfer of Wealth 29

Talking Points 31

chapter 4 **Inflating the Bubble:
The Financial Value Chain** 33

The Financial Value Chain 33

Diagramming the Financial Value Chain 35

When Economic and Financial Value Diverge 38

Why the Huge Valuations for Internet Companies? 40

How the Financial Value Chain Should Have Worked 42

Defending Enormous Valuations 43

Talking Points 45

chapter 5 **What it Meant to "Do the Right Thing"
at Enron** 47

Enron as an Internet Company 48

Inflating the Enron Bubble 49

Wall Street's Involvement 49

The Key Role of the Accountants 50

Equity Analysts Promote the Company 51

Politicians Lend Their Aid 52

Evaporating Employee Pensions 53

Unethical, Unfair, but Illegal? 53

Enron's Significance   54
Talking Points   54

Part III   **Inexperienced Leaders**   57

chapter 6   Dumb Kids?   59
Blaming the Entrepreneur—He's Dumb   59
Amazon.com's Miracle   60
How Amazon Flouted the Rules   61
The Learning Failure   62
Talking Points   73

chapter 7   How Some VCs and Bankers Led
Entrepreneurs in the Wrong Direction   75
Having to Go to the Venture Firms   75
Pressure to Spend   79
A Strategy's Limitations   81
Like Sheep to the Slaughter   83
Get-It-Right Instead of Get-Big-Fast   83
Talking Points   90

Part IV   **How Venture Firms Changed
Their Criteria**   91

chapter 8   Building to Flip   93
Venture Capital   93
Rushing to an IPO   94
Exiting an Investment   95
How Their Own Rules Were Changed
by the Venture Capital Firms   96
The Baby Goes Out with the Bathwater   97
Talking Points   105

chapter 9   Choosing the Wrong People   107
Whom to Back   107
Garden.com: A Mistake from the Get-go   108

Boo.com   *111*

Did the Venture Firms Make Money from the Bubble?   *113*

Talking Points   *114*

Part V   **Taking Start-ups to the Public**   *117*

chapter 10   How Investment Banks
              Inflated the Bubble   *119*

The Banks Bend the Rules   *119*

The Investment Banks and Institutional Investors   *121*

Who Brought Those Duds to Market?   *121*

Mass Hysteria or Fraud   *123*

The Blame Game   *125*

Mass Hysteria   *126*

What Did the Venture Firms Know?   *127*

Did Wall Street Cross the Line?   *128*

If You Can't Sue City Hall, Can You Sue Wall Street?   *129*

Beware of "Buyer Beware"   *132*

Talking Points   *134*

chapter 11   The Retail Investor: Victim or Fool?   *135*

The Buyers' Side of the Capital Market   *135*

Why Mutual Funds Got on the Bandwagon   *136*

Speculating with Pension Money   *138*

Momentum Investors in Disguise   *139*

Blaming the Investor—She's a Pig   *140*

How Important Is the Freedom to Speculate?   *142*

Talking Points   *143*

chapter 12   Influencing Factors:
              Where Does Responsibility Lie?   *145*

What the Accountants Should Have Done and Didn't   *145*

The Hype Machine   *146*

The Fed Was Also at Fault   *147*

Talking Points   *156*

Part VI   **The Road Kill of Capitalism**   *157*

chapter 13   Sell, Sell, Sell!   *159*

    theglobe.com   *160*

    Not a Smart Thing to Do   *166*

    Young People Succeeding Early   *169*

    The Return of Big Company Values   *170*

    Talking Points   *172*

chapter 14   Dire Consequences   *173*

    Creating a New Business Cycle   *173*

    Economic Losses Caused by the Bubbles   *175*

    Starving Entrepreneurs of Capital   *176*

    Setting Back Technological Innovation   *179*

    What Happened in e-learning   *180*

    Meanwhile, in Germany…   *183*

    Another Wave of Internet Companies Is Coming   *188*

    A List of the Economic Consequences of the Bubble   *188*

    Insuring Public Confidence   *189*

    Talking Points   *190*

Part VII   **A Troubled System**   *193*

chapter 15   Can America Lead?   *195*

    The United States as the World's Financial Leader   *196*

    Should American Leadership Be Followed?   *197*

    Dare We Privatize Social Security?   *199*

    Why Current Regulation Isn't Working Well Enough   *200*

    Talking Points   *206*

chapter 16   Reforms to Protect Small Investors   *207*

    The German Experience   *207*

    Every Investor a Qualified Investor   *209*

    Extending Fiduciary Responsibility   *210*

    Improving Disclosure and Governance at Mutual Funds   *212*

    A Return to a More Restrictive Prudent Person Rule   *213*

Preventing Another Enron   *215*

New Regulations to Protect Investors in IPOs   *216*

Nine Reforms to Restore Confidence
   and Rebuild the Economy   *219*

Talking Points   *221*

Part VIII   **Less Damage Next Time**   *223*

chapter 17   What Does the Future Hold?   *225*

Do We Want Another Bubble?   *225*

Will There Be Another Bubble?   *230*

Smaller Bubbles and Less Damage   *232*

Appendix A NEMAX (The German New Market)
         and NASDAQ   *235*

Appendix B Financial Value Chain Influencers   *237*

Contributors   *249*

Endnotes   *251*

Index   *257*

Acknowledgments

I am deeply indebted to several people for assistance on this book. Most importantly, I owe much to the small team that helped me do the research and design of the book: Kirstin Hornby, Dr. Dirk Seifert, and Mark Cicerelli.

Many of my colleagues on the faculty of the Harvard Business School were very generous in their responses to my inquiries about the bubble and its consequences, including Joseph Bower, Thomas Eisenmann, Paul Gompers, Samuel Hayes, Josh Lerner, Jay Light, Robert Merton, Krishna Palepu, William Sahlman, Howard Stevenson, Peter Tufano, and Michael Yoshino. I also benefited from the kind help of several of our students, including Gad Caspy, Mark Cicerelli, Kevin Greene, and Daniel Hawkins. I am indebted as well to our Dean, Kim Clark, and to John Dunlop, University Professor at Harvard, for their generosity in reviewing a draft of this book.

I appreciate the assistance of the following in this study: Gilbert Butler, Kim Davis, Ted Dintersmith, Robert R. Glauber, Torrence Harder, Samuel L. Hayes III, Karl Jacob, Edward C. Johnson III, Arthur Levitt III, Phil Lochner, John Maxwell, Andrew G. Mills, Shirley Mills, Reiner Neumann, Steve Papa, Norbert Reichert, Steven Rosefielde, John Stanton, and Martin Wansleben.

I am grateful to the Harvard Business School Division of Research for its support of my work.

All interpretations and any errors are my responsibility alone.

Daniel Quinn Mills
Boston, Mass.
May 2, 2002

The Bubble and Capital Markets

The great Internet bubble in the stock market burst in the spring of 2000, but the repercussions of the mania continue. Even today, companies that have held on since the bubble are finally collapsing. Far from the bubble being gone, it and its consequences are with us still.

1 How to Use This Book

Why This Book Has Been Written

I've written this book because of what happened to a friend of mine. She was in her 50s, and had painfully accumulated over her working life a nest egg. When she lost her job, she received the money in a lump sum. It was to help support her old age. She visited the Web site of one of the largest mutual fund companies and studied the performance record of the 15 or so funds they offered for annuity contracts. She identified those with the best returns. She then called a representative at the company to ask about an investment. He told her that she had picked the two best funds, just what she should do, and he arranged for her to make the investment. She now had an annuity contract with the mutual fund company with her capital invested in a single fund.

Three months later the fund began a rapid collapse. She called the company and was told that the decline was temporary, and that the proper long-term strategy was to remain invested. She did, and the fund fell to about 30 percent of its level at which she had bought it. It turned out that the fund had been heavily invested in Internet stocks.

"Why did I lose my money?" she asked me. "Why was my pension money invested in such speculative stocks? Who got the money I lost?"

How This Book Was Written

So a small team and I went to work studying the great Internet bubble. We looked at the various players who were involved in the process by which venture funds and entrepreneurs built companies, and then with the investment banks, took them public. We made a list of how the venture funds changed their investment criteria as the bubble developed, and how investment banks changed their criteria for taking firms public. We looked at how the mutual funds shifted their investment criteria so that many funds became loaded with dot-com and telecom stocks. We looked at Alan Greenspan's warnings, and at the inflation and then bursting of the bubble. We looked at who made money in the outcome, and who lost.

We have read the literature on financial manias and explored the explanations being given for the recent bubble. The key explanations are that (1) it was an accident: A group of forces came together like the perfect storm—new technology, an affluent investing public, and a booming economy—and then blew themselves out; (2) it was engineered: The incentive structures in financial service firms made their blowing up into a bubble a certainty; (3) it was a result of inexperience: Investment professionals (including the business press) were young and inexperienced, and believed that the New Economy was qualitatively different from the Old Economy so that valuations weren't recognized as inflated; and (4) it was another example of the madness of crowds—individual investors were prone to mass hysteria and didn't do their homework and so drove stock prices to unreasonable levels, and when the bubble burst, got what they deserved.

We also asked whether or not the entrepreneurs, venture firms, investment banks, brokerages, and mutual funds really thought that the companies they sold the retail investor were legitimate firms; and we looked at the litigation now underway about how IPO sales were conducted.

We asked whether or not a bubble was a necessary consequence of the operation of our free markets—the way western economies raise capital to fund technological innovation? Or, alternatively, whether the bubble was a dangerous aberration that should be avoided if possible?

Our research convinces us it is the latter, so we asked what might prevent another bubble, or at least help protect retail investors from the worst ravages of one if it occurs.

We also looked at Germany, which had a somewhat similar bubble in Internet stocks, but with a very different outcome for small investors, and asked why. In this book, several times we provide German examples of what happened in the Internet bubble; they provide important supplementary material showing how the bubble leapt international boundaries, and how its elements were often the same but sometimes different. But in this book, to avoid confusion we usually are talking about the American experience, except where Germany is explicitly cited.

We were fortunate to find many knowledgeable people willing to talk with us about the bubble. Some were willing to do so for attribution; others were unwilling to let themselves be identified, in part because litigation about events during the bubble is gathering force today, and many people are either involved in or hoping to stay out of the legal fray.

Regardless of whether or not people were willing to be identified in print, they provided us with an ongoing dialogue from which this book emerged. It's the hope of our research team that readers will engage their own friends and acquaintances in a discussion of the important issues which arise in this book. To encourage such a dialogue, we have provided a small group of talking points at the end of each chapter—not a summary of the chapter, but rather the key points that a person might want to take from it to a discussion with others.

An Unusual Feature of This Book: Contributions from Others

An unusual feature of this book is that it includes short contributions from people other than the author and his team. Several American and German participants in the bubble have consented to give their experiences and their views about the issues with which this book is concerned, so that this book provides a forum within which some of the players in the Financial Value Chain can discuss what occurred during the bubble. Sometimes contributors to this book don't agree with the author, but differences in opinion will help the reader make up his or her own mind about what happened in the Internet financial mania and what it means for each of us.

The Message of This Book: How to Avoid Another Bubble and How to Protect Yourself If It Occurs

From our inquiry, we've developed a set of suggestions as noted in Chapter 16, "Reforms to Protect Small Investors," about how entrepreneurs and investors can help avoid another bubble or protect themselves from it if it occurs, including proposed regulatory reforms that would provide much more protection for investors in the event of another bubble.

Talking Points

Many investors took heavy losses during the Internet bubble. How did that happen and what, if anything, should be done about it?

2 Destroyed by the Bubble

The room was full of people, some of whom controlled large amounts of investors' money. David Perry stood nervously as he prepared to step to the front and address the group during the Harvard Business School new business competition. It was for this that he had come to the Harvard Business School, but he could not escape misgivings. What if he bombed? Still, he'd prepared well, and as the final seconds sped by before it was his turn to present, excitement at the prospect before him pushed aside other emotions.

Perry stepped to the front of the room, wiped a bead of sweat from his forehead, and began, "I'd like to introduce a new concept to you. I call the company Chemdex." He went on to discuss a new forum for B2B exchange in the life-science and medical equipment industries. B2B had never been done before, but it was quite impressive to the professors. In fact, it won second place in the contest. And this was good enough for Kleiner Perkins Caufield and Byers, who became the lead investor in Chemdex, and the first VC firm to fund a company of this nature.

With two million dollars of seed money in his pocket, a lot of courage in his heart, and a few weeks of life in the "real world" post-Harvard Business School, in June 1997, Perry hopped into his car, sped out to the West coast, and started Chemdex. Perry began the company in September 1997, with co-founder Jeff Leane (who left the company in late 1999), and launched the Web site in 1998. Perry was thrilled to secure about $13 million in VC funding from Kleiner

Perkins Caufield and Byers, along with CMGI and Bay City Capital, by May 1998, and an additional $30 million by April 1999.[2]

At this point, Perry was encouraged to build the business quickly and to proceed to the IPO, whether or not he was ready. Perry was again nervous, and remembered the day of his presentation. But all had gone well so far, and thus, nine months after the launch, in July 1999, Perry turned over the financial reports of the company to Morgan Stanley, BankBoston, Robertson Stephens, and Volpe Brown Whelan & Company, LLC to execute the IPO with a suggested per share price of $15.

It turned out he had no need to worry. Less than one year later, in June 2000, his stock was up 1,620 percent, to $243.50 per share. This was a bit overwhelming for Perry. He was out of business school for three years, and, at age 32, found himself almost a billionaire. But Perry wasn't worried about saving for a rainy day. He had a lot of faith in his idea, and was going to push it until it burst. He reinvested all that he received into the company.

In February 2000, when the company changed its name to Ventro, Perry held an enormous party for his employees, featuring himself lip-syncing in a rock video. He also bought a jet. He was a bit concerned that stock analysts at the Wall Street firms might look askance at a young CEO with a company that as yet had virtually no sales, not to mention any profits, spending this way, but he needn't have worried. The analysts had no problem with his actions. Mary Meeker, Morgan Stanley's Internet stock wizard, predicted that Ventro would have revenues of $129 million in 2000. So Perry saw no reason to sell any of his stock. To top it all off, in June 2000, he was named northern California's—and thereby Silicon Valley's—entrepreneur of the year.

Perry continued to grow his company, purchasing and building four new online marketplaces. He used his company's soaring stock to buy Promedix, an online marketplace for specialty medical supplies. He hired a staff of highly regarded executives, including Robin Abrams, president of Palm Inc., as his COO.

Though Perry was delighted with the growth of his stock and his business, he had a few misgivings. Building marketplaces was expensive, about $45 million for the first one, and about $7 million for the second, and for some reason, the revenue numbers just were not coming in as he, and Wall Street's analysts, had predicted. With the company's continued expansion, encouraged by the high stock prices, Perry began to realize that things may not be as rosy as he had expected. By the second quarter of 2000, Chemdex only had 144 corporate customers, and was generating considerably less revenue than Wall Street was forecasting. Perry tried to figure why the revenue numbers were so low. Potential customers simply were not buying. Later reporters would write that "Analysts said Perry's B2B dreams have collapsed largely because of a flaw in his business plan. Ventro 'attempted to get between the suppliers and buyers of mainstream products,' said John Bermudez, analyst with AMR Research, which studies online business markets. 'Suppliers don't really want anyone between them and their customers.'"[3]

Further, though Perry knew his company's costs were enormous, he had not paid much attention because none of his venture capital backers, upon whom he relied for business direction, had expressed concern about costs. But with his firm's rapid expansion and high costs, losses started to get so out of control that Ventro's board of directors, against Perry's wishes, ordered a search for a buyer for Ventro. To Perry's dismay, by the end of 2000, Ventro closed down the original Chemdex chemical marketplace. By now the company had lost almost $618 million, and soon after, it lost most of its top executives. Then he had to do what to him was almost unthinkable—cut his staff in half. Perry saw his dreams dissolve. In June 2001, matters got worse when Ventro faced a shareholder lawsuit filed in federal court in San Francisco alleging securities fraud by Ventro executives. It had been two years since he'd taken the company public, and three years since he had founded it. The collapse of Ventro's stock price can be seen in Figure 2–1.

How did this happen? How was Ventro allowed to raise all this money, only to see it disappear? Did Perry lack experienced advisors? It wouldn't seem so. Brook Byers, who is the managing director at Kleiner Perkins Caufield and Byers, one of our nation's most experienced and successful venture capital firms, served as a director on Ventro's board, and as its chairman. Jon Callaghan has served on the board for years while a general partner at CMGI Ventures.

Today Ventro is holding on despite the fact that its stock is now listed at about $.30 per share. Perry himself, however, has been left in a most serious situation. Near the height of the company's share price he had exercised some options, buying shares of his company's stock at a price much lower than the

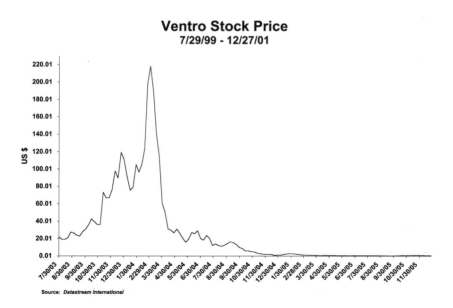

Figure 2–1   Ventro stock price, 7/29/99–12/7/01.

price in the public market. Expecting the stock to go higher, Perry did not sell the shares but put them in his personal portfolio. When the stock price started to fall, he held on to his shares to demonstrate his confidence in its ultimate rebound to his investors. But by a quirk of American tax law, the Internal Revenue Service assessed him a tax on the difference between what he'd paid for the shares and their price in the public market on the day he'd purchased them (a so-called phantom gain). The amount of his tax liability was some $50 million—although he had never received a penny by selling any of the shares he'd purchased. Nor was there any escape for him via personal bankruptcy—bankruptcy does not discharge a debt to IRS.

Ventro struggles along today, still losing money and abandoned by its erstwhile supporters on Wall Street. A company that had in February 2000 been valued by investors at some $8 billion, was worth only a few million little more than a year later. A young entrepreneur who had been in February 2000 a very wealthy man was, a year later, so far in debt to Uncle Sam that never again could he reasonably hope to have any financial security.

Young entrepreneurs are not unique to America, nor is it only in America that they were able in recent years to obtain financing for their business ideas. Peter Kabel was 22 years old, a student at Hamburg University and a ticket seller at a motion picture theatre when he started his first venture, a graphic design company. Several years later, when he was 29 and had finished his studies, Kabel founded Kabel New Media, describing it as a full service e-business enabler. In March, 1998 KNM began operating a professional tennis tour Web site, taking responsibility for obtaining advertising revenues, and thus becoming a multimedia advertising agency. This became the basis of a story about potential sales and profits which strongly stimulated the imagination of the financial markets and future investors. A handsome, dark-haired young man, Kabel quickly became a favorite of brokers and investors in Germany.

On June 15, 1999, shares in KNM were sold ("floated") to the public on the new market segment of the Frankfurt Stock Exchange, underwritten by two major banks: BNP Paribas and DG Bank. The share price peaked within six months at more than 13 times the IPO price. The company attracted several significant corporate clients. At its peak, more than 800 people were employed by KNM. Meanwhile, Kabel decided that the title "Professor" would enhance his reputation, and became a part-time professor at the College of Media Design in Hamburg.

Soon, however, financial results were disappointing, especially compared to the high valuation of the company. Beginning in March 2000, the company's share price entered a precipitous decline. Shortly, KNM announced a cessation of payments, essentially insolvency, and by August 2001, Peter Kabel left his position as CEO. On that same day prosecutors began an investigation of Kabel, because up to two weeks before the company declared insolvency he had been assuring investors that it would reach break-even at the end of 2001. Soon thereafter, Paribas ceased to sponsor the stock of the company. (See Table 2–1).

Table 2–1 Timeline for Kabel New Media.

Year	Events
1986	Founding of Peter Kabel's first company: Buero fuer grafische Gestaltung.
1991	Founding of two additional companies: Kabel Hamburg and Buero Hamburg.
1993	End of Kabel's studies and founding of Kabel New Media.
June 15, 1999	KNM goes public on the Frankfurt stock exchange (price: 6.15 Euro).
July 1999	First takeover of competitor "Cutup codes."
March 2000	KNM reaches share price peak: over 80 Euro (worth: 1.3 billion Euro).
March 1, 2000	Acquisition of the Team4 (CRM specialist).
May 11, 2000	Acquisition of the Austrian IT consultant Scope.
May 16, 2000	Acquisition of the Swedish IT consultant Lexor.
May 24, 2000	Peter Kabel voted entrepreneur of the year 2000.
June 28, 2001	Temporary cessation of payment.
August 1, 2001	KNM's CFO and deputy chairman steps back.
August 28, 2001	KNM sells subsidiary in Vienna.
August 31, 2001	Peter Kabel announces his resignation.
August 31, 2001	Prosecutors start their investigations.
September 1, 2001	Insolvency proceedings for KNM formally commenced.
September 4, 2001	BNP Paribas announces its withdrawal from its position as designated sponsor of KNM.
November 2, 2001	The German stock exchange excludes KNM from the market (last price: 0.08 Euro).

Over the short period from June 1999 to September 2001, some $1.2 billion (the March 2000 value of the company on the Frankfurt exchange) of value had been created and had then disappeared.

It had taken about 18 months from its inception for KNM to become a publicly listed company. It had taken nine months for the company to reach a billion dollar valuation, and then it had taken 15 months for the company to become valueless. A promising entrepreneurial venture which, given a decade, might have become a major company, had instead been caught up in a financial bubble. The bubble first wildly exaggerated the company's value, inducing the firm's leaders to expand far too rapidly, and then, like a balloon when the nozzle was suddenly released, quickly deflated, causing employees at the company to lose their jobs and the investors their money.

The Capital Markets as an Engine of Progress

The dot-com bubble was the result of the introduction of a new technology (the Internet as a platform for doing business) to the investing public. The capital markets' role according to economic theorists is to channel money into companies that support new technology through products and services, and thus build the new platform. To do this, capital markets raise money and bring promising new companies—via initial public offerings once companies are out of the high risk venture capital stage—to the general public that gets involved as investors. The public is also involved as customers to many of the new companies.

The capital markets are serviced by banks, mutual funds, and other financial institutions that raise money for corporations and governments, and provide investment vehicles in which people place their savings and pensions. The capital markets are made up of some of the largest businesses and best-known names in the economic world, including, for example, Chase, Goldman Sachs, Fidelity, Deutsche Bank, and so forth. All of the large firms and many of the smaller ones are also intermediaries between entrepreneurs and the individual investors, whom Wall Street labels "retail investors." The banks are linked to the mutual funds and other financial companies that will determine which investors ultimately own a company's stock.

The role of the financial companies is to facilitate the transactions by which shares in a new company are sold to the public—giving worthy companies the sort of solid, long-term investor base that every company wants. Financial companies are also supposed to provide retail investors with reasonably secure shares that increase in value over time, and to provide diversification to small investors because any individual stock may, of course, go down in value. If investments on the whole were not to increase in value, investors would not invest, and capital markets would not exist. So capital markets exist to provide capital to firms that will use it to create value, which is then shared with those who have invested in the companies.

The Social and Economic Utility of Capital Markets

Economic activity is not simply for the benefit of those involved; it also serves a social purpose, or it is ordinarily not permitted. For example, dealing in heroin is an economic activity that the United States believes serves no social purpose and so prohibits. People who participate in capital markets assert that capital markets serve several major social purposes—including that they are crucial to innovation and therefore improving living standards. Capital markets are said to fund innovation, and innovation to drive our economy, an argument given its modern formulation by Joseph Schumpeter in the 1920s and 1930s. Innovation improves living standards either directly, through new products and services, or indirectly, by driving up productivity in producing existing products and services.

Western capital markets, especially those in America and Europe, claim to be the best in the world at allocating capital to competing uses, especially among likely innovations. The markets are said to be large, highly developed, efficient, and transparent (and thereby worthy of investors' trust). Because of these features, western capital markets are able to pour investment dollars into innovations and push them ahead much faster than would otherwise be possible.

Since innovation drives progress, and capital is said to drive innovation, the role which is claimed for the capital markets is as significant as any which can be imagined. This is the core of capitalism. It's the economic mechanism widely acknowledged now to be the most effective at creating wealth and thereby improving living standards for large numbers of people.

The capital market firms that are engaged in supporting innovation, and building a link between entrepreneurs and the investing public, are more complex than might be expected because they have two functions: They must not only help embody promising technologies in products and services, they must also embody the products and services in financially successful firms.

Not every institution that funds innovation has this requirement. We'll see later that the Internet, for example, was initially supported by government funding, and this funding had no requirement of a successful commercial application. The government sought only the success of the technology and its use in research.

But capital market intermediaries had not only the obligation to develop the technology and its applications successfully, but the additional substantial obligation to do this in a way which promised to bring private investors a return on their investments in firms which brought innovations to the market. That is, an innovation backed by capital market institutions has not only to be useful but profitable.

The Internet, Capital Markets, and Innovation

The Internet is a classic example of the application of capital markets to innovation. Money was initially denied to the developers of Internet technology. Then it was dumped on them. Some of it was used to develop important technology, useful products, and viable companies. Much of it was wasted.

As excitement grew about the potential of the new technology and its commercial applications, the price of shares in Internet companies soared. Soon the price far outdistanced long-term real value. When the public perceived this inconsistency, the share market collapsed, taking with it many firms, many of which were not ever likely to be viable. However, the collapse also took down some promising companies that had strong management teams, good products, and were simply at too early a stage financially to survive the collapse of their share prices.

What does it all mean? It can be argued that the money that went into dot-com companies wasn't wasted; that the technology has promise, but the business models of many early firms did not. Now that the early firms have been culled by the stock market bust, new firms will emerge with better economic models for exploiting the technology.

Some therefore conclude the process of innovation is always inefficient—lots of people are trying to develop similar things at the same time. This process is expensive and inefficient, but it works, and therefore is sensible.

To the disciples of Schumpeter, this is what capitalism is about and it is all to the good.

But how much expense and inefficiency is necessary? Is it possible that we are now exceeding what makes sense? How much damage to the entire economy does innovation require? How much dislocation for people? How much loss of investors' money?

The Early-Stage Financing of the Internet

Despite the role of the capital markets in supporting innovation in capitalist economies, many promising technologies do not get support. The Internet, for example, was developed in two major stages, neither of which had capital market funding. It was only years later, when the technologies were commercialized, that private capital came in. This was despite efforts of the original builders of the technologies to get private financial support for their capitalization.

In the late 1960s, Bolt, Braneck and Newman (BBN), a private research firm in Cambridge, Mass., received a contract from the American Defense Department's Defense Advanced Research Project Agency (DARPA) to build a network that would connect the computers of research agencies of the government and of government contractors. BBN used packet switching technology to build the network, the Internet. This was the network that was called DARPANET, and building it was a major technological stretch. At the time Bell Labs thought it couldn't be done, and so didn't bid on the Defense Department contract. BBN also developed the server that made the network possible, and labeled it the Interface Message Processor.

In the early 1970s, there were four servers at different universities that were Defense Department contractors, and one at BBN. This was the early Internet.

BBN saw the potential commercial application of the Net and sought to raise capital to build the network. The notion was to sell access to the network to business for various purposes. As part of its effort at commercialization, BBN applied to the Federal Communications Commission and received an exclusive carrier's license for three years. Then BBN sought private equity investment to commercialize the Internet.

But the venture capital community wasn't interested. Principals in the venture firms didn't understand the concept, and the telephone companies recognized a potential competitor and didn't like it. So the venture firms wouldn't invest.

BBN pressed ahead with development of the concept via a research trust limited partnership, but there was neither enough capital nor enough market understanding to make a breakthrough into significant commercial use. The Internet would have to wait for another 20 years for the capital markets to become interested.

Meanwhile the research and defense community continued to use and improve the network. In Switzerland, at the high-speed particle accelerator (CERN), Tim Berners-Lee and his associates needed a way to find items on the computers connected to the Internet and developed the World Wide Web. Again, there was no private capital involved.

Thereafter, young engineers at the University of Illinois, in particular Mark Andriesson, developed a program—the first search engine—to find items on the Web for various purposes, and soon it was in use by the public, especially at universities, for a variety of purposes. It was at this late date, in 1994, that private equity entered the development of the technology via the foundation of Netscape.

Netscape was the first search engine but the public needed a way to access the Web to be able to use it. Along came America Online, and then other competitors, and thus the Internet as we know it today, with its availability to the public, its millions of Web sites, and its commercial applications. All this was some 20 years after just such a network had first been envisioned by the builders of DARPANET. Yet within just a few years after the founding of Netscape and AOL, billions of dollars of venture funds were pouring into hundreds of companies set up to exploit the new technology—leading, in not so many additional years, to the Internet bubble and its bursting.

The System Hits a Glitch

Ventro and Kabel New Media are but two of literally hundreds of examples showing what happened to entrepreneurs and investors during the great bubble of the turn of the 21st century. A vast amount of wealth was apparently created, then disappeared. How did it happen, and why? And what are the consequences?

Significantly, the bubble was similar in Germany and America, but the impact on small investors was not, as we'll see later.

The bubble was the consequence of interaction between capital markets and the innovation process. That this interaction took the form of a bubble raises important questions regarding the role of the capital markets in the innovation and investment processes in Western economies.

In the recent bubble, the system which links technological innovation to the investor via capital markets seems to have hit a glitch. Instead of investor's financial support providing the basis for the long-term growth of new companies, many start-up companies ended bankrupt. Instead of their investments appreciating, many small investors (though not only they) lost large portions of their savings and of their pension assets.

Talking Points

We've looked at two companies, one American, one German, that were both part of the dot-com bubble. They are examples of how the system seems to have had a glitch. Instead of investors' financial support providing the basis for the long-term growth of new companies, many ended up bankrupt. Instead of their investments appreciating, many small investors lost large portions of their savings and of their pension assets.

The capital markets serve two purposes: to drive innovation and to support financially successful businesses. The Internet was one means by which money was provided for progress, but much of the money was wasted through this process.

The slow progress of the Internet from its Defense research beginnings to its commercial application illustrates how early development continues to be the domain of government funding and academic and research people; how private capital is, at the beginning, often limited in technological understanding and commercial imagination; how private capital flows in only slowly, and often only when the public has already seen potential and begun to find ways to get access to systems developed by government and research organizations; and how private capital finally jumps in, and with it, excessive enthusiasm about the commercial value of applications of the new technology. Years of disinterest give way almost overnight to wild excitement.

How did this happen? What caused new companies to go awry? Did the companies embody serious business ideas in which responsible people had confidence and worked hard to achieve, but fell down due to good reasons? Or were they screwy notions that never should have been funded, and certainly not sold to retail investors? Were they ideas in which neither the founders nor the investors had confidence, but were simply hyped to make a killing in a public market? If so, who's to blame? Is it likely to happen again? Do we want it to? If not, can it be stopped?

These are among the key questions that this book will answer.

How the Bubble Happened

The Internet bubble was like a great storm—many different forces had to come together for it to happen.

3 Causing the Bubble

The Technology Bull Market

The last two decades have seen a global technology revolution that began with the personal computer (PC) and led to the Internet era. Companies like Apple, Microsoft, Intel, and Dell Computer were at the forefront of this new wave of technology that promised to enhance productivity and efficiency through the computerization and automation of many processes.

The capital markets recognized the value that was being created by these companies. Microsoft, which was founded in 1975, had a market capitalization of over $600 billion by the beginning of 2000, making it the world's most valuable company, and its founder, Bill Gates, one of the richest men in the world. High values were also given by the market to many of the other blue-chip technology firms such as Intel and Dell (Table 3–1). It was in this environment of highly valued technology companies that the Internet mania reached its peak.

Table 3–1 Market capitalization of major technology companies, January 2000.

Company	Market Capitalization ($ billions)[a]	Stock Price (January 3, 2000)
Microsoft	603	116.56
Intel	290	87.00
IBM	218	116.00
Dell Computer	131	50.88
Hewlett Packard	117	117.44
Compaq Computer	53	31.00
Apple Computer	18	111.94

Sources: Yahoo! Finance, Edgar Online.
[a] Based on share price close on January 3, 2000, and reported shares outstanding.

There developed a widely accepted belief that the Internet would profoundly change the way business is done because of increasing computing power, ease of communication, and the host of technologies that could be built upon it. The benefits of the Internet were expected to translate into greater economic productivity through the lowering of communication and transaction costs. It was thought to be a revolution, like that of the railway or the automobile. Not only did this make sense logically, but trusted research sources, such as Forrester, consultants, and even business school professors were endorsing this view and labeling it a new economy.

The pressure to buy into this vision should not be underestimated. When it seems that thousands around us, some of whom have superior experience and education and others of whom are our coworkers and friends, are getting rich by buying into these concepts, there seems little choice but to get involved, lest we appear to ourselves and others like idiots for not taking advantage of the situation.

Thus it came to seem obvious that lucky investors would be able to capitalize upon new opportunities in the financial markets, and that the next Microsoft would soon appear. People who missed out on the original opportunity to invest in Microsoft didn't want to miss a similar opportunity the second time around.

The Bubble

The stock market bubble associated with the Internet was arguably the biggest financial mania in history. "At the 2000 peak of the titanic bull market... the value of all stocks as a percentage of the American gross domestic product reached 183 percent, more than twice the level before the crash in 1929."[4] By early fall 2001, virtually the entire gain in the value of the NASDAQ which had been made since 1995 had evaporated. The bubble lasted about a year and a half, in 1999 and 2000, though it had deep roots in the earlier 1990s. Appendix A charts the bubble on America's NASDAQ and Germany's Nemax.

Though it is convenient to speak of one bubble, there were in fact four bubbles, one rapidly following another. This helped account for the remarkable overall size of the craze that is now referred to as a single entity: the Internet bubble. The first bubble consisted of the stocks of companies that were trying to use the Internet to help businesses reach consumers (B2C). When the bloom began to fade on this rose, the second bubble, consisting of stocks for firms trying to use the Net to conduct commerce among businesses (B2B), blossomed. As promise slipped in this area, and the lack of key infrastructure elements became evident as a cause of the limited success of B2C and C2C, a bubble began in the shares of firms building infrastructure for the Net. Finally, to connect everyone to the Net, a significant element of infrastructure building, a bubble developed in the telecom sector.

In retrospect, it might be asked why bubble followed bubble, but the earlier enthusiasms had not yet resulted in disaster, and each new enthusiasm was simply a way of extending the excitement further. In effect, as one element of the Internet excitement became satisfied by new companies doing that thing, and valuations of the stocks of those companies got very high so that they looked expensive to investors, then a new arena for investors opened.

There have been previous booms and periods of inflated share prices, including one for leasing companies in the 1960s, for disk drive firms in the 1980s, and for land development firms in the late 1980s. But the bubble of the late 1990s was distinguished by its great size and excesses. For example, shares of some companies were selling for brief periods at almost 300 times sales (in the case of Sycamore, the company wasn't profitable). Companies which were profitable sold at as much as 350 times operating profits. These were remarkable valuations by any standards, and in retrospect, it is not at all surprising that they collapsed.

New economy companies, as opposed to old economy ones (exemplified by companies in traditional manufacturing, retail, and commodities), based their business models around exploiting the Internet. They were usually small compared to their old economy counterparts, with little need for their real-world "bricks and mortar" structures. Instead, they preferred to outsource much of the capital intensive parts of the business and concentrate on what they believed to be the higher value-added, information-intensive elements. Traditional companies, finding their market shares and business models attacked by a host of seemingly nimble, specialized dot-com start-up companies, lived in danger of "being Amazoned." To many, including the capital markets, the new economy was the future, and old economy companies would become less and less relevant. From July 1999 to February 2000, as the Nasdaq Composite Index (which was heavily weighted with technology and Internet stocks) rose by 74.4 percent, the Dow Jones Industrial Average (which was composed mainly of old economy stocks) fell by 7.7 percent. Investors no longer seemed interested in anything that was not new economy. Very substantial financial valuations were being given at the top of the bubble to companies that were sustaining considerable losses, but which were darlings of the new economy.

Venture capitalists invested about $80 billion in start-up companies, about one-third of which went into dot-com companies, another one-quarter into telecom companies, and the remainder into companies in other industries.

Why Did the Bubble Form?

The bubble formed when many venture firms and investment banks altered their decision rules to exploit a growing public enthusiasm. The VCs gave up their traditional rules for making investments; the accountants began to accept questionable revenue booked by the dot-com companies; the investment banks abandoned their traditional rules for deciding which companies to take public. Finally, large investors such as mutual funds changed their own rules—their spending habits and attitudes toward risk. The Internet boom was greatly facilitated when many financial firms veered from their traditional operating requirements.

The excuse offered by each of these companies for the changes it made is that the circumstances demanded the changes. Those financial firms which were getting into the Internet game were showing much higher rates of return on their investments, so that those firms which were not began to lose the interest of the investing public. Every venture firm, every accountant, every bank had to get in to the dot-com game in order to be able to stay in its business—to get clients and make money. If others were doing it, those who didn't would get left behind—money would go elsewhere. So the rules changed and the bubble expanded.

In the modern world, a financial bubble is made by professional players who take advantage of public excitement to realize profit opportunities. This is a different view of bubbles than one that blames the investor or stresses irrational crowd behavior which sweeps up both professionals and the public.[5] It isn't that public excitement wasn't a factor in the bubble, it was. But it alone was insufficient to drive the inflation of the bubble, and would in fact quickly have subsided had the fires of excitement not been fanned by financial market professionals. That is, financial professionals were not so much caught up in a public frenzy, as fanning the flames of the frenzy in order to profit from it.

Market professionals are well aware of the dynamics of a financial frenzy and how to exploit it. In a book widely known among professionals, Charles

Kindleberger of MIT described the three phases of speculative bubbles: mania, distress, and panic. And he noted that speculative bubbles are triggered by market shocks such as major technological changes. Kenneth Galbraith also discussed mania in his study of the stock market boom that preceded the great depression of the 1930s—a book also familiar to financial professionals.[6]

When the advent of Internet technology began to generate public excitement, professionals in the financial markets saw an opportunity. It is true that during the bubble, many younger people in the venture firms, the investment banks, and the financial press lacked the experience of markets which went down as well as up, and lacked historical perspective as well, but this simply isn't true of the seasoned executives who ran the businesses and were responsible for what the younger professionals did. They knew the mania was ill-founded, but many, though not all, were content to profit by it nonetheless.

Day Trading and the Source of the Bubble

It's a fundamental rule of market economics, but one too little understood by most people, that prices are determined at the margin—or in the case of the Internet bubble, by the margin. This means that for some stocks a small increase in demand can create a big price increase, just as only a small decrease in demand can cause the price of a product to take a steep fall.

This situation emerged in the market for Internet stocks with the advent of a new player—the day trader. With the ability to trade online, quickly and continuously, the day trader created a whole new category of demand, to which the market quickly responded. Analysts estimated that at its height, day trading made up almost 18 percent of the trading volume of the New York Stock Exchange and the Nasdaq in 2000.[7] Sites such as Yahoo! Finance grew in popularity, while chat rooms devoted to stocks and trading proliferated.[8]

Observers pointed out that day trading was made possible by high margin loans made by brokerage firms to traders, and asked the SEC to restrict the margins. It studied the question, but ultimately didn't act. Thus it was that the buying power lent to day traders created the margin in the market that drove dot-com stock prices up sharply, dramatically augmenting the bubble. See Table 3–2 for valuations given to money-losing dot-com companies during the height of the bubble.

Soon financial products of the desired nature (especially shares in new companies)—linking investors to companies supplying Internet technology—were forthcoming, and a steady stream of IPOs began to satisfy the new demand. And the market began to create substantial financial values for more and more companies.

Table 3–2 Market Valuations given to loss-making dot-coms.

Company	Net Income ('99/'00)[a] ($ millions)	Market Capitalization ($ billions)[b]	Stock Price (January 3, 2000)
Amazon.com	−720	30.8	89.38
DoubleClick	−56	30.1	268.00
Akamai Technologies	−58	29.7	321.25
VerticalNet	−53	12.4	172.63
Priceline.com	−1,055	8.4	51.25
E*Trade	−57	7.1	28.06
EarthLink	−174	5.2	44.75
Drugstore.com	−116	1.6	37.13

Sources: Edgar Online, Yahoo! Finance.
[a] As of end of 1999 or early 2000, depending on fiscal year end.
[b] Based on share price close on January 3, 2000, and reported shares outstanding.

Other Bubbles in History

As suggested earlier, the Internet stock mania was a financial bubble. A bubble is formally defined as an exceptionally rapid rise in prices in which a commodity's price far outstrips what it is worth to anyone except a speculator.

Bubbles are usually caused by a shift in a technological paradigm, so it's easy to make a story about fantastic opportunities for investors who have no ready frame of reference to place the story in context. Bubbles are funded by easy credit so that in a modern economy, a central bank is involved one way or another.

The Internet bubble was in many respects a typical bubble. For example, the tulip bubble in the Netherlands in the 17th century—during which individual bulbs of rare tulips rose in price to astronomical levels—involved a series of florists who were neither growers nor connoisseurs, but became bulb traders and drove the market to excess through speculation. The "greed, inexperience and short-sightedness of the florists were all that was required to turn tulip trading into tulip mania…"[9] The mechanism of the mania was speculative trading.

It wasn't flowers that were traded in the tulip mania, but contracts for flowers, often kept only a single day by traders. That is, speculators didn't want tulips, they wanted contracts for tulips.

Similar things occurred in the dot-com bubble 350 years later. Speculators often held on to dot-com shares for a very short time. It wasn't connoisseurship that drove the tulip mania, and it wasn't technological knowledge that drove the dot-com bubble. In both instances, it was short-term and naïve speculation.

What had been needed to generate the tulip mania were a new and inexperienced group of traders, a new place to trade (the taverns of the Netherlands), and an exciting new product with multiple variations (the tulips—newly introduced to western Europe from Turkey).

The dot-com bubble had the same elements—day traders (new and inexperienced), the Internet (a new place to trade) and an exciting new product (dot-com company shares) in multiple variations (different firms with different business models, etc).

But there were also important differences in the two bubbles hundreds of years apart. Unlike the tulip mania, the dot-com bubble had well-established players (venture capitalists, investment banks, and brokerage houses), and trading over established exchanges (NYSE, ASE, NASDAQ). Where the tulip mania "was a craze of the poor and the ambitious that ... had virtually no impact on the Dutch economy,"[10] the dot-com bubble dramatically impacted a key infrastructure element of the U.S. economy (the Internet and the telecom system), and the bursting of the Internet bubble helped drive the American economy into recession. Further, the tulip mania occurred in an unregulated market, while the dot-com bubble occurred in one of the most regulated of U.S. markets (the stock market). The dot-com bubble was therefore not a typical bubble, in comparison with the tulip mania, and had more lasting economic effects.

At the height of the dot-com bubble, people looked for something similar in the past in order to obtain some perspective and perhaps a glimpse into the future. The spotlight immediately fell on a period at the end of the 1960s and the beginning of the 1970s when a group of largely technology stocks, including Polaroid and Xerox, became the darlings of investors (the so-called Nifty Fifty). In 1972, for example, Polaroid commanded a share price of more than 90 times earnings per share[11]—something not repeated until the late 1990s, when share prices went even wilder. During the Internet bubble, companies without any earnings sometimes commanded stock prices that were as much as 300 times revenues/share. The enthusiasm of the early 1970s didn't last, of course, and years later, in 2001, Polaroid sought bankruptcy protection.

The Software Cycle

The significance of the comparison of 1970 and the late 1990s is the appearance of a market cycle in technology stocks. For example, today, software seems to be beset by such a cycle. In a sense, the cycle is the stuff of disappointment and disillusionment. New products come along supplied by a new company. As word of the products and the underlying technology gets out, the shares of the company leap in price. The company has momentum; people come to work for it and it compensates them with options to buy shares in the future. (In the past, options were ordinarily restricted to a company's executives. During the dot-com bubble, share options were frequently extended by companies to most and sometimes all their employees.) The share price continues to rise. The company's initial products do well. Then it has to migrate to a new generation of devices and starts development. Along comes a major stock market correction. The price of the company's shares dive. Soon top programmers and project managers have options that are worthless—"under water." They leave. Also, the low share price undermines the credibility of the company with customers.

Because entry to the software industry is relatively easy—just personal computers for programming and a loft or garage or kitchen to work in—and there is often venture money available (at the right time in the cycle)—top programmers who leave are likely to find opportunities to start their own companies. If successful, a new company hires top managers and takes it public during the next boom for a huge valuation.

There are multiple examples of this dynamic. Enktomi, one of the first of the Internet infrastructure firms, saw its share price rise to a peak of about 180. Then the stock market soured on its shares. This could have happened for reasons associated with the company, or with its industry, or for unrelated reasons. In Enktomi's case, the share price plunged to $3. The company is still active—it has more than $150 million in annual sales. Perhaps it will resume its growth and its shares will again be hot. But often companies in such situations never become a major force again. Once they've fallen off the growth track, they aren't likely to get the next generation of product, both because of difficulty raising money to build the new products and because of difficulties attracting and retaining talented people.

Rising share prices of start-ups were widely viewed as a great advantage early in the bubble. It permitted start-ups to pay lower salaries for talented people and to compensate them with share options. But the picture was never this one-sided. In fact, when start-ups adopted stock options for key employees (or for all employees for that matter), the bubble damaged them in two ways. When the bubble was expanding, it allowed people to cash out and leave; when it burst, it left people with valueless options and disillusioned. In the first instance, valuable people were lost; in the second, they ceased to be motivated.

Akamai would have been a better company except for the financial bubble and the wild ride the company got from it. Defenders of bubbles as the price American-style capitalism pays for innovation should look carefully at the example of this company.

In 1995, Tim Berners-Lee, now a professor at MIT, approached another MIT faculty member, who then approached one of his top graduate students, for a solution to the growing problem of congestion on the Internet. A student from MIT's Sloan School of Management joined the team, and after raising venture capital, launched Akamai Technologies in August 1998. The MIT team, recognizing that it needed top managerial talent, went to its venture investors, who found for it a former top IBM sales executive, George Conrades. Conrades became CEO of Akamai and pulled together a strong management team. With Akamai now led by business people and with exciting technology protected by licenses, patent applications, and copyrights, the company sought a public offering of its stock. In October 1999, the company went public so successfully that it soon became a model for other aspiring firms. Akamai's shares had been originally priced at $26 per share; not more than a few months later, the company's share price had risen to a remarkable $345.

By spring 2001, the company had some 1,300 employees managing some 9,700 servers in 56 countries directly connected within over 650 different telecommunications networks.[12]

But though the company's sales were rising, they were not yet high enough to offset the operating costs, and the company remained unprofitable. The capital markets turned down, and Akamai fell out of favor. By fall 2001, the share price was less than $4. The company had become a victim of the capital market cycle, and it was rumored that it was being offered for sale.

Akamai is a company led by seasoned managers, with excellent technology and technical people. The bubble permitted it to raise a substantial amount of capital early in its history and therefore to be well financed to build its business. But the bubble also bid the stock price of the company up to very high levels very quickly, levels not at all merited by the economic value which the company had been able to build at the time. In the crash, the share price of the company declined to such a low level that customers' and suppliers' confidence in the company was impaired, and good people, their options way under water, left the company. In effect, it was crippled by the gyration of the financial markets. So we must balance the early availability of capital to the company against its crippling at a later stage. What is the net contribution of the financial market—did it get the technology of Akamai to market successfully? Did it allow a company to be built? Did it reward shareholders?

The answers are negative in each instance. Probably Akamai would have done better, and its technology been better developed and distributed, with another round of venture funding before it went public. In part this is because Akamai's executives seem to have overestimated both the market for its products and the price at which they could be sold. They seem to have accepted the prevalent notion of the time, that first mover advantage would guarantee a continuing high level of market share, and to have underestimated the competition which would come from investments being made simultaneously by others in data centers. Akamai would better have been taken public after it became profitable, several years after it was actually sold to the public, so that the true value of the company could have been better assessed. Today Akamai is unlikely to survive as an independent company, and late-stage investors have lost a lot of money. It's hard to see that this process contributed anything of value to the company itself or to the American economy as a whole.

When the bubble burst, the sudden shift in the attitude of the financial markets regarding what supports financial value—from revenue growth prospects to actual profits—caught Akamai at an unfavorable stage in its development. It needed an additional year or two of investment to get enough sales volume to become profitable. The financial markets had been impatient about growth, and now they were equally impatient about profitability, and the company got killed in the switch. At no time were the expectations of the capital markets in any way compatible with the development experience of the start-up. That is, the economic reality of the company in its growth cycle, and the expectations of the financial markets, were never in sync. It's hard to argue from this experience that the capital markets are effectively promoting innovation in the U.S. economy. What they give with one hand, in funding entrepreneurial companies—they take away with the other hand, by virtue of unreasonable expectations and shifts in expectations—and the result is not effective innovation and strong companies, but slowed and set-back innovation and crippled firms.

There is an additional and somewhat subtle point that Akamai's experience well illustrates. Suppose that Akamai were to survive these difficult times and become profitable in two years. Would the company then regain favor in the capital markets? Probably not. The reason is a sort of delusion that affects companies after their shares have been caught up in a bubble. Akamai's price rose to great heights, then fell into a pit, and all the while the company was successfully executing its business plan. Nothing in what the company was doing justified its high valuation at the top of the bubble, nor its low valuation in the bust. But many investors didn't perceive that. They presumed that when the company's share price was high it was somehow merited, and when the price collapsed, that something had gone wrong in the company's performance. So they were reluctant to buy shares even as the company made progress in its business. The result is that such a company isn't ever likely again to see a rapid rise in its share price, and therefore ambitious potential employees are likely to go elsewhere. And since entry to the software business is easy, they will find other places to go. So a company has not simply received a set-back as a result of the impact of the bubble on its share price; it has been seriously damaged for what is likely to be a long period of time.

Other examples of how the financial markets appeared to give but in fact took away are easy to find. One is Exodus, once one of the best of the Web-hosting companies. Its shares took a ride similar to those of Akamai. Because of the easy availability of capital during the early stages of the bubble, Exodus over invested in its capacity and then found itself overloaded with debt and sinking fast. This was a management miscalculation, of course, but one which was motivated by false signals being sent by the capital markets. Here, the financial markets supplied not the right amount of capital to the young company, but too much. Akamai was damaged by the wild swings of its share price that destroyed the people side of its business. Exodus was damaged by the too easy availability of capital, which caused it to overinvest and then stumble under the weight of too much debt.

It will surely be argued by some that the management teams at the two companies were to blame for the ultimate difficulties of the companies, not the financial markets. Akamai's management should have tried to talk down its share price, it will be said; Exodus's management should have borrowed less money and expanded less aggressively. But these arguments are not persuasive. The price of shares cannot be readily controlled by management, especially for a small company. During the bubble, Akamai was successfully following its business plan—but for a time the capital markets blessed that, and then turned quickly against it. It can be argued that Akamai's business plan was flawed because it didn't correctly anticipate the impact changes in the financial markets would have on its business prospects. But this seems a great deal to ask of management, since its business isn't financial forecasting but rather software. In reality, Akamai's management couldn't anticipate or control this change in its environment effected by the capital markets. As for Exodus, it took, as economists would say it should, the capital offered to it as a signal from the market that it should expand, and did so. That the market was so wrong, or was going to change its mind so quickly, cannot be expected to have been evident to the management.

In fact, almost the only way a company could successfully avoid being badly damaged by the bubble was to have stayed out of the public market entirely. Privately held start-ups, including many which failed to be accepted for underwritten funding during the bubble, were the least damaged by the bubble. This suggests that in a long-term perspective, the public financial markets are not doing a good job of supporting that part of innovation in our economy which occurs via venture funding and start-up firms.

The Transfer of Wealth

What were the consequences of the bubble? Much wealth was created and then destroyed. Easy come, easy go. On balance, after the great bubble, no wealth was created. This is a difficult judgment because the numbers are not complete; yet it appears to be justified. For example, an analysis by *The Wall Street Journal* showed that between 1996 and 2001, all the profits reported by some 4000 companies listed on the NASDAQ were offset by losses reported by the same companies—net profits appearing in 1996 through 2000, and net losses in 2001.[13] With no profits on balance for the period, it's reasonable to expect that the valuations of the 4,000 companies should not have increased—although other factors might have caused that to occur.

Does this mean that nothing happened? Not at all. There was a huge gain in wealth by some, and a huge loss of wealth by others—it was as if the government had imposed a large tax for the purpose of redistributing wealth, and in so doing had slowed the long-term growth and development of the economy as a whole.

The transfer of wealth came at the expense of the living standards of the entire nation, for a significant part of the resources of the nation—human talent, business effort, capital—were diverted into activities whose ultimate result was not economic growth but merely redistribution. In effect, the capital markets did what they tell the government not to do: They intervened in the economy, at great cost in resources, to redistribute wealth. Though this was the fact, this process is never cited as the role for capital markets, nor is it cited as a justification for their significance in the economy. It perverts responsible peoples' perception of the purpose of capital markets.

It is sometimes argued that our economy is better off because of an allegedly accelerated pace of development of the Internet caused by all the money thrown at the sector during the bubble. But it is precisely this assertion that is in doubt. Was the pace of development of the Internet increased by the bubble, or was it decreased? The patient needed to be fed, yes, but did he or she have to have food forced down his or her throat for days on end, and then be denied any food at all for a long period? Was the patient better off for gorging and then starving, than for a simple, regular series of meals? The Internet needed a steady supply of capital accompanied by slowly rising valuations of its companies which reflected its pace of economic progress. It got something very different from the capital markets. On balance, was the Internet better or worse off for its actual experience? The answer seems to me to be that it was worse off. That is, the pace of development of the Internet was not increased by the bubble and the excessive capital thrown at dot-coms and telecoms, but rather the contrary—its pace of development was slowed.

During the bubble, people took huge losses on mutual funds in which they had invested pension money. Commentators at the time were expressing concern that individual investors could have retirement savings invested completely in aggressive growth funds full of technology and dot-com stocks, and lose their savings. But the mutual fund companies went right ahead and recommended such funds to people, who then lost their shirts.

This is significant. It's well-known since the German inflation after World War I that rapid inflation destroys the savings of the middle class and thereby social stability. But a bubble like ours that gobbles up the retirement savings of the middle class threatens to do the same. If the bubble is now followed by a deep recession, as it may be, we may find the political fallout of the bubble to be quite significant.

And the transfer of wealth came at the expense of the average investor, and occurred in many ways. In fact, we might ask in how many ways is the average investor being made to pay for the bubble? She paid directly by the collapse of the value of the dot-com and telecom shares she held, or which were held by mutual funds or pension plans on her behalf. She paid indirectly by the decline of the economy—which reduced the value of other shares she owned or which were owned for her, and by losing her job, or a promotion, or not getting an expected wage increase—or by these things happening to her loved ones. She paid in a lot of ways, and paid a stiff price.

In the aftermath of the bubble, many people lost their retirement savings, others lost their jobs; the entire global economy was tipped into recession. "… it was not appreciated [last year]," admitted *The Economist*, "that this was much more than just a narrow bubble in Internet stocks. Instead, 'new economy' hype had distorted the global tech sector and unbalanced the entire American economy… Over-exuberance about future profits and cheap capital had encouraged a lot of over-investment… The plunge in share prices has seriously dented business confidence and investment plans… As the world economy has become more integrated, a downturn in one economy spreads faster to another."[14]

These are the consequences of the dot-com and telecom financial bubbles; they are severe.

Talking Points

What is today called the Internet bubble was actually an amalgam of four consecutive bubbles, creating an enormous rise and fall in the value of stocks. The bubble was fueled by a global revolution in technology and by the notion that the Internet would profoundly change the way we do business. The bubble intensified as key players, such as investment banks and venture capital firms, changed their own rules to take advantage of the public excitement. This was not the first bubble in history, but it's the largest we have seen so far.

The bubble was supposed to be part of a process by which the capital markets provided funding to emerging companies so that they could advance their business prospects. The outcome was quite different. Rather than support innovation, the bubble permanently damaged some very good companies.

The capital markets are supposed to provide returns on investment to those who buy shares in innovative firms. But again the outcome of the bubble was very different. Many investors who lost money lost a great deal of money. Looking back it seems that there was no net value creation at all during the up and down of the bubble.

4 Inflating the Bubble: the Financial Value Chain

A chain of specialized institutions links entrepreneurs to the capital markets and thereby facilitates innovation. The emergence of this chain in financial services is part of a major aspect of free economies, noted two centuries ago by economists—the increasing specialization of firms as markets grow larger.

But extending the chain of middlemen between entrepreneurs and the investing public appears to be associated with ever wilder spasms of excitement and despair among investors. The greatest of these—so far—was the Internet boom of the late 1990s.

The Financial Value Chain

The economic value that a company creates by producing and/or marketing goods and services does not automatically translate into financial value—the market value of its shares. The translation from one to the other is the role of a different set of institutions in our economy—including, in addition to others, banks, venture funds, and brokerage houses. This group of financial institutions constitutes the financial value chain. It's the mechanism by which the great Internet bubble was born, and the mechanism by which it died.

The system of specialized institutions and professionals who make up the financial value chain work to convert the economic value of a firm into financial value. Economic value doesn't transfer directly in the short-run into financial value, as theorists who believe in perfect markets predict, and ironically, for the very reason they focus on—that the transfer of the economic value of a firm into financial value requires a market, which makes the transfer subject to all the emotions and inefficiencies of all markets, at least in the short run.

Financial value is the current price of a company in the capital markets. Economic value is the long-term value of the company as measured by what the expected profits of the company over years to come are worth to investors today—formally, this means the discounted present value of the expected income stream based on reasonable assumptions. In perfectly functioning markets, the two are identical. There is a theory, called by economists the *efficient market hypothesis*, which holds that every day the capital market discovers the discounted present value of each financial instrument—including stocks, bonds, derivatives, and so forth—and values each correctly. But recent years have been very difficult ones for efficient market believers—financial values have departed too widely from economic values for efficiency of markets to be credible.

It may be argued that what the financial markets do not accomplish in the short term, they may accomplish in the longer term. That is, the markets do not accurately incorporate new information in the price of a stock in the short term, but over the longer term they do so. In the longer term, then, they are efficient.

This may be so, but it has little or no significance for our examination of the Internet bubble, since it is the short term with which we are concerned.

In the short term, the financial value of a company is in the eye of the beholder, and the financial marketplace exists to permit people with different views to buy and sell shares in companies. The price of a financial instrument, like a share of stock, is the amount of money at which financial value is currently available. Every transaction requires both a buyer and seller. Often the buyer looks at a stock with a different discount factor than the seller, so the buyer is willing to pay more than the seller is for the stock, so a trade occurs. For new companies which are generally small and untested, there is usually a great divergence of opinion about the future of the company, so that people discount the expected earnings of the firm in the future at very different rates. So there is often a wide spread between what a buyer will pay for the shares and what a seller hopes to get. Hence, there is potentially much volatility in the price of the stock. As a company gets larger and more experience accumulates with its financial performance, then the discount rates applied by different people converge, and the spread between offers and asking prices narrows.

The financial value chain exists because of an asymmetry in information (some people have more and better information than others), because of differences in perception about risk and value, and because there are conflicts of interest. Entrepreneurs and insiders know much more about a firm than investors can; managers have different interests than shareholders. Investors usually lack enough information to know of opportunities to support start-ups, and even if they know of opportunities, they lack information and expertise to determine the good investments from the bad.

So both entrepreneurs and investors rely on specialized intermediaries, including accountants, lawyers, regulatory bodies, investment banks, venture capitalists, money management firms, and the media, to link them together and thereby to turn the economic value created by entrepreneurs into financial value.

Diagramming the Financial Value Chain

Figure 4–1 is of the Financial Value Chain—the group of specialized companies that together cause the capital market to function and which translate the economic value of a firm into financial value.

The chain begins with start-up firms and the entrepreneurs who run them. Next are the venture firms and/or angels who finance early-stage firms in return for an ownership stake (usually in the form of preferred stock) and who also have contacts to the investment banks. Accountants play a crucial role because they verify the honesty of the information upon which transactions are based. Without confidence that the representations of a seller about the financial condition of a company are correct, buyers would hesitate to buy, and a market would be difficult to create. But accountants have a divided, even ambiguous responsibility—

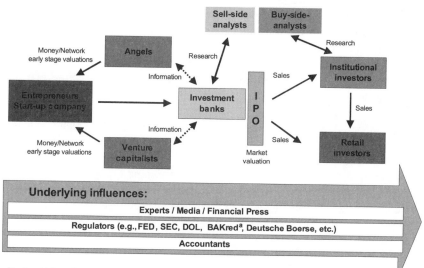

Figure 4–1 The Financial Value Chain.

partly to the company that pays their fees, and partly to the investors who depend on the veracity of their reports.

Entrepreneurs rely on investment banks (such as Goldman Sachs, Morgan Stanley Dean Witter, and Credit Suisse First Boston) to raise money through an initial public offering, or "going public." Investment banks provide advisory financial services, and help a company sell itself to investors, often in the form of a road show. For these services, investment banks are paid a commission based on the amount of money that the company manages to raise in its offering, typically on the order of seven percent,[15] a very high-margin source of business for the investment banks.

During the IPO process, banks undertake a publicity campaign to potential investors and then sell the shares, at least for a fully marketed offering. (Other offerings might be made to only a small set of investors, and so not fully marketed.) During the dot-com bubble, Goldman Sachs and Morgan Stanley together did about 70 percent of all good (or so it seemed at the time) quality IPOs. It appears that entrepreneurs and venture firms gave great importance to the stronger brand names among the investment banks.

The banks, though they represent client firms, and are paid by them, also have some responsibility to investors to be sure that shares sold to investors do not immediately become worthless. So banks traditionally exercise a gatekeeping function controlling which companies get taken to the public market. It may be hard to believe that the banks actually turned anything down during the dot-com bubble—but not every company that applied to the banks was taken public, and there was tremendous competition among the banks to get the best of the bunch to take to IPOs.

At the end of the Financial Value Chain are the investors, both institutional (such as corporate or public employee pension funds, and mutual funds) and retail (individual investors via their savings or self-managed pension funds). Retail investors may buy shares in a new company directly from the banks via IPOs, or indirectly through buying shares in mutual funds that have bought IPO shares. Small investors may end up holding IPO shares via corporate pension funds by which they are covered, or via shares in their own companies if they work for firms which have IPOs.

The Financial Value Chain is complex, involving many participants with different functions, interests, and incentives, and with different relationships among one another. This book is not the place to discuss or describe it in great detail. Appendix B at the back of this book gives a tabular summary of the chain that is more detailed than our discussion here. The appendix gives a snapshot of the entire chain and of the influences exerted on and by each of the participants.

Figure 4–2 (The Ordinary Relationship of Economic and Financial Value) shows what should be the relationship between the growth of economic value in a start-up and the growth of the financial value of the firm. The start-up begins slowly and over years builds products, services, and customers, begins to generate revenues, and ultimately becomes profitable. This is a tale of success. Many start-ups, of course, fail along the way.

While the start-up is building economic value, financial value is increasing also, and at roughly the same rate. In the ordinary course of events, a start-up gets successive infusions of capital from investors at points in its development which are milestones. At each of these times, the valuation of the company is typically increased. This is valuation via a step-function. When the company has an IPO, a valuation is placed on the company that is the last step of the step-function. After the IPO, the capital market values the company anew again each day. Again, if markets are reasonably efficient, financial value should be increasing at roughly the same rate as the company is building economic value via increased sales and profits.

The formal functioning of the Financial Value Chain during the Internet bubble was not unusual. The Financial Value Chain connected start-up companies to retail investors via investment banks and mutual funds, with the deep involvement of venture funds, financial angels, accountants, the financial press, and pension funds, and always—after the venture and angel investment stage—under the supposedly watchful eyes of government regulators. By virtue of the Financial Value Chain, the economic value being built by start-ups was converted into financial value for investors. The Financial Value Chain is intended to provide information to buyers for the purpose of facilitating investment, but during the bubble the system appears to have given out information that proved wrong about the financial situation and viability of dot-com and telecom businesses, and the consequences hurt both entrepreneurs and investors. How did the system generate results so out of whack?

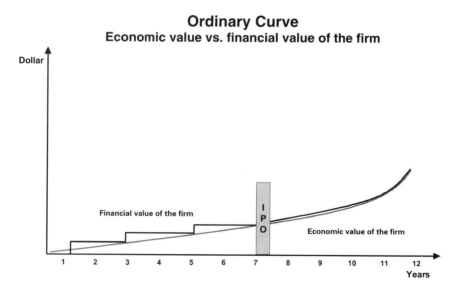

Figure 4–2 The ordinary relationship of economic and financial value.

When Economic and Financial Value Diverge

For a number of reasons, financial value can be well above, or well below, economic value. During the great bubble, financial values became enormously inflated compared to economic values, and when that was finally realized by investors, financial values collapsed well below the economic values

Figure 4–3 (The Bubble Curve) illustrates the divergence of economic and financial value for a single start-up. While the company is slowly building economic value, the financial markets accord it increasingly large financial value. Expectations far outrun actual performance. Then suddenly the financial markets realize their mistake, and the financial value of the firm comes tumbling down. As it overshot in the upward direction, now the Financial Value Chain overshoots in the downward direction, and financial value falls below economic value for the firm. From the point of view of the firm, nothing has happened to justify either the rapid inflation of its financial value, or the sudden collapse of financial value—all along the company has been executing successfully its business plan. The wild ride is all in the stock market.

Figure 4–4 (NASDAQ) shows that, in fact, a wide divergence between economic value and financial value occurred during the bubble for the entire NASDAQ. The long-term growth trend of the price of NASDAQ securities is used as a surrogate for the economic value of the firms. During the bubble, the "Era of Irrational Exuberance" in the chart, the price of shares increased dramatically above their long-term growth rate (the measure, imperfect though it is, of economic value). And as if in compensation, after the bursting of the bubble, financial value fell below economic value (the long-term growth trend).

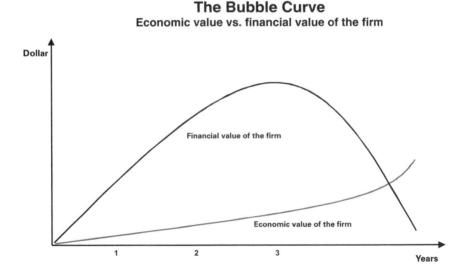

The Bubble Curve
Economic value vs. financial value of the firm

Figure 4–3 The bubble curve.

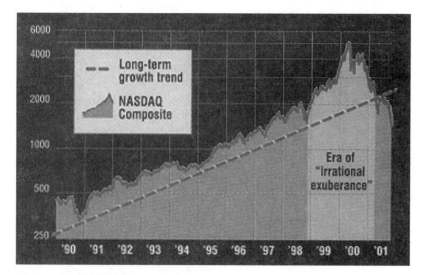

Figure 4–4 NASDAQ versus long-term growth trend.

Source: Bloomberg in Michael Sivy, "First, Do Nothing," *Money*, November 2001,
© 2001 Time, Inc. All rights reserved.

As said previously, in normal times financial value is usually connected, if loosely, to economic value. The Economic Supply Chain creates economic value; the Financial Value Chain turns economic value into financial value. During the dot-com bubble, the two were quickly decoupled. The Financial Value Chain was selling to the public, companies for which the Economic Value Chain had not yet worked its magic; but the financial institutions were treating possible economic value as already certain. A company might have great prospects, but they are only that. Economic value is the turning of prospects into reality. When financial markets treat prospects as reality and discount enormous hoped-for future income streams into present value as if they are reasonably assured, then financial value and economic value diverge. Buyers of IPO issues who thought they were getting companies that had economic value were not; hype gave the companies financial value in the market for the moment, but neither hype nor the millions raised for the companies in IPOs could give the companies sufficient economic value to justify the prices investors were paying.

Hype can sometimes create economic value for a firm. For example, a motion picture firm releases a movie which gets great reviews, becomes talked about, and soon is all the rage. Viewers stream into the theatres and ticket sale receipts pour into the distributors and producers. This stream of income is real economic value. But this is not what was happening during the bubble except in some unusual instances—especially that of Amazon.com. Instead, the hype was about the stocks, not about the products of the companies issuing the stocks. The hype was creating financial value, not economic value.

The distinction made here between economic value and financial value is new, though it has strong roots in a financial literature which tries to decide if prices in the financial markets reflect actual value of companies. It's important to give an illustration of how financial value can diverge from economic value.

Investors get excited about the prospects for a company. They are told by various people that the company's growth rate is increasing and will stay at that level for years. So the investors bid up the price of the company's stock. But there is no real basis for the rumors, and soon the company announces that its expected growth rate is the same as it has been for the past two years. Investors' inflated expectations are deflated, and the company's stock tumbles. This process happens all the time. To believers in efficient markets, it should be said that the inaccurate rumors that drove the stock up are not entitled to the label "information," and share price that resulted from investors believing the rumor does not reflect real economic value, but only the financial value of the stock at the time.

Why the Huge Valuations for Internet Companies?

People who have an interest in driving up the prices of stocks understand that financial value cannot be made to exceed economic value for very long. Generally, accurate information about the company will emerge, its economic value can then be determined, and if the share price is too high, it will fall. Hence, to get and hold a financial price, it must be made to appear that the economic price is at that level. To inflate financial value over real value requires that real value be measured as more than it is, and there are often imaginative schemes to achieve this. In fact, this is a frequent practice in the capital markets.

For example, during the late 1980s, manufacturers spun off money-losing divisions as independent companies, and bank analysts repeatedly came up with positive reports for investors on the new firms. This was also done to support recapitalizations of airlines and other types of firms. The method of obtaining positive recommendations was to assume that labor productivity at the division or the airline would rise dramatically in the future. The rationale for this assumption was usually new management or an employee stock incentive plan. Enhanced productivity would result in lower costs to the company, which would then generate a profit. The profit could be forecast to grow in the future, permitting a positive discounted present value to give economic and hopefully financial value to the firm. Shares in the firms or bonds were then issued and sold to the public. In the actual event, however, most of the assumed productivity improvements never occurred, the companies made no profits, and therefore had no economic value so that their financial value collapsed. Investors took a bath.

During the dot-com bubble, a similar process occurred. Analysts made two crucial assumptions—rapid growth in Internet usage, and rapid growth in payments made to Internet companies—for use of the site or for advertising or for purchase of products, or for all of the above, according to the business model of the firm. Analysts also assumed moderate cost growth for the firm. They tried to justify these assumptions by reliance on experts who projected these things. With these favorable assumptions, a company could be argued to have a strong future income stream—so it didn't matter that it was currently losing money—and the discounted present value of the stream made the company appear to have real economic value. Further, if these two assumptions weren't enough to give the desired result, then the discounted cash flow could always be increased by lowering the interest rate used to discount future earnings. In a time in which the federal budget was going from deficit to surplus, and interest rates were beginning a long fall, an analyst could make an argument for using assumed low future interest rates to discount future assumed earnings so that the net present value was much increased.

There is disagreement among experts as to whether discounted present value calculations were actually being made for most of the start-up companies that were sold to the public during the bubble. In the experience of some knowledgeable observers, the calculations were often not actually made; when they were, they sometimes revealed that the prices at which IPOs were coming to market were outlandishly high, to say nothing of the higher post-IPO prices at which the companies' shares traded for a while.

Either way, however, the discounted present value calculations were not serving as a brake on the mania. Either the calculations were not made, or they were made in such a fashion, with the necessary favorable assumptions, that they could be used to justify financial valuations which were out of step with actual economic value.

Asked to justify high valuations for companies with few sales and no profits, analysts would give as an example an oil company with lots of oil in the ground but no production at the moment. So the company has no sales and no profits now, but because of its oil reserves, an investor can have confidence that there will be both sales and profits in the future. Having a position to do business on the Internet was said to be like having oil in the ground.

They would also point to the unusual strength of the world economy in the 1990s, especially that of the American economy. "In the last few years of the 1990s the data just kept getting better, culminating in an estimated five percent growth rate for real GDP in 2000—not an unusual growth rate for a poor country playing catch-up, or an economy recovering from a recession, but amazing for an advanced economy late in an economic expansion."[16] Analysts argued that the economy would continue to expand, and as it did, Internet business would grow very rapidly.

In any event, the favorable assumptions that gave dot-coms high valuations proved to be erroneous—even the growth rates of the American economy which had been so exciting were revised downward in 2001 so that it was clear that the economy hadn't been growing that fast at all. Hence the new economy companies had no real prospects for a favorable income stream. There was no oil in the ground. The true economic value of the firms was far below what the analysts had forecast, and when investors finally realized this, the financial value of the firms collapsed.

How the Financial Value Chain Should Have Worked

The way the Financial Value Chain operated during the bubble is not the way it is supposed to have operated, nor the way we expect it to operate day after day, month after month, year after year. The proper operation of the Financial Value Chain is as follows:

Venture capitalists, who typically demand a very high return on investment because the risk of failure is very high, do their best to ensure that the companies they've backed will have good management teams and a sustainable business model that will stand the test of time. Otherwise, the capital markets should put a relatively low value, consistent with their uncertain future stream of earnings, on venture-backed companies when they are offered for sale to the public. Likewise, investment bankers take public only companies with sound strategies and business models that provide the likelihood of giving investors a decent return.

On the other side of the process, portfolio managers, acting on behalf of investors, try to buy companies that are fairly priced in line with their economic value, and sell companies if they become overvalued, since buying or holding an overvalued stock will inevitably result in a loss. The job of the sell-side analysts—who work for investment banks and brokerage houses—is to objectively monitor the performance of public companies and determine whether or not their stocks are good or bad investments at any point in time, and recommend to investors to buy or sell those companies accordingly. This is what sell-side analysts are supposed to be doing. Accountants carefully audit the financial statements of companies, ensuring that they comply with established standards and represent the true situation of the firms' finances. This is what accountants should be doing because it gives investors and analysts the confidence to make decisions based on financial documents.

As we said before, this is how the system is supposed to work. But during the bubble, the system became quite dysfunctional.

What happened is that venture capitalists and investment bankers were not long in realizing that the Internet might provide the key to a whole new Gold Rush. They were quickly joined by entrepreneurs. Before long, the capital markets were spewing out new issues of stock for an increasingly excited market of investors.

The Financial Value Chain should have worked by having the investment banks make reasonably accurate projections of the future earnings of firms, and from those projections, deriving the net present economic value of firms—which is the basis for financial value. But how could it be done with a new technology involved?

The answer was that analysts made wildly optimistic projections of future earnings. In retrospect, rather than jumping to a conclusion that new firms would be wildly successful, analysts needed to do just the opposite. They had several ways to do this.

First, by being conservative in assumptions: It is common knowledge among analysts that every business plan presented to a venture capitalist, and every set of pro forma financials presented by a firm to its investment bank as the basis for raising capital, has an alternative set of sales and earnings estimates. Some are described as conservative, others as more likely, and still others as hopeful. The estimates which are conservative are generally exaggerated, and those which are more aggressive are said to be more likely than the conservative ones. An analyst quickly learns to expect this and to deflate the forecasts by applying more reasonable assumptions about the future. During the Internet boom, analysts accepted sales and earnings estimates, and conveyed them to the public, that were strikingly exaggerated.

Second, analysts, and the banks for which they work, could have generated more accurate estimates of future sales and earnings by giving a company enough time before taking it public for its income stream to become reasonably well defined. This was one of the reasons for what we shall see was a long-standing rule of thumb among the banks—which went by the wayside during the bubble—that a company shouldn't be offered to the public before having experienced a certain number of quarters of profitability.

Defending Enormous Valuations

The bubble years were not marked by either conservative assumptions or by patience. So analysts made extremely optimistic assumptions about market growth, buyers' behavior, and interest rates, and they invented large streams of profits that were discounted to the present to give substantial economic value to firms that had hardly been started. These estimates were a part of the valuation of the dot-coms when they were offered to the public.

Many, probably most, academics who developed and teach the discounted present value methodology are appalled at the perversion of the methodology which occurred in the investment banks. They observe that there is no real or honest use of present value methodology in all this.

Yet analysts defended themselves from criticism about their valuations. Responding to media criticism of financial analysts, a Wall Street analyst who followed Internet consulting firms stated: "It is too easy as they do on CNBC to slam the analysts for recommending stocks when they were very expensive. In the case of the Internet consulting firms, looking back before the correction in April 2000, the fundamentals were nothing short of pristine. The companies were growing at astronomical rates, and it looked as though they would continue to do so for quite a while. Under these assumptions, if you modeled out the financials for these companies and discounted them back at a reasonable rate, they did not seem all that highly valued."[17]

The other part of the valuation of a new IPO was relative. Once some companies had gone public and were getting substantial valuations, the value of other companies could be based on theirs. This was probably a much more common method of valuation than actually working through a discounted present value analysis. It was via this method of relative valuation that dot-com valuations began to exceed by wild margins those of older, already established firms. The market developed two categories—new economy firms and old economy firms. It's often said that the methods of valuation were different between the two. This isn't strictly correct. The methods were the same: discounted present value of the expected income stream, and comparisons of the relative value of different firms. But relative valuation was the favored method for new economy companies, and discounted present value for old economy companies. Further, when discounted present value calculations were used for new economy companies, the assumptions made were more favorable than when used for old economy companies. The expected income streams of old economy companies were based on experience and unfavorable assumptions (for example, that they would lose market share rapidly to new economy competitors), while the expected income streams for new economy companies were based not on experience but hope, and on favorable assumptions (for example, that they would rapidly build market share). Once the two categories—old and new economy—were established, a firm got a larger valuation if it could get itself considered to be in the new economy category. Many imaginative efforts were spent by what were in fact old economy companies trying to find a way into the new economy category (including, for example, spinning off dot-com versions of themselves).

The most successful such transformation of an old economy company into a new economy company was by Enron (and is described later in Chapter 5). The result was an enormous inflation of the value of the company's stock, supported by accounting which was at best misleading and at worst fraudulent. The collapse of the company was one of the most dramatic incidents of the bubble's aftermath.

Once a company was placed in the new economy category by a bank analyst, then the fundamental notion of valuation became to find another company with identical cash flows and circumstances which already was public and had a value in the market. Then the two companies should have the same value, so the company that wasn't yet public could be valued. Hence analysts were always looking for comparables. If companies had no profits, and even no sales (the company was giving away its services), then an analyst would ask how many hits or eyeballs it had on its Web site, and use that as the basis of comparison.

An analyst might value a company without profits and without sales by saying, "Here's a company that's similar and is public and has a valuation of $100 million, so this company which is like it except that it has only 80 percent of the number of hits on its Web site, must be worth $80 million."

"We were all on the inside of the bubble," said a representative of a large venture firm. "From there, it looked rational. All the valuations were relative." This observation may claim to be the key to the psychology of valuation that drove the entire bubble.

Is relative valuation of this sort rational? Some would say not at all—look at the ridiculous consequences of it: the vastly overvalued dot-coms and telecoms. But on the other hand, it often makes sense to value a company by looking at its peers. Still, during the Internet bubble the whole relative valuation exercise for new company stocks was in the wrong place—that is, all the similar companies were valued incorrectly. Further, the whole new economy was valued wrongly, but that went unnoticed by very many professionals and ordinary investors. U.S. productivity growth was not what it was thought to be during the new economy enthusiasm. Revisions in the figures in the summer of 2001 lowered the annual rates of productivity growth for 1998–2000 to much closer to the long run average growth rate for the U.S. economy, though 1996–2000 remains the best period since the 1960s, and in particular, dropped the spike in productivity growth reported for 2000 from 4.5 to 3 percent.[18] Probably, there never was a real new economy. But it wasn't only analysts who pretended there was—the government's statisticians contributed greatly to the error.

Talking Points

Various specialized financial firms work together to turn economic value created by operating companies into financial value for investors. During the bubble the Financial Value Chain worked like this: New economy companies were subject to the same method of valuation as old economy companies, but with very different assumptions. So favorable were the assumptions for new economy firms that their valuations bore little resemblance to reality, and soon financial values had diverged dramatically from economic values. This is how the bubble was blown up, and why it ultimately had to burst.

5 What it Meant to "Do the Right Thing" at Enron

"We're going to do the right thing and make money without having to do anything but the right thing."

—Andrew S. Fastow, Chief Financial Officer, Enron[19]

Most of the stories in this book are about entrepreneurs and start-up companies that are somewhat outside the mainstream of established companies in the economy. The entrepreneurial sector of the economy is very important to technological progress, and it involves somewhat specialized economic institutions that are designed to support innovation—including, most importantly, angel investors, venture capital firms, and the IPO process. But while this sector was at the core of the Internet bubble, the bubble was not limited to it; instead, in crucial instances, the bubble reached directly into the mainstream of the economy—into old and established firms and into traditional industries. These companies have long-established customer and supplier relationships, are well-known to regulators, and have distinguished outside directors, highly compensated executives, and familiar relations with accountants and bankers. There is none of the newness of the start-up and none of the excuses for missteps that accompany new firms, new technologies, and new business models. Yet some situations that occurred in the mainstream of the economy were enough to make most start-ups—and their role in the bubble—look to be models of propriety.

The scandals involving mainstream firms involved not the misuse of the IPO process, but the perversion of the most fundamental elements of U.S. capitalism: the systematic manipulation of accounting rules which apply to all firms, whatever their size, industry, and longevity; the corruption of the national political and regulatory processes; and the cynical abuse of advise to investors by bankers in order to gain fees from the companies whose stock they recommended.

At Enron, the bubble and its abuses reached into the heart of U.S. capitalism.

Enron as an Internet Company

Before 1990 Enron was a rather ordinary company selling natural gas. At that time Enron Chairman Kenneth Lay brought in McKinsey and Company to study the firm's prospects. McKinsey recommended that Enron move into financial products and services, and over time Enron became an energy trader using modern information technology to build markets. McKinsey partner Jeffrey K. Skilling joined Enron and later became its CEO.

Along with its shift to energy trading, Enron announced that it was also adopting a more highly delegated management system—a nontraditional, flatter organization in which people were paid substantial sums via bonuses and stock options. Thus Enron not only claimed to be a new economy company by virtue of the innovative use of information technology, it remade itself to look like a new economy company.

On June 12, 2001, Jeff Skilling, then CEO of Enron, was the final speaker at the Strategic Directions technology conference in Las Vegas, where he shared with his audience his vision of Enron as the center of trading in cyberspace. As described by Kurt Eichenwald and Diana B. Henriques in *The New York Times*, "The executive who introduced Skilling noted that Enron was being hailed as 'America's most innovative company' and that Mr. Skilling had been declared 'the Number One C.E.O. in the entire country.'" With that, as a videotape played, Mr. Skilling bounded onto the stage, tieless and in a sports coat. The Internet, he told the crowd, had barely begun to show its usefulness to business. U.S. industry would be transformed by its prowess, and the future of Enron would be found there, he said. "We couldn't do what we're doing now without the technology of the Internet."[20] Thus Enron, by changing its management structure, shifting the majority of its business to trading on the Internet, and by claiming to be a new economy company, made itself into an Internet company.

And it participated in the bubble. Its stock price rose rapidly as it announced striking increases in revenues and profits. However, it didn't collapse with the majority of the bubble companies when the bust began in early 2000. Instead, Enron was able to keep going well beyond the bursting of the bubble by taking steps that misled investors as to its financial situation and prospects. That it was an older company—not a dot-com start-up—and apparently a very large company kept away, the suspicions which investors directed at dot-coms.

Enron was also unusual in that it gave substantial sums to politicians and thereby obtained favorable legislation and regulatory rulings. Particularly valuable to the company were rulings permitting it to do certain things as it shifted its business from the old to the new economy; also very useful were rulings about what financial reporting was required of the company, and about the kind of accounting it was permitted to utilize. Political access helped Enron to grow more rapidly than other Internet companies, and deception enabled it to continue increasing its stock market value long after the bubble had burst for most new economy firms.

Inflating the Enron Bubble

A striking aspect of the Enron story is that the company's success in deceiving the investing public into believing that it was both growing very rapidly and profitable was made possible only by the energetic cooperation of many key elements of the Financial Value Chain, especially investment banks, accounting firms, and regulatory agencies.

Enron used several means to give its revenues and profits the appearance of enormous growth during the years of the bubble and beyond into late 2001. Its key methods were:

- A shift in Enron's business model to Internet-based trading suggested by consultants;

- Imaginative financing vehicles provided by investment banks;

- Favorable accounting treatment accorded by auditors; and

- Advantageous rulings by regulatory agencies.

So successful was Enron with its approach that it was believed to be one of the 10 largest companies in the United States. Yet late in 2001 most of the company's favorable financials suddenly appeared to investors to be a sham. Early in 2002 the Petroleum Finance Company recalculated Enron's total revenue for the year 2000 and reduced it from 100.8 billion dollars to about 9 billion dollars.[21]

Wall Street's Involvement

Investment banks conceived and created financial instruments (especially derivatives contracts) that allowed Enron to inflate its reported sales and profits to the extent that it appeared to be one of America's largest companies. Enron conceived and created other entities (especially partnerships) that allowed it to not reveal to the investing public the full extent of its liabilities. Enron paid substantial fees to the investment banks for the creation of these entities.

"Investment bankers at some big Wall Street firms," wrote a reporter for *The New York Times,* "helped create and find investors for complex partnerships that the Enron Corporation used to mask its true financial condition...After hatching that idea, some of those bankers...sold it to other corporations that wanted to make their financial statements look better too."[22]

Enron executives, especially Andrew S. Fastow, its Chief Financial Officer, and other financial executives who reported to the CFO, took personal positions in the financial partnerships and thereby made substantial sums for themselves. This created a conflict of interest in which some Enron managers were negotiating on behalf of Enron with other Enron managers who were negotiating on behalf of the partnerships. When Fastow said that at Enron he was going to do the right thing—as quoted at the outset of this chapter—was he engaging in hypocrisy or was it self-delusion?

Enron gave us the spectacle of a company in which some executives were able to exploit the company for personal gain, while others were left to carry the ultimate costs of the collapse of the company. It looks like one set of rules—very favorable ones—for those on top, and another set of rules—very much less favorable—for all the rest, including employees and investors.

The Key Role of the Accountants

Enron's accountants could have put a stop to the machinations promoted by Wall Street by refusing to let Enron record them in its financial statements in ways that essentially concealed them and their consequences from investors. But its accountants instead accepted the entities, and the financial statements that made use of them, as consistent with generally accepted accounting principles. The auditors also accepted other financial devices which inflated sales figures and understated expenses, thereby increasing reported profits. It seems that Enron was even allowed by its auditors to borrow money and report the money as operating cash flow.[23]

Why did they do it? Perhaps because Enron was a major customer of the accounting firm Arthur Andersen for consulting services as well. Such services tend to be far more lucrative to the accounting firms than are their auditing services.

Enron's accounting was full of devices to exaggerate revenues, minimize costs, and hide liabilities. Among the more important was market to market accounting by which Enron booked as immediate revenue the full amount of the expected cash flow of contracts that would yield money in the future.

Also significant were transactions between Enron and other companies and partnerships that had no real economic character but which served to inflate revenues and profits. "Over 15 months, from the beginning of the third quarter of 2000 through the third quarter of 2001, Enron reported pretax profits of $1.5 billion. Had Enron not used the [financial] artifices, the figure would have been 72 percent lower: $429 million...There was a large transfer of wealth to the Fastow partnerships, which were guaranteed huge profits while taking no risks. Those transactions helped provide $30 million for Mr. Fastow and millions for other Enron insiders."[24]

What had happened to the company's accountants? How could they accept devices so riddled with conflicts of interest and so potentially damaging to the company? How could they not require Enron to clearly divulge these transactions to investors and admit their impact on the company's revenues and its risks?

The answer is that accounting had changed subtly but significantly over the years. The objective of the accountants became not to provide proper information to investors, but to go as far as possible with accounting interpretations favorable to client companies. Thus, the critical questions for the accountants became: Can we make a case for this favorable interpretation? Can we defend it if called upon to do so? Can we rationalize it?

The proper question, "What is the right way to support the overall objective of transparency to the investor?", which is what accounting is supposed to provide to the financial markets, was asked only in passing, if at all, and with little or no impact on the numbers ultimately released. Accounting became a game in which both the company and its accountants tried to provide as little—not as much—transparency as possible.

This development did not occur only at Enron. This sort of accounting had its roots many years before the Internet bubble and had reached into many of the major corporate entities in U.S. business. Enron leapt more fully into the Internet enthusiasm than other large, long-established companies, and it was thereby the more damaged when its own bubble finally burst, but the financial tools it used to inflate its revenues, and profits and thereby its stock price, were being used at many other mainstream companies. Enron might have felt more compelled to stretch accounting rules because it was in the bubble, and so it needed to maintain the appearance of very rapid growth even more than if it were just a mainstream company.

Equity Analysts Promote the Company

Analysts at investment banks recommended Enron for purchase by investors and continued recommending it in many instances even as its stock crashed in value in the fall of 2001. In some instances, the recommendations to buy continued and even became stronger as the company's share price declined from the low $80s to less than a dollar. For example, Alliance Capital is reported to have bought Enron shares on behalf of the Florida State Pension Fund in large amounts as the share price declined from $22 to $9 and then to have sold the shares at $.28 each.[25]

In principle, the analyst's reasoning could have been justifiable. The financial markets do sometimes experience share price declines that are unmerited and which will be reversed. When share prices decline, therefore, sometimes real buying opportunities are created. When seeking a buying opportunity, analysts might recommend a stock whose price doesn't turn around, and thus the purchase causes losses for the investor. This is the ordinary operation of the market.

But when there is a conflict of interest, it's hard to accept that a mere mistake was made. That is, when an analyst for a bank recommends shares in a company to the public while the bank is receiving substantial fees from the company, or while the bank is dumping shares in the company that it owns itself, or while it is dumping shares owned by its preferred clients, then it is likely more than a neutral mistake. In effect, conflicts of interest undermine the credibility of the entire system of analyst recommendations.

Politicians Lend Their Aid

Enron made substantial campaign contributions to many politicians of both parties. Reporters looking for specific favors that office holders provided to Enron in return have apparently found little. But this doesn't mean that Enron received nothing for its political contributions.

There were, in fact, decisions of regulatory agencies that were favorable to Enron, and Congress played a role in championing these. Perhaps favorable decisions would have been made in the absence of political contributions, but perhaps not.

"Let's get real, folks," wrote Rich Karlgaard, Publisher of *Forbes*, in discussing the Enron collapse. "Tax and accounting laws are written as favors to one group or another and are manipulated with impunity in practice."[26] Certainly Enron received tax and accounting advantages and manipulated the regulations with years of impunity in practice.

Further, Enron pursued its transformation into a fast-growing Internet company without interference from the many regulatory commissions—including the Securities and Exchange Commission, the Treasury, the Federal Energy Regulatory Commission, the Fed, the Labor Department, and others—any of which were in a position to challenge it. "While each agency was doing its narrowly defined job, nobody was protecting shareholders," wrote a commentator for a new economy magazine.[27]

Evaporating Employee Pensions

For years Enron maintained a pension plan for employees in which thousands of Enron workers kept substantial amounts of their investment in the form of Enron stock. In the months before the company's stock collapse, its chairman assured employees that the company's finances were sound. And for a critical period in the decline of the company's stock during the fall of 2001, the company changed plan administrators and prohibited employees from selling the stock, even as executives whose holdings of company stock were outside the plan were in many instances selling their shares. The consequence of several factors—including the heavy investment by employees in company stock, the transaction freeze, and the collapse of the company's share price—was that many employees lost virtually the entire value of their pension accounts.

Today State Street Corporation is assuming the oversight of Enron's retirement plans at the behest of the U.S. Department of Labor. State Street had itself held some 16 million shares of Enron stock at the end of September 2001, when the company's meltdown began, and as of the end of 2001, it had reduced its holdings to about half a million shares. [28]

Unethical, Unfair, but Illegal?

Whether any or all of what was done by Enron and its executives was illegal is a matter that will concern the courts for years. Illegality will depend not only on the possible violation of specific regulations, but more generally—and regardless of the legality of specific actions—on whether or not there was intent by the company and its executives to conceal information and deceive investors.

Further, according to U.S. law, literal compliance with accounting principles is not a sufficient defense against prosection if it creates a fraudulent or misleading impression in the minds of shareholders. [29]

It appears that prosecutors see criminality in the Enron story. "At the foundation of the company's downfall was a series of multimillion dollar crimes, legal experts and former prosecutors said…These include false valuation of assets, bogus deals between related parties, and millions of dollars pocketed by participants along the way." [30] But whether or not this indictment can be proven in court remains to be seen.

Enron's Significance

Enron was already an established corporation long before the Internet was conceived. It had much greater ability than a start-up to conceal what was really happening in the firm and thereby was able to hold on long after the Internet bubble had burst and start-ups were collapsing on every side. It was some 18 months after the crash had begun that Enron began its tumble, but when it came, it came quickly. And because this was the heart of the economy, the shock was profound, bringing with it:

- The collapse of the company itself;

- The destruction of one of the nation's major accounting firms;

- The besmirching of the reputation of the accounting profession generally;

- The embarrassment of many of the nation's most important political leaders;

- A shock to citizens' confidence in the reliability of the U.S. financial system as a whole, and especially in the integrity of the information upon which that confidence was based;

- The revelation of the inefficacy of regulators, who missed the big picture for the details and who caught small violators while large-scale violations went unnoticed for lengthy periods and were finally brought to public view not by the regulators but by suspicious investors;

- The loss of hundreds of millions of dollars invested in Enron; and

- The loss of jobs and pensions of thousands of Enron employees.

Talking Points

Enron was different from most of the other companies that are discussed in this book because it wasn't a start-up but instead was an old, established company. Nevertheless, Enron played an important part in the Internet bubble.

Enron transformed its image in the public mind from a natural gas company into an energy trader, much of whose business was done on the Internet. With the help of investment banks it created financial entities, often partnerships, that allowed it to magnify its revenues and reduce its expenses in ways that gave it rapid growth and profitability, and made it very difficult for investors to keep track of its debts. Its own executives and partners in some of its banks participated financially as individuals in these entities. Its accountants accepted these devices, while contributions to politicians helped result in favorable regulatory decisions.

It created the appearance of a corporate culture—of work habits, organizational structure, delegation, and incentive compensation—which supposedly drove creativity and performance among its employees. In consequence, it appeared to grow financially much more than it actually did, and its stock price rose dramatically. By mid-2001 it appeared to be one of the largest companies in the United States.

Enron outlasted the collapse of the Internet bubble by more than a year because of its great size and financial resources. When it collapsed, many small investors were very badly hurt, especially its own employees. Because many executives seemed to have been able to sell before the stock value collapsed, a public scandal was created.

The debacle at Enron occurred because of the willingness of consultants, bankers, accountants, regulators, and politicians to take actions that had the effect of misleading the public about the financial state of the company. Most of what was done at Enron is also done at other large companies, perhaps in some cases even on the same scale, so there may be more Enrons waiting to happen.

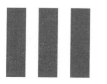 # Inexperienced Leaders

In the business press it's become common to refer to dot-com and telecom executives as dopes who managed their companies so poorly that they drove them to collapse. For example, "With the dumb dot-com money gone," wrote the editors of a major new economy magazine after the bubble burst and many dot-coms were failing, "the ... race [for efficient and effective business performance] begins in earnest."[31]

But is this really the core of the matter—were dot-com and telecom managers simply dumb? And if so, why did so many sophisticated investors—especially venture capitalists and institutional investors—give them so much money? Or was something more at work—was the behavior of dot-com entrepreneurs often in response to directions or incentives provided by their financial backers?

6   Dumb Kids?

Blaming the Entrepreneur—He's Dumb

The stereotype is a kid in his 20s running an Internet start-up on other people's money, living the high life, and in the end blowing it all. But what about the older, more experienced people who gave him all that money? Did they just turn away in blissful ignorance while he tried to figure out how the company should spend investors' money?

Not likely. Far more likely was a situation in which the investors gave advice and direction to young entrepreneurs. This was, in fact, often the case. In instance after instance, venture firms encouraged dot-com entrepreneurs to follow a get-big-fast strategy and provided, as an incentive for the entrepreneur to do so, funding for his or her company.

In essence, the advent of Internet technology allowed financial firms to take advantage of public excitement, to the ultimate detriment of both the new companies and their late-stage investors.

The conclusion should be that many of the dot-com entrepreneurs weren't very smart about how they managed their companies, but they certainly didn't create the financial bubble. This isn't to say that many entrepreneurs were not willing partners with the financial institutions in inflating the bubble and trying to profit from it. In fact, some dot-coms and some telecom start-ups were founded by people from financial institutions, and their primary purpose was not to build companies, but instead to create a vehicle for a public offering. In a sense this was their role, at least while they were in the investment banks. But when they left the banks to start companies which were not really intended to be viable businesses, but merely vehicles for financial manipulations, they stepped over a line.

Most dot-com entrepreneurs were not of this type, however, but were people trying to build businesses, that is, to create economic value. They were not focused on the capital markets, and certainly lacked the know-how and resources to take a company public. The entrepreneur's role was to build the company's economic value; the role of the financial institutions was to build its financial value.

This is not to say that there is a simple division of responsibility between the management of a firm and its financial backers—one responsible for economic value, and the other for financial value. It cannot be so simple. The CEO of a firm is responsible for the firm in its entirety and must listen to the financial markets, for they change continually. In fact, all markets—product, supply, labor, and financial—change continually—that's what business is about. So it's inappropriate for entrepreneurs to complain that the financial markets changed on them, and to blame their financial backers for the changes. There is an unpleasant whiff of the attitude of entitlement when some entrepreneurs complain that the rules of the financial game changed on them midcourse—as if the rules shouldn't have changed, and it was unfair that they did. But how could the rules not change when start-ups had been so greatly overvalued? It was the responsibility of the CEOs to anticipate and adapt to the changes.

But nothing in what the entrepreneur was able to do created the bubble or brought it to an end. The entrepreneur is affected by the financial markets—he or she doesn't drive the financial markets. The entrepreneur takes the price of his or her firm that the financial markets place on it; the entrepreneur doesn't determine the price in the financial markets, and he or she has influence, little though it is, on financial value mainly by building the economic value of the firm.

Financial market value is, however, affected by the financial institutions which make up the Financial Value Chain. They are not merely price takers in the market, but have more influence than that. The great Internet bubble occurred in financial value, and was the responsibility primarily of the financial institutions who sensed the opportunity and exploited it.

Amazon.com's Miracle

Amazon.com led the way. Jeff Bezos at Amazon.com pulled off a sort of miracle, violating all the prescriptions for how to build a company in his market context, and afterwards, everyone else wanted to do the same. They had all learned a wrong lesson—believing that Bezos had it right—especially the venture capitalists, who spread the misconceptions widely. They were quickly joined by investment bankers who were looking for firms to take to market. Venture capitalists pushed and investment bankers pulled entrepreneurs toward the public market much too fast, adapting Amazon's strategy to multiple settings. Only a handful of the entrepreneurs who adopted the advice were successful; while in pursuing the strategy other entrepreneurs spent great sums of money, and led late investors to a financial slaughter.

Bezos had adopted a strategy that shouldn't have worked, but because it was the early days of the Internet, he was able to pull it off for years. Essentially the strategy was one of prodigious spending to build wide brand recognition among the public, and to acquire market share without regard to profitability.

The strategy stressed so-called first mover advantage: Brand building and growth above all other aspects of a business. Although if was an old strategy, and had a Japanese flavor—it was the strategy many Japanese manufacturers had used to break into the American market—it received a label for the Internet age: GET-BIG-FAST! "Tossing aside just about every experience-honed tenet of business to build business in a methodical fashion, Internet businesses have adopted a grow-at-any-cost, without-any-revenue, claim-as-much-market-real-estate-before-any-one-moves-in approach to business. This mentality has come to be known as 'Get Big Fast.'"[32] In pursuit of this strategy, venture firms pushed much more money on entrepreneurs than they wanted or could use effectively, and bankers pulled their clients toward IPOs much more rapidly than the business progress of the companies warranted.

How Amazon Flouted the Rules

Amazon's importance lay in the fact that its strategy appeared to work despite the absence of the conditions that were thought to be necessary for its success. Hence, Amazon suggested to the financial community that the ordinary rules didn't apply to Internet space.

One of the conditions for the success of the get-big-fast strategy did apply to Amazon. Its strategy did require large up-front investments, and Amazon made them. But the other two conditions didn't apply. There are no network effects of significance; that is, it doesn't matter to a customer where another customer purchases books or any of the myriad of other products Amazon now sells. And book selling has large established players who have defended their established customer relations, even becoming online retailers, and have thereby kept Amazon's profit margins so low that it has never yet been profitable.

Even at the beginning of the excitement in the financial markets over Amazon, some analysts pointed out the weakness in its strategy. Where is Amazon's long-term competitive advantage—something every business plan proposed to early-stage investors must have—it was asked with suspicion. "Amazon.com is not a technology company, it is not a software company..." wrote Jonathan Cohen of Merrill Lynch.[33]

Established booksellers, large and small, have always watched Amazon in amazement. How could a company which essentially sells below total cost continue in business? How could it obtain a valuation in the billions and raise hundreds of millions of dollars from investors so that year by year it could expand, while continuing to lose money?

In part the answer lies in its very novelty. Amazon was the first of the online retailers and as such attracted substantial publicity. It was called to the attention of investors the world over early in its existence by a favorable article in the lead column of the front page of *The Wall Street Journal*. Amazon was widely hailed as the forerunner of a new breed of e-retailers (e-tailers) which would displace existing brick and mortar firms. As such, Amazon was at the center of one of the first streams of enthusiasm which fed into the great river of hype which was building about Internet businesses. Amazon gained greatly from this.

In addition, book selling appeals to many investors as a business made for the Internet. A customer can merely visit the Amazon site, locate a book, pay for it online, and have it shipped to her or him, avoiding an inconvenient trip to a bookstore which may not have the book in stock. Some people will wish to go to a store to browse and to inspect books, of course, and they can continue to do so. But for those who seek the convenience of online shopping, it provides real value. When Amazon offered prices competitive with or better than bookstore competitors, the advantage of the e-tailer was even more evident.

So Amazon defied the rules because it was first, and because book selling seemed to investors unusually suited to the Internet. It also succeeded because Jeff Bezos raised as much money as he could whenever he could, so that when the bloom fell off the Internet rose, Amazon was not destroyed by inability to get additional capital to fund its continuing operating losses. At least that is the story so far.

The Learning Failure

A serious deficiency of the get-big-fast strategy is that it doesn't allow the trial-and-error method of determining the right business plan, and in a market space as new as the Internet, entrepreneurs' early presumptions about successful business models were often wrong. But growing fast and spending lots of money almost foreclosed a significant shift of model midstream. It was possible for a management team to learn from experience, of course, and to modify certain tactics in the marketplace, but that was about all. An example of this weakness of the get-big-fast approach is eToys.

eToys had a great deal going for it. Its founder, Toby Lenk, was a top graduate of Harvard Business School and had been a corporate vice president for strategic planning at Disney. At the time he founded eToys he was in his midthirties and possessed great energy and endurance. One venture investor in eToys told me in mid-1999 how Lenk had flown from San Jose to Los Angeles to deal with a last-minute problem with an acquisition, worked all night, returned to San Jose the next morning and resumed his schedule without sleep. "That's the kind of drive and commitment a successful entrepreneur must have," the venture capitalist told me with conviction.

Another key member of the leadership team, Steven Schoch, CFO, had earned an MBA from Dartmouth, and had been vice president and treasurer of the *Times/Mirror* in Los Angeles. He was in his late thirties. Before coming to eToys he had put together a $100 million financing for the *Times*.

It was a leadership team in which venture investors could have confidence and take pride.

With his training in strategic planning at Disney, Lenk was able to present a persuasive story to investors. eToys was not simply an online retailer, as he told it. It would revolutionize the retail business in toys by building a wholly modern distribution system based on new warehouses.

Lenk saw the success of his company as a given: the opportunity to save parents from having to drag their kids to Toys R Us; the variety and availability of thousands of products at their fingertips; an insightful Web site, with suggestions by age, gender, interest, and wish lists, indicating exactly what the children wanted. This was a Web site for adults. The concept seemed infallible, especially to Lenk. He stated it best, "It's a labor of love. I know this sounds silly, but we have soul. This site has soul."

In late 1996, Lenk got an investment from Bill Gross of Idealab to start eToys. In October 1997 eToys launched its Web site. Before long the Web site was winning awards for its design and ease of use, and substantial traffic. Revenues in 1998 were about $15 million—more than Lenk had forecast. In the fall of that year, Lenk had added to toys the sale of music videos, software, and video games to the eToys site.

Toby Lenk envisioned that eToys would be a Web destination, not unlike that of his old employer Disney: a premier destination for families with kid-related needs. His plan was to start small, build eToys into a brand, and then expand into other kid-related categories. "From Disney, I knew that once you have a relationship with a family, you have them for 10 years," he said.

eToys received enormous favorable publicity. It topped most of the Web site lists, and was seen as a savvy, user-friendly Web site. Forrester, Jupiter, and other market research companies were 100 percent behind them. "They'll have a very strong showing," said Nicole Vanderbilt, an analyst at Jupiter communications in New York in March 1999. "eToys is one of the top dozen online-only retailers. eToys sells a product that people want to buy over the Web, and the company has executed exceptionally well, recently placing first in a ranking of e-shopping experiences compiled by online research firm resource marketing."

As a poster child for e-tailing, there was overwhelming support by the stock market, the public, and research groups, giving investors and the CEO too much confidence. This overconfidence was clear in Lenk's business plan: to hit an unprecedented $750 to $900 million in revenues in order to make a profit. It was clear in the $50 million invested by venture capital firms upfront, for a company that did not plan to be profitable for five years. And it was clear in the approach—to spend large amounts of money on advertising in order to obtain customers to achieve sales goals.

In May 1999, Goldman Sachs led the underwriting of a public offering of stock. It had been about 18 months from founding to IPO.

The company used the proceeds of the IPO to make acquisitions, to enter the British market, and to cover rising operating losses.

Within five months of its IPO, eToys had reached a peak market cap of $10.3 billion, two and one-half times that of Toys R Us, its counterpart in the brick and-mortar universe. So what if Toys R Us had 40 years' more experience and $1.6 billion more in sales?

Lenk did not lack confidence. "We have perhaps the best consumer experience on the Web. We went from nothing to $150 million in revenue last year in a completely new space that we created, in a very crazy environment with 10 competitors spending $200 million against us. And we beat everybody hands down because we're so good."

But from the start, eToys encountered competition. Its well-established old economy rival, Toys R Us, created a Web site in June 1998, but eToys stayed ahead. In the Christmas season of 1999, eToys had more than $100 million in sales, about three times Toys R Us' online sales. That year the Toys R Us' Web site was marred by site crashes and delivery delays, so that it was forced to give some customers gift certificates to try to hold their loyalty.

eToys was never able to become profitable. In fact, its apparently successful 1999 Christmas season was the beginning of its undoing. Overall, the bricks and mortar companies had strong advantages in costs (for example, they didn't have to ship their products—customers came to pick them up). They had established relationships with suppliers. And as other online retailers, such as Amazon.com, got into the toy business by teaming with Toys R Us, pressure was put on eToys' profit margins. Once investors realized this, availability of new investment to fund continuing growth and operating losses dried up. When the company did obtain financing, it was on ruinous terms. At the end of February 2001, the company filed for bankruptcy; in early March it closed its Web site, and on April 6, 2001, it closed its doors owing creditors some $200 million.

In the end there simply was not sufficient profit margin in the online toy business to support eToys, or at least not in the way Lenk had approached the business. Whether or not a different business model might have succeeded cannot be known, because with growth the dominant objective, there was no time to learn.

eToys had gone from inception to IPO in 18 months, and from IPO to bankruptcy in 21 months. It had been a wild ride.

Early investors had bet on an unproven business model, and had given Lenk only a year and a half to prove it. But the underwriters of its IPO didn't ask for proof—growing sales at whatever cost was enough to persuade them to offer shares to the public. The public bought shares in an IPO only six months before the Christmas season of 1999 revealed the inadequacy of the company's business model to careful observers (the profit margin wasn't there) and, in fact, the public kept bidding up the stock for yet a few more months early in 2000 until the entire dot-com bubble began to burst.

eToys had tried to do a lot very quickly. It had to build brand recognition, an efficient Web site, a chain of suppliers, a new physical distribution system for toys, and an effectively operating company, all at once. Inevitably, the company had to make plans based on suppositions rather than market experience, and later when market experience suggested changes in the plan, only limited changes could be made. The pressure to grow quickly meant a certain rigidity of plan that kept the company from adjusting to what it was learning in the marketplace.

But almost none of these concerns made their way into the reports analysts did on the company until well after its stock was in full decline. In fact, looking back on how bank analysts evaluated eToys, it's hard to see any analysis, rather the reports were only providing justification for investment at very high share prices. From the start, data was available on the toy market in America, and criticism of eToys was available from its bricks and mortar competitors, which permitted an analyst, if he or she were so inclined, to identify the fatal weaknesses in eToys' business model. Being charitable to the analysts, one could say that perhaps they disregarded the criticism of eToys from its competitors because they recognized that the competitors were biased in their own behalf. Yet, the competitors were right, and the role of analysts is to understand the business models of the firms they follow and evaluate them. To reject legitimate criticism because of its possible bias is to blind one to what may be valuable insights. Hence, the issue with respect to the criticism of eToys was not its source, biased or not, but its validity. And the criticism was valid. The analysts were wrong to ignore it. Perhaps the motivation for rejecting it was that the banks for whom the analysts worked were profiting in various ways from both eToys and from other new economy firms, and didn't want to upset the apple cart.

So why didn't analysts torpedo the stock early on? They were either stupid, or they were willing to be taken into what was not much different from a confidence game. Analysts are not stupid. I once had the CEO of a very large retailer tell me that the most difficult part of his job was meeting with Wall Street analysts who followed his company. He described them as young, pushy, very smart, and as knowing more about his company than he did. "They ask questions which are right to the point, and usually know more about the answer than I do," he complained.

Since analysts are not stupid, but much to the contrary, it's hard to escape the conclusion that they were engaged in what was merely momentum analysis (that is, discovering what stocks had prices which were rising rapidly in the market, for whatever reason) which they disguised as value analysis (discovering firms for which the financial markets were not yet giving full financial value for the economic value being created). This sleight of hand, never disclosed to the public, mislead small investors.

At the very time that Wall Street analysts were issuing buy recommendations for Amazon.com and Webvan, for example, there were strong criticisms of the business models of the two companies in the quarterly journals of major consulting firms. Did the analysts not read them? Or did they dismiss them because they weren't relevant to momentum analysis? If the analysts weren't doing value analysis, then why did they not so inform their reading public? Certainly they would seem to have had a duty of disclosure on such a crucial point.

The story was different for Webmiles, the subject of our first in-depth contribution. The firm had a great idea, attracted money, but got caught in the bubble's deflation. Then the entrepreneurs discovered that investors can get tricked by the mirage of easy money—offered a good sale-out price by a major German company, Webmiles' investors insisted it wasn't enough and turned it down. Only by adept managing of investors' expectations was the management team of Webmiles able to revive the offer and obtain investor approval for the sale.

Contribution: Webmiles

Patrick Boos, founder and former CEO of Webmiles
The Ups and Downs of Webmiles

The Idea

We sat in front of the credit card terminal pulling our hair out. Only five orders had been placed in the last 24 hours, and one of the credit cards was obviously no good. From experience, we knew that we would never be able to collect the money on that order. Our dream of moonlighting as online booksellers was in danger. Loretta was an attorney in Munich, and I worked for a television network in Berlin. Late in 1998, neither of us could resist the siren song of the rapid development of the Internet. Five thousand DM of seed capital, a working agreement with a book distributor, and no shortage of enthusiasm. With that, we had an excellent chance of challenging Amazon—or so we thought! In fact, however, orders remained at around five per day.

Quite honestly, we were amazed that even one customer had found our Web site, considering that we had done no advertising since it had not been calculated in our start-up budget. That brought us unavoidably to the question of how we would deal with our small competitors—we had long since forgotten about Amazon. We needed a clever idea that would bring customers to us exclusively.

Loretta and I were both passionate about accumulating Frequent Flyer Miles, which always influenced our purchase decisions. That led us to the idea to purchase "miles" from Lufthansa and to pass them on to our customers. We arrived at an idea to create a new form of Frequent Flyer Miles, namely "miles" for shopping on the Internet. We would give shoppers Frequent Flyer Miles on key airlines for purchases made on the Internet. We would sell that capability to Internet-based vendors. And so Webmiles was born.

The next morning I investigated the availability of the domain name: "Webmiles." In view of the fact that a short time later domain names were being bought and sold for seven-figure sums, it seems absurd in retrospect that we waited a few days before acting because we considered 100 DM to be too expensive. Besides that, we were not so sure that our idea was a good one.

We reserved the domain name and began to think about our business plan. The result was a written abstract of our plan. We sent this to potential customers where I had contacts through previous jobs. One of those was Conrad Elektronik, Germany's largest electronics distributor, who gave us an opportunity to present our concept. We could hardly believe it upon receiving confirmation of the appointment. What exactly should we present? How would we field questions from the experts? We had neither experience with bonus programs and customer loyalty, nor had we even thought about a technical solution which would allow us to realize our idea.

What can one do in such a situation other than to shamelessly exaggerate and thereby suggest that the platform is nearly complete, other clients are about to sign a contract, the financing is all sewn up, and that success is practically guaranteed? So that's what we did. Our representations were supported by a punchy presentation on a laptop loudly betraying itself as the property of my employer via a large inventory sticker. Despite all of that, the presentation was a complete success. The Director of New Media for Conrad Elektronik was thrilled and committed himself to participate. We left his office, ambled coolly and nonchalantly down the street, fearful that he was watching us through the window. Once within the safe confines of our auto the joy burst out of us like an explosion. We had lined up our first client. Webmiles **had** to be a success.

Seed Funding

Having returned to earth, we asked ourselves: how do we really get the financing we need to get started? To begin, we did our homework and began to write a business plan. With it we planned to approach banks in order to get things moving. We anticipated that we would have to put up all of our parent's earthly possessions as collateral, since we ourselves had little.

To our surprise, we remained lucky. A few days later, in the middle of the night, Loretta called me, her voice full of excitement. On that same evening at dinner, she had let on to another guest in a roundabout way what we were planning. As it turned out, this gentleman was a consultant to young venture capitalists. Loretta couldn't exactly tell me what venture capital was, but her fellow diner had said it would be the answer to our problems and that I must come to Munich immediately. Two days later, I flew to Munich. We met the gentleman, Dominik von Ribbentropp. By and by we told him of our idea. Beforehand however, we saw to it that he signed a nondisclosure agreement. We were fearful our idea might fall into the wrong hands.

After our meeting with Dominik, he told us that it was clear to him that our idea had immense potential, and that without difficulty we would receive several millions in start-up money. How would that work? A couple of sassy young people have an idea, write up a business plan, and receive therefore, several million marks. For me, it was inconceivable.

But why not? We made an agreement with Dominik: If he would support us in the search for capital, we would make him a partner in Webmiles. From there on out, everything went very quickly. A week later, we had six presentations with VC firms scheduled within two days. Beforehand we had business cards printed in a copy shop and completed the business plan. Dominik sent me the latest figures, in which terms like "sales multiple" and "capital at risk" appeared, but which meant nothing to me. The best part however was that Dominik's spreadsheet showed our yet-to-be-founded enterprise to have a value in the range of eight figures (DM). In preparation for our meetings with the VCs we needed only to rehearse briefly before we were using these expressions and valuations as though we had never done anything else.

The investors were quickly convinced. Five of six firms were interested in financing our idea. We decided in favor of a firm that had been the swiftest to get things moving. Looking back, this was indeed our most unbelievable experience in the New Economy. We could pick and choose who would be allowed to invest.

After the first presentation, our VC did a cursory check of our projections on market potential and realization. There were a few questions posed about competition, legal concerns, and the completeness of our team. That was it. In regard to the last question, it was clear to Loretta and me that we wanted Dominik on board as our CFO. After a further meeting, we drafted a letter of intent. Ten days later, on March 15, 1999, we sat with a notary public and signed the partnership documents. I thought I was dreaming. We had received a commitment for financing, including a subsidy of four million DM. For what? It came down to a dashing presentation, 60 pages of text, and a vision. We quit our jobs. We had finally become entrepreneurs.

Start-Up

Before we could begin, we needed an appropriate office. Ideally we imagined a spacious loft with large windows, hardwood floors, and without question, a terrace. We quickly found something: an ideal space in an old factory. The real estate agent collected a commission of 35,000 DM. No problem, we had enough money, not only for the space, but for the architect as well who designed our new digs. In the meantime, we had to consign ourselves to something less comfortable. The search for qualified people occupied the following weeks and months. The market was tight: a rapidly growing number of start-ups were already competing for the top talent. Our first priority was to recruit the leaders of our six business lines, which we had identified in our business plan. Our investors remained distant from day-to-day operations, yet constantly emphasized the importance of the "equity story." That meant above all: growth, growth, growth. Hire whoever was available and develop as many products as possible for as many markets as possible. We thought little about complexity and cost consciousness, and neglected thereby some of the fundamental rules of good business.

Nine months after the founding of Webmiles, 50 people were working for us. Our office was bursting at the seams. The noise level was on par with an airport. We had to rent space in a neighboring building. Nevertheless, enthusiasm and dedication among the employees was incomparable. They had all contracted Webmiles fever, working until midnight and then going out to party afterwards. Not only the employees, but the "in-crowd" as well, took to Webmiles t-shirts and baseball caps. They developed a unique culture.

Our investor was extremely pleased. The Web site was developing beautifully. We were signing new large and midsize clients, and firms without an Internet presence as well. In contrast to many other start-ups, we had revenues of more than two million DM in our first nine months of operation. We were ahead of plan on other points as well. Our burn-rate accelerated in parallel to these developments. The expansion abroad, the talent we had lured from top consulting firms, and the investment in technology meant we would need more money before year's end.

Luckily, we had presented our concept to a number of venture capitalists. Among the most enthusiastic candidates was a top-drawer investment bank and one of the leading sources of venture capital worldwide. Our goal was to raise 10 to 20 million DM through a very positive evaluation of our company. That meant a funding of five times our seed capital. At the same time, we broke the nine-figure barrier. As negotiations with our "eager" investor were dragging and we urgently needed cash, we returned to our first round investor and arranged for interim financing. With five million DM in fresh capital, we could breathe again and go to the bargaining table with more confidence. In the first quarter of 2000, we received a commitment for 15 million DM from our preferred investor.

Growth

Webmiles became Germany's model start-up. Success, visibility, and a five million DM television and radio campaign encouraged much attention in the media. On top of that came the story of Loretta: a very young and successful cofounder, an example of the rise of a new generation, which led to unprecedented press coverage.

Meanwhile, there were 100 employees, who in part were sharing desks. The secretary working for Loretta and me sat at the gap between our two desks. Besides our conference room, there was only one other closed space, originally intended as a boardroom. As the IT team needed quiet however, its eight members were put in the board room along with an air filtering system, without which it would have been unbearable. Because the conference room was constantly occupied by employees, we were always improvising places for conferences. Meetings took place in the tiny kitchen, on the terrace, in the café across the street, or in the apartments of the employees.

Thanks to the new financing, we were able to push our expansion even further. Our investors spurred us on, particularly towards international expansion, with the idea of taking the company public looming in the background. In a few months we built teams in England, France, Italy, Spain, and Sweden. Loretta and I did nothing but fly around Europe, recruiting people, finding collaborative partners, and accelerating further the burn-rate to an even more frightful level. The equity story, however, was still in line. The concept appeared to have proven itself, and there was great interest from clients abroad. The vision of a company with worldwide presence was near at hand.

In Germany, sales were going well too. As the Internet and e-commerce developed at breakneck pace, companies such as booksellers and online banks were dependent on an instrument like Webmiles to keep competitors at bay and to foster customer loyalty. With the average value of a signed contract topping 100,000 DM, our expectations had been thoroughly exceeded. We had quickly accumulated a portfolio of 50 firms in Germany and again as many internationally. Our largest client had contractually bound himself to a minimum purchase of 2.4 million DM worth of Webmiles for a one-year period. That convinced every investor of the value of our business model. From their point of view it was now time to make their exit, taking their profits, via an IPO. Webmiles was an ideal candidate for the German new stock market (the New Market), in which comparable companies had enjoyed unbelievable growth in valuations.

IPO

We began planning the beauty contest, and agreed to invite six investment banks to hear our pitch. The presentation took place over two days. Some bankers appeared with as many as seven companions. The projected value of our company rose to a level unimaginable to us. The average was around 300 million DM prior to any additional investment. Most noteworthy was that all of the banks were exclusively interested in the upside potential—risks were not discussed.

Of course every invited bank considered itself our best choice. Each bank offered sufficient reasons why we should choose it. Because of their excellent research department, we chose Schroders-Salomon-Smith-Barney.

In April 2000, as we were choosing our investment bank, the first signs of a downturn by publicly held Internet companies appeared in the U.S. and directly thereafter in Europe. Initially we did not give this much attention, and the Bankers too regarded it as a short-term correction.

We marched on according to plan. A meeting to discuss the Webmiles IPO turned out to be a significant day for us. About 35 people—among them investors, bankers, attorneys, accountants, people from the advertising and investor relations agencies, and we three partners—met to discuss the necessary steps for an IPO, which had been planned for July 2000.

In connection with the kick-off, teams were formed, beginning their work immediately: a prospectus had to be produced; a presentation for admission to the New Market and a road show prepared. Meanwhile the stabilization of the overall share market predicted by the analysts and us had yet to materialize. On the contrary, the mood continued to darken. We founders began to discuss whether or not the time was right for taking the company public. Suddenly we no longer had a set date from the bank. It was clear to us that the bank was intent on not taking any risk. That meant that they would sign the sales agreement a few days before the IPO, if at all. We remained optimistic and continued with business as usual.

We made a successful presentation to the New Market, and a few days later, we received notice of our admission. Then there appeared the first signs of an impending crash in the capital markets. Now it became clear that the time was not right for a Webmiles IPO. We decided not to cancel our entry into the market, merely to put it on the shelf. In any event, we had an enormous finance problem—namely our dwindling liquidity. We were going through considerably more than two million DM per month, not including the costs associated with taking the company public.

We reactivated our contact to the VCs we had been neglecting, only to quickly discover that their appetite for Internet investment was not what it had been at the beginning of the year. Companies comparable to ours had taken a dive on the NASDAQ. One of the few possibilities for a quick infusion of cash appeared to lie with private equity firms which usually invested at a later stage in a company's development than did strictly venture firms. To that end, we and our investment bankers took our road show to just such a firm in London. Against the backdrop of sinking technology stocks, the initially positive responses turned to retractions and cancellation, and thereby the death-knell of our IPO.

The Storm

The situation had become serious. We had only two months of liquidity remaining and urgently needed money. Even though we held a Letter Of Intent to Invest from a VC firm, we had a painful down round in which we were asked to accept payment objectives that were coupled to specific milestones. For us spoiled founders, that was unacceptable. The alternative was intermediary financing from our present investors. The question was: Where would this bridge loan take us? The IPO had just been cancelled and was therefore unlikely. So we were going to have to look for further financing from a VC, and perhaps seek to sell our company to another business. We accepted certain binding conditions in a bridge loan from an investment company and were again able to catch our breath. It was clearly necessary to give serious thought to our strategy.

The intense push we initially received to expand Webmiles was above all at the behest of our investors, who believed that a presence throughout Europe was essential to taking the company public. But now, of their own recommendations to "Hire anyone we could get" and to "Establish a pan-European presence as quickly as possible," they wanted to hear no more. The new commentary became, "How did you end up so over-staffed?" and "What are you seeking in Spain?" It was now our assignment to work out cost-saving measures and downsizing strategies.

With that, the original dream of unbounded growth was gone. The future did not look so bright; the euphoria had been dampened. Our gloom was deepened by the similar plight of other Internet companies, which were drastically reducing their marketing expenditures, thereby depressing our sales. We were without a plan, until one day in June we received a telephone call that was supposed to change everything.

Trade-Sale

On the other end of the line was a representative of Bertelsmann, who expressed interest in meeting us, and, we hoped, possibly acquiring Webmiles. We knew that Bertelsmann had been working on a concept that was very similar to Webmiles for some time. We met a week later for our first discussion.

The first meeting was extremely similar to an unpleasant recent discussion we had had with our first-round investor, whose willingness to support Webmiles, now a large and expensive company, had seriously waned. The initially friendly climate in the meeting quickly changed. We were considered arrogant for not considering unattractive offers more seriously.

This discussion was not exactly a good starting point for what was to follow. Despite low spirits, we collected ourselves in order to make a self-confident presentation to the top brass of Bertelsmann. Obviously we made an impression on them, for they signaled to us at the conclusion of our presentation that they were very interested in discussing an acquisition of Webmiles. We pretended to be unimpressed and attempted to suggest that this was not the first offer we had received.

There followed further discussions. We were enlivened and saw again good things in our future. In order to create competition, we decided to approach other potential buyers and in effect create an auction. To this end we retained Goldman Sachs to identify and contact possible candidates.

As it turned out, Bertelsmann was prepared to pay a price, which for the times, was very attractive. Despite that, the price was too low for our investors.

Loretta, Dominik, and I struggled to make use of the opportunity provided by Bertelsmann's interest and to reconcile our squabbling investors to a sale of the company. As the candidates Goldman Sachs had produced were only willing to pay considerably less than the investors were willing to accept, we were growing desperate.

At the next round of negotiations, in which Bertelsmann, the investors, and we the founders met, our investors were the first to present their case. They confidently demanded a sum for Webmiles which in my opinion was inappropriately high. All three of us founders had an uneasy feeling, and saw our much desired sale of the company to be in danger.

A day later, our fears were confirmed by a fax from Bertelsmann. They informed us that they intended to rescind their offer to buy Webmiles. We were petrified and imagined all sorts of horrible scenarios. To prevent spreading gloom among our employees and other involved parties, we acted as though everything remained on track, but were ourselves terribly uncertain.

What saved us was a courageous maneuver through which we were able to change our tack. With a great deal of sensitivity we managed to revive the discussions with Bertelsmann and obtain a certain readiness for sacrifice on the part of all hands on board our ship. Finally this led to an agreement. In October 2000, after nearly five months of negotiation and the signing of contracts, Webmiles moved to a new phase of development.

Through the entry of Bertelsmann, with corporate synergies and extensive financial commitments, it was possible to save Webmiles. Via its incorporation into Bertelsmann, Webmiles has very good prospects. Our brand of corporate culture has, no doubt, suffered in the process. The fever has given way to profit motive. Emotionally, this is a loss. Observed rationally, however, all parties know that this is the only way that the firm's survival can be assured.

Webmiles experience exemplifies that of many dot-com companies. Two inexperienced people with an interesting idea found too receptive a financial market and were encouraged to build their company fast, spending lots of money and engaging many people. But they had no proprietary technology, and were facing much greater risks than they realized. When other companies, similarly started and similarly financed, though not in the same business niche, began to lose favor with the financial markets, Webmiles got caught in the downdraft. But Webmiles was lucky—it found a safe haven in a larger old economy firm and has been able to continue to operate.

Talking Points

The bubble allowed financial firms to take advantage of public excitement through the creation of companies for the sole purpose of going public. They did this by encouraging entrepreneurs whom they funded to get-big-fast. This seemed to make sense when the entrepreneurs observed companies, such as Amazon.com, that employed the get-big-fast strategy and appeared to succeed. Unfortunately, with this strategy, there was no opportunity for learning, and none to get-it-right as opposed to get-big-fast. Although some entrepreneurs were at fault for not knowing enough about business, or building companies simply as a vehicle to take public, their primary role was to build the company's economic value. The role of the financial institutions was to build its financial value. The bubble occurred in financial value, and was the responsibility primarily of the financial institutions.

7   How Some VCs and Bankers Led Entrepreneurs in the Wrong Direction

Having to Go to the Venture Firms

In the United States, entrepreneurs have limited sources of capital. They may finance a new company themselves, but since most have little wealth, this can usually be done only on a shoestring. The result is that most start-ups are funded by entrepreneurs for only a short time, which carries the company only a short distance. More capital can be obtained from friends or acquaintances, or even wealthy individuals, so-called "angels." But again, most entrepreneurs cannot obtain sufficient funding from these sources. A major source of funds available for many business purposes is ordinarily closed to early-stage start-ups: banks.

Investment banks rarely invest in start-ups, and then only in very large ones created by people they know well. Commercial banks rarely provide loans because start-ups usually don't meet their loan criteria, which often base the amount to be loaned on the volume of sales of the company in the previous years. For most early-stage companies, there were no sales or only insignificant amounts—so there can be no loan. This is true even when an entrepreneur, or a friend or acquaintance, agrees to co-sign a note with the company, and thereby take responsibility for the loan.

An entrepreneur and family or friends could, of course, borrow money against a home or other property and invest in the company, but this is very different from the company obtaining a loan from a bank.

So other than angels, American start-ups are usually forced to venture funds for capital, and those that don't get funded usually disappear.

In Germany, banks will lend to entrepreneurs, and for many, banks are a preferred source of capital. A contribution to this book from Christoph Pech explains how bank loans are an alternative source of funding in Germany, and why they are often preferred by entrepreneurs. It's less the terms of the loans than the lack of interference from the venture funds that seems to be the key to this attitude.

The point of view that the venture capitalist is to be avoided, not sought out, because he or she is likely to be meddlesome rather than helpful, and is likely to demand an unreasonably large share of ownership in a new firm, turns a commonly expressed American point of view on its head. In America, venture firms assert that they bring more value to a company than money alone, and in many instances there is evidence from both the VC and the entrepreneur that this is correct. But in many other instances, especially in the hectic days of the bubble, and especially in the fiasco of the bubble's bursting, this was not at all the case. In Pech's contribution that follows, we see why a German entrepreneur, who has an opportunity to go to a commercial bank for capital, an opportunity his or her American counterpart lacks, may prefer to deal with banks rather than VCs.

Contribution: Bank Credit Versus VC Financing Management Angels Case

Christoph Pech, Co-founder and Managing Director at Management Angels GmbH

Although a vast number of start-ups are financed by venture capital firms, there are many companies which are financed exclusively by bank loans. In the following case study, the practical advantages of such an approach are summarized.

The Management Angels GmbH specializes in placing interim managers with companies in the innovative economy. The company was founded by Thorsten Becker and Christoph Pech in Hamburg, Germany, in autumn 2000. Up until today, the company had been financed only through its equity and loan bank capital.

Compared to Great Britain, the Netherlands, Switzerland, and of course the U.S.A., the market for interim management in Germany is still in its early stage of development. On the other hand, the United Kingdom already combines 25 key interim management companies, some of which are independent intermediaries, and others of which belong to portfolios of the big chartered accountant companies and consultancies like Ernst & Young or Price Waterhouse Coopers. In spite of their long market presence, the German market providers have fallen short, generating an over-proportional growth until now. After a more detailed analysis, one discovers that the current interim management companies focus their recruiting activities only on the older segment of interim managers. Most of the managers who belong to these pools have already passed the zenith of their managerial careers. Consequently, it seems to be particularly difficult for young and innovative entrepreneurs to integrate a "senior" into the team; the fear of a culture-clash is too high.

To better fit the needs of this high growth segment, the founders of the Management Angels GmbH decided to target their service towards experienced and high performance managers of lower age segments, from 30 to 45 years of age. Thereby a new interim management segment was conceived. This first-to-the-market-strategy helped to gain an outstanding competitive advantage over the other market players. The Management Angels' additional competitive advantage stems from their service profile. They attempt to run not merely a "body leasing" business, but to be a permanent partner, at both the manager's and the client company's disposal, during the whole extent of the project. In this view, the mediation itself is a mere component of the whole process.

The founding partners of the company met for the first time at Frankfurt University and both continued their business studies at the Leipzig Graduate School of Management. Having obtained their diplomas, they joined Procter & Gamble and Bertelsmann, respectively, and came together again at a B2B marketplace conference two years ago. While setting up the German subsidiary of the company, they quickly became aware of growth bottlenecks for companies that were having trouble hiring new personnel. This deficiency was felt especially sharply in development projects, where it was necessary to assign highly skilled experts on an interim basis. Furthermore, this growth constraint was reinforced by a relatively long period of notice required of employees by strict German labor legislation that prevented an employee from changing jobs frequently in short periods of time.

After various market analyses, we recognized that there were no interim management providers responding to the needs of expansion sectors of the German economy. Hence, the idea of the Management Angels GmbH was conceived.

At this point, both founders had built a pool of managers in the triple digits, and helped a number of clients to overcome their immediate personnel constraints. The growing popularity of interim management, both among companies and experienced managers acting as freelance consultants, and liberalizing labor legislation in Germany, predicted encouraging expansion opportunities for the company. Unfortunately, those indices and ventures into such a prospecting niche market did not necessarily guarantee success. The proper form of financing is an equally important success factor.

As mentioned at the beginning, Management Angels was self-financed and backed exclusively by loan capital. One of the reasons for this lies in the business concept. The service offered is not capital intensive; the running costs grow more or less proportionally to expanding operations. Nevertheless, the company had to rely on some amenities of VC-financed companies. The owners took on comparatively low salaries, and relied on public transportation rather than expensive company cars. They were very conscious of their financial responsibility both to themselves and their employees, reinforced by the fact that they were liable for providing financing to the extent of their private property. Nevertheless, the question regarding the advantages of a genuine bank loan financing needs to be tackled.

A lot of start-ups remain adamant about capital budgeting by wrong estimated and target figures, and they try to find a proper balance between public funds and VC financing. But there is a lot working against this approach. In order to run a business free from guidelines imposed by external investment companies, which would not guarantee refinancing in case of capital shortage, the Management Angels counted on the above cited method of financing.

For instance, in 2000, the expansion of start-ups in Germany was driven in this way, mainly by transaction-oriented B2B and B2C company concepts. As a European Business School study revealed, those already stood for 40 percent of all funding in that year. Increasingly covered product categories and the present criticism towards B2C will dampen further growth in this segment. Even now, this recognition brings many venture capital companies, especially those that are not acting as corporate VCs, to the edge, and lets them sell off seminal shares.

Secondly, Becker and Pech did not want to incur this kind of an Orwellian "Big Brother is watching you" debt because they previously relied on, and still rely on, a planned network and account management. For example, it is not market-economy advantageous for both to open new subsidiaries in locations where there is no netting of clients. To revise this disadvantage and to generate slow but steady internal growth, they find it more reasonable to celebrate the marriage with strategic partners.

The third and last argument which speaks against a VC financing in the eyes of the founders is the fact that they do not have to render an account towards the bank in regard to business segments, acquisitions etc. As a result, they are free to set their autonomous business policy.

To summarize the given criteria, the following points speak against a financing with VC capital from the point of view of Management Angels:

- With bank loan financing, the decision-making power and influence in the company stay in the hands of the founders.

- Based on the experience from day-to-day operations, the founders are competent to properly judge further expansion and investment opportunities.

- A great amount of equity available may lead to euphoria and misrouted spending.

Finally, a properly deliberated long-term strategy, in congruence with realistic target figures, is much more important than the question of proper choice between credit and VC financing.

In Germany, commercial bank credit may sometimes be found by entrepreneurs to finance their companies, rather than having to resort to venture funding. Bank credit is much cheaper, and banks are also likely to be more hands-off in their dealings with entrepreneurs. During the Internet bubble, hands-off dealings were an advantage to entrepreneurs because venture firms had begun to give bad advice—the get-big-fast strategy when it wasn't appropriate. In the past, before the venture firms had changed their patterns of behavior and advice to take advantage of the Internet mania, close support from venture firms had been an advantage to entrepreneurs.

Americans wonder why German banks will back early-stage companies; banks won't in America. In part, it is because German banks are allowed to assume ownership positions in German firms in ways uncommon in the United States.

Pressure to Spend

In America, why did so many VCs press the get-big-fast model on entrepreneurs? Were they not aware of its limitations? That's unlikely. For decades, venture firms and investment banks had cautioned entrepreneurs about trying to do too much too fast, had doled out money sparingly, and imposed long waiting for access to the public market, in order to limit the natural ambition of entrepreneurs. But suddenly this all changed. In the mid-1990s when entrepreneurs went in to see venture firms, they often found themselves being told that they were far too modest in their requests for funding and in the pacing of their business plans. One reason for this is that as VCs raised larger funds—much of the money flowing in from corporate and public employee pension funds—they wanted to put larger investments into the same number of deals, and for this reason pressed spend-a-lot-fast programs on entrepreneurs.

I recall a meeting I attended in 1998 between some young entrepreneurs and a partner of a major venture firm. The entrepreneur, who was a seasoned executive from high technology, took in a business plan for an Internet training company calling for an initial investment of $3 million, and providing carefully measured growth for the company so that it would have time to perfect its business model. The venture partner replied that this was the wrong way to do the start-up, and insisted that he himself knew how it should be done. The entrepreneur should take $40 million in investment immediately, spending 80 percent of it on mass media advertising to build brand recognition; the remainder should be used to ramp up the organization much more quickly than the existing plan. The strategy the VC was promoting was simple and soon became very well-known to entrepreneurs—it was get-big-fast.

How venture capitalists were insisting that their investment money was to be spent by entrepreneurs is revealing, since the venture firms were providing money which had ordinarily in the past been used primarily for hiring people and to develop technology. Now, during the bubble, this changed. Venture firms were pouring money into start-ups to be spent on marketing. There was a Ponzi scheme flavor to this—spend the marketing dollars on banner ads on other dot-com sites. So money went from one dot-com to another, inflating the supposed revenues of the recipient companies. In the past, it had been the IPO stage at which money was sought for taking a product to a wider market.

Was large-scale marketing a sensible use of venture investments in start-ups? The answer is that not many successful brands have been built in a short time via large-scale marketing. There are a few exceptions, and during the Internet bubble venture capitalists seem to have believed that almost every new firm was going to be an exception. But of course that couldn't be the case. Big marketing expenditures for start-up firms were usually a road to nowhere.

Perhaps the venture firms were just ignorant of this likely outcome. Mostly venture firms had built themselves by investing in technology companies, and now they were advising companies that were focused on marketing. A venture firm that had been a success at building disk drive companies wasn't well prepared by experience to lead online retail companies.

But venture firms were being flooded with investors' money, and they pressed entrepreneurs to accept it. In the mid-90s Mike Lannon founded a company which was intended to revolutionize how gifts were given in America: *Sendwine.com*. Lannon decided to approach venture capitalists during the successful 1998 Christmas season. Initially, he only was seeking to raise about $1 million from one or two VC firms. Lannon said that seemed like a lot of money at the time. "It took me a while to get used to saying, I need one million dollars." To his surprise, the VCs kept pushing him to raise more money, telling him that $1 million was "merely a drop in the bucket." By March, Sendwine.com had secured financing totaling $10 million from four top-tier VC firms: Greylock Management Corp., Highland Capital Partners, Charles River Ventures, and Benchmark Capital. Accepting $10 million that December, his question was "How should I spend my VC money?"[34] Years later, Sendwine.com still exists, though not as a separate company. But many other dot-coms, which were urged by investors to spend much more money than they were ready to, have collapsed.

It's important to remember that not all venture firms and not all venture capitalists pushed start-ups at a hectic pace toward IPOs. In fact, today many venture partners remember themselves as having been skeptical of the Internet mania all along. Yet the same people often say immediately that all the venture firms which wanted to be in the game had to play—that is, had to make investments at high valuations and try to exit as quickly as possible. In other words, many venture players may have had reservations about the bubble and the role of venture in it, a few may have stayed out of the game, but most, with or without reservations, played by the new rules of the time.

A Strategy's Limitations

For a start-up, the get-big-fast strategy has its place; there are circumstances in which it makes sense. They have recently been defined with admirable clarity by Thomas Eisenmann of the Harvard Business School in two books.[35] The appropriate setting for such a strategy is one in which large up-front investments are required, there is the likelihood of network economics (meaning that the customer prefers one provider to several, usually because when all customers are using the same provider, they can communicate with one another—the most dramatic current example is the preference for a Microsoft operating system by most personal computer users—perhaps some people would say today that customers now have little choice), and where there are not well-established competitors to contest the market. These conditions create a winner-take-all dynamic in which a start-up can be the winner if it can get-big-fast enough.

Incidentally, America Online (AOL) has been another widely watched example of the successful application of a get-big-fast strategy. AOL acquired more than 20 million subscribers by the fall of 2000 after "carpet bombing" the United States for years with disks containing free software for installing AOL.

But in the case of AOL, unlike Amazon, the conditions for a successful use of the strategy are largely met. The business requires large start-up investments (a barrier to entry); it has definite network effects (seen in AOL's Instant Messaging product). And AOL had no well-established competitor—though companies like ADT later tried to contest the space.

A key condition for a successful get-big-fast strategy is that there be few competitors—showing the firm really has a head start on potential rivals. Venture investing's "best known law," wrote an observer of the venture world, "is 'Market risk is inversely proportional to technical risk...' If the product is easy, presumably others will come up with it and crowd the marketplace."[36] When investing in dot-coms, venture firms were picking companies with low technical and high market risk. Yet they seemed to ignore the virtual certainty of competitors.

In the bubble period, the supposed advantage of being first in the market came to be labeled a first-mover advantage. But such a situation usually did not exist. For example, four major start-ups, each using a get-big-fast strategy, and each backed by venture funds, contested the pet supply market. Together the firms raised and spent some $400 million in investment capital, each following a get-big-fast strategy. For each company, the get-big-fast strategy was flawed from the start because all the companies tried to do it simultaneously, and thus today all have collapsed. Did they know at the time that each company was pursuing the same strategy? It's hard to believe that they didn't, if they paid any attention to competitors at all. Each venture firm was pushing the get-big-fast strategy on the start-ups in which it had invested, and this fact was being widely discussed in the business media.

To a degree, this is just normal competition. However, in the arena of new technology and start-ups, because the risk to investors is so high, in the past, venture firms have tried to work together to avoid duplication of effort. Venture firms exchanged information about start-ups' proposals and prospects, and tried to select the most promising for support, and often combined into a syndicate to finance the efforts. But during the bubble, such care was abandoned, and venture firms sponsored many competing start-ups in the same market space, their efforts canceling each other's out.

"In the fall of 1999, the senior management team of Petstore.com sat in a conference room with their investment bankers, high above Manhattan. The group was debating whether to raise $40 million to fund an aggressive customer acquisition campaign. Just then, a biplane passed close by their conference room window, towing a banner that read, 'PETS.COM—SAVE 50% ON DOG FOOD.' That fly-by ended any debate over the need for a bigger marketing budget."[37] The company determined to raise the money.

Experiences like this were apparently repeated hundreds of times for entrepreneurs. In part it was because venture firms had lots of money to invest and wanted to get it out quickly, and because investment banks were finding it easy to raise money for dot-com companies. In part it was because the experience of Amazon.com had convinced the financial community that the old rules didn't apply. But in part it was simply a race to the IPO.

Professor Eisenmann has done a statistical analysis (thus far unpublished) for publicly held dot-coms and telecom companies of their business models versus quarterly changes in the stock price. He found that the capital markets were nondiscriminating in what they were prepared to buy, so that the get-big-fast strategy was not rewarded in the financial market.

Why then did venture firms and bankers so often choose the get-big-fast strategy for start-ups, especially when the conditions to make it successful were so often absent? The answer is that venture firms and bankers were pressing entrepreneurs to get-big-fast so that the firms could be launched as quickly as possible onto the IPO market. Gone was the venture firms' traditional concern for building a viable business; gone was the bankers' traditional concern for being sure that viable businesses were offered to the public. The goal was to create paper and move it onto the public market as fast as possible, and the entrepreneur had to cooperate by ramping up his or her firm as quickly as possible.

The result was that many firms were condemned to failure from the outset by virtue of a mistaken strategy. This need not have happened. Many firms were potentially viable if allowed a different business strategy than get-big-fast. But financial backers demanded this single strategy, and the result was a disaster both for the entrepreneurs and their public investors when the companies failed.

Like Sheep to the Slaughter

The full story is a bit more complicated than this, of course, but the fundamentals do not change. Entrepreneurs were often not unwilling adopters of the get-big-fast strategy. As a group, entrepreneurs are optimistic and in a hurry. So when their financial backers and potential underwriters urged them to go for it fast, many entrepreneurs were happy to do exactly that.

After Amazon.com got an 18-month lead on its old economy competitors, VCs and entrepreneurs were alerted to a potential opportunity in every other product category.

This was the game, and entrepreneurs quickly perceived it. The bubble had created perverse incentives. For example, when online retailers spent many times the amount of their bricks and mortar competitor, the financial market rewarded them. An additional dollar of sales to the online retailer (even if purchased for $100 to acquire the customer) was worth $300 to them in the valuation of their firm on the public market. So while it made no economic sense to spend that much to acquire a customer, it made short-term financial valuation sense. Of course, when the bubble burst and the online retailer was left with high costs and little revenue, it soon went under and the financial value of the firm went to zero.

Further, for an entrepreneur, the biggest question about a get-big-fast strategy is whether or not he or she can get it funded. Lots of capital is required. In normal times, the capital markets are reluctant to put large sums behind a novel idea, no matter how attractive the idea and the entrepreneurs who are sponsoring it. But during the bubble, money was readily available, so numerous entrepreneurs who wouldn't have considered the strategy because they couldn't finance it, suddenly saw money available and pursued the strategy.

But nothing that entrepreneurs did changes in any way the fundamental point—that in the rush to get to the public market, VCs and bankers pressed on entrepreneurs an inappropriate strategy, which in the end doomed the companies and their late stage investors to financial disaster.

Get-It-Right Instead of Get-Big-Fast

A few start-ups bucked the trend by trying to get-it-right before they tried to get-big-fast. A key example is Streamline, another start-up in the online grocery, or home-delivered grocery, market. Seeing that it made no sense economically to send pickers into the crowded aisles of grocery stores, and less to try to take an unproven concept across all demographic segments and areas of the country, Streamline's executives refined their business model in Boston's well-heeled suburbs before trying to expand rapidly. When it worked, they decided it was time to get-big-fast. But they had taken too long. The company expanded rapidly out of the Boston area, but the taste of investors for get-big-fast had evaporated with the bursting of the stock market bubble. Streamline had discovered the right business model for building economic value, in part by taking more time than its competitors like Webvan, but the capital markets had lost interest.

The bubble period involved a disconnection between economic value built by firms and financial value created by the Financial Value Chain. Many start-ups that were not creating economic value were given huge financial value by the capital markets. Streamline was an example of the opposite: a firm that was creating economic value, but which was given almost no financial value by the Financial Value Chain.

Why did this happen? The answer is that during the bubble the Financial Value Chain had no patience. There was little interest in a company that was working in the traditional fashion to get a business model right before spending lots of money and trying to go public. The get-big-fast strategy was dominant. And after the bubble burst, there was little interest in an Internet company, even if it now had the model right. This is how the bubble drove good companies into the background in favor of companies with far less real promise.

Two Stanford graduates started FastResponse, and when it didn't succeed, started Altimum. They never got it funded by a venture firm, but did find an angel to support Altimum. But by the time the company was ready for more funding, the bubble had burst and nothing was available.

Contribution: FastResponse and Altimum

Julian Kurz, Co-founder, FastResponse and Altimum

It was our big moment. Over the last three months, Baldemar, Anand and I had taken a class in Entrepreneurship at Stanford's School of Engineering and we had worked extremely hard on our business plan. Yet, this effort had meant much more to us than a regular class project, since we were seriously planning to start this business. Our idea was promising, and we had already signed up a number of friends and contacts to help us get started.

Now we presented our pitch to a group of angel investors and venture capitalists. The presentation went extremely well, our audience got really excited. Especially one guy had caught fire, a partner of one the Valley's most reputable VC firms. After the event, he confirmed his interest and invited us to give a presentation at his firm.

At that point, our decision was made: We would go forward and start our business.

FASTRESPONSE—HOW NOT TO ACQUIRE FUNDING

The Company

Two weeks later, in June 1998, we received our master's degrees and could move full steam ahead. We were striving for a sizable opportunity: We wanted to develop software that would help companies to utilize the Internet to serve their customers better. In particular, large companies with consumer-type customers at the time were struggling with the growing numbers of customer e-mails.

Accordingly, we called our company FastResponse. Our software would help companies to manage these customer e-mails by recognizing the e-mails' content, sorting and forwarding them to the right customer service representative, and automating the process of replying to the customer's request. Using the software, companies could be much more responsive to their customers and also capture valuable customer information.

A small number of companies were already competing in this space, a segment of a market that would later be consolidated and known as the Customer Relationship Management (CRM) software market. Our competitors were ahead of us, yet we felt the window of opportunity was still open and we could leapfrog them in the long-term.

Still operating out of a Stanford dorm room, we quickly defined the initial team. We were three founders: Baldemar Fuentes, originally an engineer from MIT, had worked for HP for seven years. With his management experience and his excellent people skills, he clearly was to be our CEO. Ramgopal "Anand" Vidyanand would be the CTO. He was from India, a software engineer by background, and had recently worked as a development manager for a software company. I myself would take the COO position, heading company operations, and initially, marketing. As an industrial engineer, that role perfectly suited my strengths in project management and "getting things done" quickly and reliably.

In addition, we gathered a team of three software developers to build the 1.0 version of our software. The developers were friends of ours, who were all excited about being part of the company. Just like the founders, they did not receive any cash compensation—cash was the one thing we did not have—but they were granted equity stakes in the company.

As a team, we were poised to tackle this opportunity. Unlike many other entrepreneurs, we were not driven by getting rich, instead we wanted to build an organization, a company that would successfully serve its customers and that would be a great place to work for its employees. One might call us idealistic and inexperienced, and probably that is what we were at the time.

The Funding Game—Round One

In order to grow our company beyond its current scope, we obviously needed to attract some early-stage financing. We estimated the funding requirements for the first year at about $1.5 to $2 million, and given the positive feedback we had received, we decided to directly approach the local VC community. We had made a number of initial VC contacts, but our favorite was one of the well-known firms in the Valley and, as mentioned above, one of the partners had already invited us for a business plan presentation.

The meeting went well: we introduced the team, we laid out our plan, and we demonstrated a prototype. The two VCs, both partners of the firm, had a lot of questions, were very thorough in their approach, and seemed excited about our venture. They confirmed the great market opportunity we were after. They saw we had great potential as a founding team, although they made it clear that they would like to bring in some more experienced executives at a later stage, which was in line with our expectations. Also, they liked the prototype and the fact that we had signed up some pilot customers.

At the end of the meeting, the VCs were very positive. They recommended that we continue to develop our software, to work with our pilot customers, and to do more research on our competitors. They claimed to be seriously considering an investment in our company, and invited us to come back in a month for another meeting. To our surprise, they asked us not to approach other VCs, but instead to focus on our business, and they said we would certainly get things worked out.

Blind to Reality

We were psyched, and we decided to do everything we could to get the investment settled by the next meeting. We hired additional developers to expedite our efforts. Also, we did not contact any other investors, since we felt comfortable with the choice we had made.

The second meeting was again promising, but again we did not get a final commitment. Instead, the VCs identified a number of issues that they felt were critical for our business, and they asked us to sort these things out and then come back to them. Again, they showed a great deal of excitement, and again they explicitly asked us not to approach other venture capital firms.

This time we started to get a little worried. Were these guys really interested in our company? Were they involved in any of our competitors' activities? What was their real agenda? In addition, we were stretching the team's resources. We continued boot-strapping[38] our venture, and some of our developers had received attractive offers from other start-up companies. Yet, we convinced ourselves that we were on the right track and that we would meet success the next time.

We did not meet success the next time. In fact, we went through another two "cycles," and we increasingly felt that the VCs level of interest was falling off. Meetings would be delayed and rescheduled, and every time the VCs would bring up new issues that had come to their minds. We finally asked them to make a clear decision and, not surprisingly, they decided not invest in our company at that time.

The End of a Dream

Unfortunately, this decision would finally bring about the end of our company. We had been working for more than six months, some of the engineers had already left our team, and the window of opportunity was closing down. Our competitors were well funded and thriving, they had expanded their competitive edge, and new companies were entering the market. Since we had not built up an effective network of relationships in the VC community, we believed it would take us at least another three months to acquire an initial investment.

Finally, we had no choice but to close down the company. With our last efforts, we were able to sell parts of our code to a large company, but we had clearly failed to complete our mission.

We were disappointed about what had happened. The VC firm had let us down, but we really put the blame on ourselves. We had lacked the necessary experience. We had failed to ask more people for advice. We had not considered to approach any of the other VCs or angel investors. In sum, we had not committed sufficient effort to one of the basics in entrepreneurship: the funding game.

ALTIMUM—A TALE OF THE IMPOSSIBLE

The Company

Despite the unfortunate end of FastResponse, our desire to build a successful company was unbroken. After two months of endless discussions and brainstorming sessions, we decided to start another venture, and "Altimum" was born.

We had learned many lessons from our previous mistakes, so we felt comfortable about getting it right this time. Also, both Baldemar and Anand had prior experience in the area of printing and imaging, so we identified an opportunity that would allow us to leverage that experience.

Altimum's value proposition was simple: Our document printing service would be valuable to anyone who needed to print but who did not have a printer or the "right" printer (e.g., color laser printer) available. In particular we targeted mobile professionals, such as salespeople or consultants. Customers would go to our Web site, upload their documents, specify printing, finishing, and delivery options, and we would work with partners (Kinko's, FedEx, etc.) to fulfill the customers' orders.

In the long run, however, we knew we had to be more than a Kinko's service extended to the Internet. Altimum's vision was to allow customers to "print anytime, anywhere over the Internet." In order to accomplish this vision, we were to use a brand-new technology developed by Hewlett Packard. We later became an HP development partner, and we started to build an infrastructure to become the exclusive "directory of Internet-connected printers" that would allow people to identify printers and print directly via the Net.

The Funding Game—A New Approach

After deciding to pursue this opportunity, we went out to find some early-stage investors. This time, we focused our search on business angels, since we knew we were not yet ready for VC money. Also, we wanted to prove our concept, and we needed an estimated $200,000 to accomplish that goal.

We approached a broad variety of individual investors and continued to build a solid network of relationships. After approximately two months, we managed to get a commitment for investments from three angel investors, totaling $180,000.

Backed by these initial funds, we could go ahead and seriously expand our efforts. Our roles were similar to the days at FastResponse: Baldemar was the company's CEO, Anand became CTO, and I again took the role of COO. This time, I was also responsible for managing some of the development efforts, in particular some parts that were supported by a group of developers from an incubator firm.

Over the course of the next few months, Altimum made serious progress. A prototype Web site was completed quickly, and we started a trial of our service at a number of Bay Area hotels that would offer our printing services to their guests.

The outlook for the business appeared promising, so we wondered how to acquire additional funding. Should we go for a new round of angel funding or should we start talking to VCs? We were about to continue our search, when suddenly an amazing twist of events happened.

The True Angel

One Thursday afternoon, we got a call. The caller was a well-known individual, in fact he was one of the cofounders of one of the world's largest technology firms. We had tried to contact that individual a while ago, and he was now returning our call. The message was plain and simple: "Why don't you guys come to my office tonight and show me what you have?"

The adrenalin shock was huge. We got ready as quickly as possible, and finally made it on time to the appointment. We knew we would not have a lot of time in the meeting, so we jumped right into the presentation. After about ten minutes, the angel started to bombard us with questions about our business. The discussion was intense, yet we felt very comfortable about the way it went.

About twenty five minutes into the meeting, the angel stopped, paused for a few seconds, and said "You guys need to execute this plan quickly. You need to do this now! You said you have $200,000 so far... Let's do this: I will give you another $800,000, so you can go ahead quickly, and we will see how it goes. Sorry guys, but I have another appointment. See you later!" A minute later, we were back out at the parking lot.

What a feat! We were so happy, but we could hardly believe what had happened. When we told the story to the rest of our team, they would not believe us either. Yet, a few days later the money was deposited in our bank account, and "our angel" even accepted a board seat at Altimum.

Growing the Company

Finally, we could go ahead and build a "real" company. We rented some reasonable office space, over time we hired a capable team of 20+ employees, including development, sales, marketing, and business development staff, and we started executing our ambitious plan.

The angel's investment had helped us tremendously. Beyond the money, the fact that this individual had invested in our company gave us a lot more credibility towards potential hires, customers, and, of course, to new investors. In fact, our angel arranged meetings with a number of potential investors at a later stage.

One of these was a meeting with Kleiner Perkins Caufield & Byers (KP), which was another memorable experience. Being one of the top addresses on Sand Hill Road, meetings with KP are extremely hard to get. Yet, by the time we decided to pursue a another round of funding, it did not take our angel more than a couple of phone calls to provide us with just that great opportunity.

Two days later we met with KP for an 8:00 A.M. presentation, and our angel joined us there. After diving into the details of our business plan, the KP partner confirmed that we were up to a great opportunity, yet he was very frank about the potential conflict of interest with one of KP's portfolio companies. As a result, KP would not invest in Altimum, but we would take valuable recommendations, and a number of people to contact, away from the meeting.

How It All Turned Out

Over the months to follow, the funding search became increasingly difficult. By mid-2000, the climate in the Internet space had cooled down dramatically. Although we were making good progress in preparing for a major national launch for our service, investors became extremely hesitant to commit their funds. As we burned our remaining cash reserves, the situation became tighter and tighter.

By late 2000, our financial resources were finally used up, and it seemed like VC firms were completely freezing their investments. We had one final chance, but the VC firm that we hoped would save us withdrew a term sheet for a $7 million investment on the very day we were supposed to sign the document.

We finally had to file for bankruptcy. It was a tough and unpleasant experience, especially letting go our great people, who had been central in building our company and its culture.

On the other hand, we had gained a tremendous amount of experience, and we had learned our lessons in the funding game. Our experiences with the angel community had been especially positive: our angels had been involved in major business decisions, and they had provided advice and great coaching along the way. The angels had made a big difference, in fact, they had been a real blessing to our venture.

These young men who tried twice to build successful Internet companies emerged with little for their efforts but experience and a good attitude. The financial markets smiled on them for a while, then deserted them. They were able to abandon one company and start another, and to substitute an angel for venture backing, but when the financial markets turned down, their company ran out of money. In one way or another this was the experience of thousands of would-be entrepreneurs during the bubble period. But in these instances no small investors were being hurt, because the companies never got to the public market. We'll see soon what happened when shares in companies not much further along than the two started by these young men were sold to the public.

Talking Points

In the United States, entrepreneurs have few options for gaining funding beyond angels and venture capitalists. Venture firms, with a tremendous amount of capital, were looking to spend it, and so urged start-ups to spend far more money than was sensible. Although the get-big-fast strategy can work, the situation in which it will do so is rare, involving a lack of current competitors and a significant head start for a company over potential competitors.

During the bubble the Financial Value Chain had no patience. There was little interest in a company that was working in the traditional fashion to get a business model right before spending lots of money and trying to go public.

IV How Venture Firms Changed Their Criteria

"Yes it was bad, and yes, valuations were bullshit, and yes, money was free and grew on trees, and shame on us for paying all those prices for companies. Then the land grab was over that day in April 2000. One, we stopped spending recklessly, and two, we told our portfolio entrepreneurs, 'You've got to slow down here and treat this as though this may be your last round. You need to get to breakeven on this money.' We took more of that mindset. I wished we'd realized it sooner. But at least when it was blatantly obvious we caught on."

—Comment on the bubble from a top venture
capitalist who prefers not to be identified

8 Building to Flip

Venture Capital

As technology has continued to progress and economies to grow, there have been ever-larger demands for capital to fund innovation and ever-increasing sophistication of both technology and business. The result is that a new financial institution has arisen to specialize in providing capital and business expertise to early-stage technology companies. This is the venture capital fund. The public purpose of the venture fund, like that of other financial intermediaries involved with innovation, is to facilitate the introduction of new technologies and applications to the marketplace so that the economy may benefit and living standards be improved.

Because venture investing is about commerce as well as technology, being successful as a venture capitalist also meant "knowing how to play rough with entrepreneurs—playing on their inexperience and emotions, playing founders against each other, negotiating tough prices and generous ownership stakes that in hindsight infuriated the entrepreneurs."[39]

Venture firms are unusual because they are significant institutions in the financial markets, and yet are largely unregulated by the government. This is to them a substantial benefit. In the past, it has been a benefit as well to the investing public, because they have been free of bureaucratic procedures imposed by regulators, and at liberty to exercise their judgment in what innovations to back and how to nurture them.

During the Internet bubble, the venture firms engaged in investing, which was completely inconsistent with their historical charter and their area of expertise. The bubble was a wild ride for investors and entrepreneurs. Most of the companies funded ultimately failed. A major contribution to failure was made by the financial advisors of the start-ups, especially the venture firms. In general, they chose the wrong people to back, pressed upon them mistaken strategy; chose the wrong method of exit from their investments, and erred in the aftermarket support they gave the companies which they'd taken public. Companies were built not to bring new technologies to customers, but instead to appear to do so while early investors made a bundle from selling out. The companies weren't built to last, but were built to flip.

It is all the more unfortunate, therefore, to see how so many venture funds abused their liberty during the dot-com bubble. Venture funds overreached themselves, and partly as a result, gave bad advice to entrepreneurs. For example, Technology Crossover Ventures adopted a rule last year that a partner could not sit on the boards of more than eight companies. By the old standards, eight is still far too many, but that the firm adopted eight as a limit says much about the large number of boards on which venture partners had begun to sit. With a limit of eight boards, Technology Crossover Ventures expected that its professionals would spend more time guiding entrepreneurs and fine-tuning business models. James W. Breyer, managing partner of Accel Partners, used to spend 75 percent of his time on new deals and 25 percent on existing ones. Now it's the reverse, allowing him to help along the firm's existing investments. "We dropped the ball on the level of advice and strategy we were providing [to existing investments]" he said.

Rushing to an IPO

Venture firms played a crucial role in the bubble. In the past, they had served to winnow out aspiring entrepreneurs who had little experience and uncertain business models. The traditional venture rules for making an investment were tough.

The venture firm expected that it would take five to seven years for a start-up to be ready for an IPO, if things went well. Many investments were expected to fail, but one or two big winners would be sufficient to generate a healthy return. Thus the venture capitalist was not a patient investor so much as a realistic one.

For years, venture capitalists declared that their mission was to build rock-solid, sustainable businesses. They would seed start-ups with millions of dollars, betting that two out of 10 would hit it big, and they would be richly rewarded. Venture funds then made small investments at low valuations, nursed a company along to its next stage, sought new management at each stage; and expected five to seven years of building a company before its shares could be offered to the public.

In the past, venture firms did one or two deals per year per partner; by bubble time they were doing six. They couldn't be.

A reasonable time horizon for a company to develop; an entrepreneur with experience and reputation; a commitment of time by venture partners to the start-up—these sensible rules which had led the young venture industry to years of increasing prosperity were cast away in the dot-com bubble.

"The prototypical start-up that has flourished in the VC setting has a technological solution to a mass problem," wrote Rob Norton. "It produces something that has a high average selling price, high margins, and an expectation of being profitable ... in a fairly short amount of time... Many of the investments made during the boom were in companies with none of these characteristics."[40]

Exiting an Investment

A key issue for any investor is how he or she will get his or her money out of a company if it is successful. Shares in a privately held company can be very difficult to sell, often requiring the permission of other investors—and establishing a value for the shares can be difficult. Finally, finding a buyer can be difficult, since there is not much information available to potential buyers that would connect them to potential sellers.

There are a limited number of ways by which a company can provide liquidity to its investors. It can sell its shares to the public—going public via an IPO—or it can be sold itself to another firm or to another group of investors. None of these are easy or can be done on the spur of the moment. Investors can be unable to dispose of shares in privately held companies for long periods. So investors often insist that entrepreneurs be interested and willing to provide an exit for investors in a reasonable amount of time.

But, unfortunately for investors, entrepreneurs may not be interested in letting investors get out. Entrepreneurs know, or learn, that if a company goes public, it will come under rigorous scrutiny by Wall Street and by regulators, something which may damage the performance of the company. So an entrepreneur may be less interested in going public than investors. Alternatively, if the company is sold so that investors can cash out, the entrepreneur will ordinarily lose his or her role as CEO. Because entrepreneurs are often very emotionally attached to the companies they have founded, this can be a wrenching experience. Hence, entrepreneurs often have a great deal more patience about cashing in their own investment in their firms than do investors.

Yet because our capital markets are volatile and unpredictable, investors often want to get out as quickly as possible. In a bubble stage of the stock market, companies can be sold to the public that in other circumstances would not be saleable at all, or could be sold only at a very much lower value. Therefore, when the stock market is open for IPOs and is valuing new offerings generously, then investors are often anxious to sell quickly. Despite their reasons for reluctance, entrepreneurs sometimes have several reasons to agree to sell shares quickly: to obtain liquidity for their own shares, to please investors, and to get cash into the company's accounts.

During the bull market of the late 1990s, investors saw great opportunities for taking start-ups public and thereby exiting their investments. In fact, so strong was the public market and for so long that investors could finance new companies in the hope that they could be built so quickly that they could be sold before the current bull market ended. Companies could, that is, be built to flip—built for no other purpose than to be sold rapidly to benefit early investors.

During the bubble, public investors had their guard down. Early investors—angels and VCs in particular—offered to bankers, for sale to the public firms, that were not real companies nor likely to be, and whose collapse not long after an IPO left investors with substantial losses. These firms were built to flip—created to take advantage of the bubble, and for no other reason—not to bring an important new product to market, not to create a company with a future.

So during the late 1990s, the length of time between inception of a company and its going public shortened dramatically. A study of venture-backed initial public offerings showed that companies averaged 5.4 years in age when they went public in 1999, compared with eight years in 1995.[41] By early 2000, the average period seems to have been as short as 2.2 years.

Companies built to flip were not an instance of the financial community backing innovation. Such companies were nothing more than a financial manipulation—a pretend company created to sell to the public.

But even during the bubble, prominent investment bankers still tried to choose the best of the entrepreneurial firms for sale to the public, and the road show still had to have the semblance of credibility, so a firm built to flip had to look like a real business with sustainable prospects. Hence, even today, after the collapse of hundreds of the built-to-flip firms, their proponents can still point to this or that as evidence that there had been the chance of business success.

And in some cases they are right. Start-ups with real potential died in the bubble's collapse, as well as those that were only pancakes—built to flip.

How Their Own Rules Were Changed by the Venture Capital Firms

Perhaps the most important change in the traditional rules of the venture firms was the rush to take companies to IPOs. This caused VCs to alter their criteria for investment from building a sustainable business to finding a model that could be floated to the public quickly. When Net mania hit, they abandoned that approach and began rushing companies onto the public market with the ink barely dry on the business plans.

Why was this? In part it was because older venture firms had inducted many younger partners who may not have known any better and because there were many new venture firms that had no experience of the past to guide them. Among these new venture firms were many established by large corporations.

Another key factor was that some venture firms were able to create for themselves the sort of incentives familiar to investment banks, which push for IPOs rapidly, regardless of long-term consequences, because they are paid up front in fees. Venture firms were sometimes similarly able to get out quickly after an IPO either by virtue of short lockup periods or by distribution to their partners before the IPO.

The new rules for venture investment that accompanied the bubble can be stated as follows: Invest in any plan—there's no need to know the people or for them to have a track record—which meets the following criteria:

- The budget is sufficient to build a team and get some brand recognition within a year;

- The entrepreneur has a story about the business which can be sold to Wall Street and thus to investors;

- The company has a management team that can do a road show; and

- All the above can be in place for an IPO within nine months.

So to the entrepreneur the venture firm would propose, not a steady build-up of a solid business, but instead, the following:

- A big investment, fast, to give semblance of a business;

- A fast ramp up via lots of hiring, advertising, and site-building at whatever it cost;

- Focusing on creating a good story for Wall Street to build expectations of a high valuation;

- Early contact with an investment bank to drive an early IPO (within nine months); and

- A fast end to lockups so that VCs and other early investors can get their money out fast.

The Baby Goes Out with the Bathwater

The players in the Financial Value Chain had created a huge bubble in the shares of dot-com and telecom stocks, and at the start of the new century it burst. Many public companies and their late investors went down in the pop.

But during the time of the bubble, not all the companies taken public had been "pancake" companies—built merely for flipping. Instead, many entrepreneurs had been focused on building real companies with economic value. Some of these companies had been taken public; some had venture funding but had not yet been the subject of an IPO; others were seeking venture funding. Among them were many companies with strategies other than get-big-fast, including a large group of firms that had been pursuing strategies of get-it-right, and so had not been deemed suitable for IPOs by underwriters. The get-it-right companies had been especially focused on finding business models that would generate income and ultimately allow profitability.

In essence, the venture firms and investment banks had sought and funded what they said were companies which had gained a first-mover advantage in the marketplace by starting early and getting big fast, and the capital market had largely ignored all others. But after the bursting of the bubble, many first-movers disappeared into bankruptcy, and what deserved attention were those firms which remained standing in the marketplace with a possible future ahead of them.

After the bubble burst, how did these companies fare? How did the capital markets treat them?

In general, badly. Investors fled from all Internet and telecom companies as if because so many bad companies had been taken public, all were of the same ilk. But what were they really fleeing from? The technology? Not at all. Few supposed that the Internet would not be the major shift which it had been recognized to be. The issue was not the technology's ultimate impact but its timing. Undoubtedly the Internet was not going to revolutionize commerce in the very short time span so confidently predicted by much-heeded commentators just a few months before. Were they fleeing the entrepreneurs? Not really. The investors still believed in the many excellent executives, young and old, toiling in the dot-coms and telecom companies.

Instead investors were fleeing the excesses of the capital markets—public offerings of companies built only to flip, or companies with the wrong strategies, or companies headed by inadequate leadership. And retail investors were fleeing the grossly exaggerated valuations which the capital markets had placed on many companies. They were frightened by the disconnect which had proceeded so far between the economic value of companies and their financial valuations. Why panicked selling began at this point, rather than earlier, is not easy to say. The difference between economic value and financial value had been widening for some years. An important factor was the fizzle of the Y2K concern—because the Fed, which had increased the money supply to offset an expected economic downturn associated with a Y2K problem, now, since it hadn't occurred, began to tighten the money supply. As credit became less available, some share prices started to fall, and soon the upward momentum of the market was broken, and prices began to tumble.

Investors were fleeing, that is, not the real economy of technology and companies and customers, but the psychological netherworld of the capital markets.

The economic function of the capital markets, however, remained the same—to channel investment to companies to support innovation. This responsibility remained in the aftermath of the bursting of the bubble. It remained when the investing public, badly burned by the bubble, were frightened out of the market.

And many deserving entrepreneurs and companies remained, seeking capital to build innovative companies and to launch innovative products and services.

Nor were the capital markets without investible funds. The IPO market was largely closed after the bubble burst, but venture firms were still flush with cash. The year—2000—of the flameout of so many dot-com and telecom companies was also the year of the second largest inflows of investment funds to venture firms in history.

But in the aftermath of the bubble, most venture firms were like deer caught in the headlights of an approaching car. They stood immobilized in the road. They seemed to have lost their bearings—they were uncertain which way to move, or whether or not to move at all. They appeared to have lost confidence in themselves. The bursting of the bubble had caught many of them unaware. They had apparently believed the rhetoric of the capital markets—they had breathed their own exhaust, so to speak, had thought the markets perfect and the high valuations legitimate. So many of their investments were collapsing that they were no longer certain they understood the market—understood what companies to invest in and which to avoid—understood whom to back, and what strategies to endorse and whether the market wanted show or substance, a company built to flip or one with long-term viability.

Principals and managers in venture funds met frequently to decide which of the firms in which they had investments to cut off from further capital—effectively closing down many of the firms. Venture firms were generally unwilling to invest in firms which had gone public and which now needed additional capital, and to which the public markets were now closed by the adverse reaction of the investing public to the flameout.

So what had been a feast for entrepreneurs became a fast. Companies which had been cautious, and had not let spending exceed revenue by such a wide amount that they were bankrupted, and which had learned from the mistakes of their competitors and now were positioned to make a successful move in the marketplace, were denied investment.

The capital markets were now throwing the babies out with the bathwater.

Perhaps the investment banks couldn't help it. The excesses of the bubble had killed the IPO market for an unpredictable span of time ahead, and the banks were lying in the bed they had created. They had no access to capital to help deserving entrepreneurs—the IPO process was, after all, supposed to be first and foremost one by which start-up companies raised money from investors for expansion. The capital markets, and especially the venture funds, having made so many wrong investments, now fled from making better ones when they were available. And the failure was compounded because the collapse of the bubble had made good investments available to the venture community at a fraction of the valuations of only a few months ago.

Better investments were available at much lower prices, but the investing public wasn't interested, nor were the experts—the venture firms.

The collapse of the Internet frenzy meant that many venture firms had investors' money that was not yet committed to an investment, and for which traumatized venture partners saw no good prospects. At least one American venture firm, Crosspoint Partners, returned money to its investors. In Germany, a start-up did something similar but even more unusual: It returned money unspent to its investors, rather than string out its existence for as long as it could. Whether it be a venture fund or a start-up, recognizing when the game is lost and cutting one's losses, especially for one's investors, is one of the most unusual actions taken.

An interesting aspect of the story of this German company is that when the failure of the company became clear, it also emerged that the company had taken IPO proceeds to invest in other dot-coms. Investors were suitably angered. This wasn't proper. Where were the directors of the company when this was happening—why didn't they stop it? Did a different set of rules apply to Internet companies, people asked incredulously?

Contribution: From the Cradle to the Grave: buecher.de

Dr. Barbara Böhnlein, Assistant Director at ABN AMRO Rothschild (AAR), the Equity Capital Markets Joint Venture of ABN AMRO Group and Rothschild and Sons

The Short Life Cycle of a German B2C Company

When buecher.de[42] started its online business in late 1997, no one could have expected the company to have a market value of nearly EUR 400 million only one and a half years later. Attracted by the success of business models like Amazon.com in the United States and the favorable forecasts for consumer spending via the Internet, buecher.de's story began with the idea to create an alternative sales channel for printed media in Germany.

The founder of buecher.de was in the CD-ROM cataloguing business when he discovered a new niche: to sell books via an electronic platform. Using his know-how in distribution and logistics of print media in Germany, the founder invested in an attractive Web site, added the hardware, and began to offer a sizable variety of mainly German titles. The company's business model was based on two economic trends. First, Germany was considered to be the third largest market for printed media worldwide, after the United States and Japan. And German consumer spending on books had been growing throughout the 1990s. Second, the Internet had begun to be a widely used communication tool, and the number of users rose every day. U.S. experience showed that print, audio, and visual media were among those goods that were the most likely to be sold electronically. Accordingly, market researcher Datamonitor estimated Germany's U.S. $111 million online-bookmarker would rise to U.S. $1.2 billion by 2003.

In 1998, however, buecher.de was still a one-man show. CEO and founder, Richard von Rheinbaben, ran the business with some part-time employees. Sales reached only about EUR 1.5 million that year, with the Internet bookstore contributing 75 percent. The overall loss was about 50 percent of sales, driven by the costs of goods sold and marketing expenses. Since the bookseller was extremely undercapitalized, it would not have survived without external help. The company managed to find some private individuals with whom it went through a few small financing rounds, collecting about EUR 1.3 million by the end of the year. It was clear however, that buecher.de needed much more money to build a brand name, not only because it faced severe competition from Amazon.com's new German Web site, but because traditional booksellers with financial power were pushing into the promising German e-commerce business. Only an IPO could bring enough funds for buecher.de to become a serious player.

From today's viewpoint, it may be hard to believe that a start-up company with negligible sales and limited branding would have been floatable on a stock exchange. But in 1998, the Internet boom had reached new heights in Europe's equity capital markets. Following the U.S. hype, where small, loss-making Internet companies had valuations that easily surpassed the market capitalization of major industrial groups, Germany's Neuer Markt became the main platform in Europe to raise substantial money for this type of stocks. Investors blindly bought shares of any company, as long as it was labeled to be a promising growth company in the tech or Internet sector. In contrast to earlier bull markets, retail investors played a significant role in this upswing. Attracted by short-term opportunities and the introduction of online brokerage, private individuals fueled the hype. With liquidity and investor appetite extremely high, there was a shortage in supply for growth stocks. Since only a few of these companies were already listed at the exchange, people began to chase for new IPOs. This shortage caused valuations to explode, helped by extremely buoyant analyst recommendations of e-commerce companies in the U.S. Short-term gains were guaranteed for those who managed to receive new shares, since the first quote usually more than doubled the issue price.

buecher.de was riding on that hype when it floated on Neuer Markt in July 1999. The issue price was EUR 19, set at the upper end of the 16 to 19 EUR pricing range used to canvass investor interest. Investors sought 50 times the number of shares offered. This gave start-up bookseller buecher.de a valuation of over EUR 150 million, and gross proceeds of approximately EUR 38 million. Despite this obvious overpricing, the bookseller's shares closed around EUR 50 on their first day of trading. Due to the lack of European and German peers listed, analysts had compared its valuation with that of Amazon.com. The big U.S. rival's stock had soared to a market value of about U.S. $20 billion in those days. Thus, people jumped on this 'baby Amazon' hoping to ride on the ever faster running Internet train.

buecher.de said it would use its IPO proceeds to fund expansion of its product range, to make acquisitions, and for marketing. It expected sales to triple to more than EUR 5 million in 1999 and to break even at the end of 2001. buecher.de acquired three companies the same year: a virtual trading platform for antique books, then a Swiss online book retailer, and finally German online CD retailer Alphamusic. Spending for these three e-tailers was small with less than EUR 6 million,[43] but so was their contribution to growth and profitability. The antiquarian Internet bookseller covered a very tiny market by definition. The Swiss virtual bookstore signified buecher.de's first move abroad, but was of limited reach in a small country. In addition, buecher.de could have covered the Swiss market with its German language Web site directly.

The most promising deal was that of Alphamusic, because it helped diversification into other product areas. But even Alphamusic was small, with sales expected to contribute only up to EUR 3.6 million in 2000. During the same period, buecher.de spent about EUR 6 million in marketing. Branding was the task in a time when Germany's online book market was very fragmented and no e-tailer had enough customers to make profits. More competitors had arrived. One of them, newcomer buch.de, went public in November, even smaller than buecher.de at the time of the IPO. Others, like BOL[44] or Booxtra, were backed by traditional book retailers or media groups who saw opportunity in the promising e-commerce business. The battle for market share became even more fierce. Due to its early IPO and brand name, buecher.de managed to fight for Number 2 against BOL, while Amazon continued to capture the lion's share in Germany.

At the beginning of 2000, the company's shares seem to have been neglected already. buecher.de's performance did not follow the ongoing hype of Internet stocks in the United States and in Europe. Its fall had already begun in 1999. Several facts were responsible for this phenomenon. First, investors became more focused on new IPOs. More than 150 companies went public in Germany in both 1999 and 2000, with the percentage of Internet IPOs rising up to 20 percent of total issues during that time. Many investors followed a hit and run strategy, i.e., to take short-term profits and turn to new stocks immediately. Moreover, BOL was rumored to float in due time. Second, buecher.de reported gross sales for 1999 of EUR 8.1 million,[45] a huge increase compared to 1998, but 9.5 percent below its own forecasts. In March 2000, the share price moved further down towards the issue price, while the Neuer Markt Internet index enjoyed its all-time high. Fears about buecher.de loosing market share led to merger speculations. The stock could not benefit from this though. Instead, investors worried about value creation. The brand buecher.de still stood for books only, with Alphamusic requiring marketing expenses for its own brand name. Geographic reach did not extend over the German-speaking regions, and the German name was difficult to sell abroad.

In July, share price plummeted to EUR 10. The bookseller reacted by creating a new group name for all companies: Mediantis AG. It turned out to be too late, however. The party for e-tailers was over. Investor appetite shifted away from B2C companies; the fall in stock prices came even faster than the rise. Sector experts were concerned that many Internet retailers would never manage to become profitable. It turned out that consumer spending via the Internet lagged behind forecasts. Analysts significantly lowered their forecasts for Amazon.com and other online stores. In mid-2000, buecher.de's strongest German competitor, BOL, had to cancel its IPO due to poor demand for the stock.

To be a winner in the consolidating European online book market, buecher.de would have had to spend a double or even triple digit sum of million EUR in marketing. This was much higher than the actual marketing expenses of EUR 9.5 million in 2000. A successful strategy would have more than absorbed the company's cash from the IPO. The downturning capital market left no room for e-tailers to raise fresh funds. Some Internet companies that did not make it to the stock exchange had to close down. And on the Neuer Markt, companies faced default because they had invested all their funds in marketing and acquisitions without raising sales at the same pace. Even buecher.de was alleged to be one of the potential candidates to go bust. The bookseller tried to calm investors by feeding the press with positive news. It also stressed that it did not intend to use all its liquidity to push brand awareness. A vicious circle began. Lack of marketing and branding prevented buecher.de from taking the lead in the consolidation phase and to fight against competitive pressure. Investing in branding to gain market share would have surpassed the company's financial means.

In the course of the year, buecher.de had to revise its forecasts again. Profitability shifted away two years to 2003. Liquidity in the stock, which had been limited all the time, dried up more than ever. Institutional investors had been switching out of local Internet players, at the latest by the end of 2000. Due to lack of demand, analyst coverage decreased dramatically. buecher.de became an orphan stock with its price below EUR 3 at the end of the year. On March 1, 2001, buecher.de reported that the company's 2000 loss more than doubled to over EUR 12 million. Share price fell more than 30 percent to a record low of EUR 1.4. Thus, the bookseller's share price had dropped more than 80 percent in the past six months, while Neuer Markt Index had fallen by only 53 percent.

The Turning Point

A few months later, buecher.de's annual general meeting had a surprising topic on the agenda. For the first time in German history, shareholders asked a board of directors to sell a company's assets, to pay back all the cash to the investors, and to close the business. The organization of small shareholders, called SdK,[46] argued that it was doubtful whether buecher.de could ever become a profitable company. It would be preferable for the shareholders to get the cash value of the assets, instead of risking a default in due time. Sales in the first six months of 2001 rose by 13 percent only—far below business expectation. EBIT loss was reduced by over 28 percent year-over-year because buecher.de significantly reduced marketing expenses. But the bookseller still had funds from the IPO. SdK therefore claimed that it preferred to have its money back rather than see it burning in extensive marketing campaigns.

SdK's request was voted down at the meeting. A short time later, it became public that buecher.de had invested a substantial amount of the IPO proceeds in risky assets like growth funds and stakes in nonlisted companies. While it reported its cash position to be at EUR 15 million at the end of Q1, the bookseller had to write off large parts of these investments that were hit by the downturn in the stock market as well as buecher.de itself. The company thus augmented share-holder risk in acting as a portfolio manager that invested in Internet stocks during the hype. With this bad news, the share price declined to an all time low. To pre-vent the scandal from increasing, the board decided in August 2001, to follow SdK's proposal. The core asset, the Web site of buecher.de, ought to be acquired by Booxtra for up to EUR 3.5 million, about 2 percent of the value at the time of the IPO. The extraordinary shareholders' meeting approved the sale of the group to its competitors in October. The share price, which had fallen below EUR 1 dur-ing the summer, soared to EUR 1.3, the lower level the board estimated an investor to receive per share[47]. In due time, buecher.de will cease to exist.

The short life cycle of buecher.de reveals a lot about the Internet hype and its aftermath. Like many other Internet companies, buecher.de was neither mature enough to be a public company at the time it went public, nor was it ever to earn the money to justify its valuation. This was already obvious in the business plan announced at the time of the IPO. Investor negligence of this fact stemmed from the tremendous increase in share prices of Internet stocks. There seemed to be free lunch opportunities out there. And truly, one must not forget that many peo-ple made a fortune in being early in investing, then exiting around the peak of the hype. Those shareholders that did not hit the right window to exit may force Neuer Markt companies to take a route similar to that of buecher.de. Or financial investors could take over and rip off the assets. Most attractive for such under-taking are those companies with substantial cash from the IPO that did not make the mistake of investing the funds in risky assets. The most suitable targets have double digit millions of Euros in liquid funds and trade below their book value. One can find a number of these companies on Neuer Markt. The typical candi-date is in the Internet sector with its share price having dropped over 90 percent in the last 18 months. Time will tell whether more buecher.de stories will reduce Neuer Markt issuers' board in due course.

Dr. Bohnlein, in her depiction of the short and fantastic life of a German Internet company, makes the right point when she observes that it seems incred-ible today that shares in a start-up company with negligible sales and limited branding could have been sold to the public. But that is what happened again and again during the Internet bubble. In the case of buecher.de, the circumstance was especially egregious because the company was actually investing its own investors money in other companies—a double level of speculation, it seems. In the end, investors took a bath.

Talking Points

Venture firms were not slow to see the financial opportunities created by the public's interest in the Internet and by loose credit conditions. To take advantage of the situation, VCs changed their own internal rules regarding the quality of companies they would support and how fast they would push a company towards an IPO. In general, they chose the wrong people to back, pressed upon them mistaken strategies, chose the wrong method of exit from their investments, and erred in the aftermarket support they gave the companies which they'd taken public. One incentive was that the IPO is one of the few ways an investor can exit an investment quickly. In fact, some companies were "built to flip," or built solely for the purpose of being sold to the public, even if there was not a strong business model in place but simply brand recognition with a management team that could do a good road show. In the end, many good companies were lost in the bubble as they could no longer get funding once investors had soured to this prospect. Other companies realized the game was over, and that they could no longer succeed in the new market. In Germany, a company even returned money unspent to its investors, rather than string out its existence for as long as it could.

9

Choosing the Wrong People

Whom to Back

There is nothing more fundamental to a successful venture capital business than selecting the right entrepreneurs to back. Whatever the outcome for a company, its leadership will bear the major responsibility.

Andy Mills, who built a start-up, Business Research, Inc., into what became First Call and Thomson Financial Services (a multibillion dollar company) says that "Building a big business from a start-up takes 10 to 15 years." He adds that to do it, a chief executive officer has to do four things:

1. Have a long-term perspective.

2. Have a growth orientation.

3. Be people oriented.

4. Be deliberate about the culture put in place.

The role of venture capitalists is to find people to run new companies who can do these four things successfully. But during the bubble, as we shall see in more detail that follows, venture capitalists ceased to seek such people and looked instead for entrepreneurs who would rush to an IPO. The result most of the time for the entrepreneurs, their companies, and the public who bought stock in the companies after an IPO, was disaster.

It wasn't that many entrepreneurs didn't try to build large and stable businesses in the manner described by Andy Mills; they did. But for too many of them, the bubble shut off the opportunity midstream; for others, their venture backers never let them look to the long term, pushing them to do the wrong things; others saw the opportunity to get rich by appearing to be building a company, found investing partners, and did it themselves, with no attention to the preceding four factors.

For example, following is a suggestion made to *The Wall Street Journal* for a monument to the dot-com bubble: "Because we had absolutely NO communication with our management, I propose the dot-com monument should be a GIANT soda machine from our office, with statues of me and my colleagues looking at the soda price to determine if we were going out of business. First they were free, then subsidized, then face value—but when they became part of the revenue model, we knew we were in trouble."[48]

That abandoning traditional criteria for choosing whom to finance was a dangerous game was recognized by some in the venture business. For example, Richard M. Burnes, Jr., an experienced venture capitalist, told an audience of entrepreneurs in the late summer of 1999 that "What you're all talking about is really a disease that's eating this whole industry at its heart." The disease, as described by a reporter who covered the speech, was "the desire to found a dot-com business, take it public, and then take the money and run."

"I think it's really important for all of you entrepreneurs… to remember this: This will ultimately come crashing down because companies will go public too soon, they will miss their earning and the whole thing will just cascade down… The whole thing is much too oriented towards running, towards cashing-out rather than building a strong organization with good people, good products and a defensible strategy."[49]

He was exactly right.

Garden.com: A Mistake from the Get-go

Traditionally, venture investment was recognized to be a people business. The venturer backed not an idea, not a plan, but a person. The function of a written business plan was to be sure the entrepreneurs had carefully thought the project through, and to educate the venture capitalists enough about the proposed business that they could challenge the entrepreneur about the proposal. But it wasn't a plan that the venture firm backed; it was the entrepreneur.

The rule of thumb about whom to choose for an investment was: Invest in someone you know, or someone with a track record. The best investment is in someone you know who has a track record. And never invest in someone you don't know who has no track record.

In May 1995, three MBA graduates of Northwestern University's Kellogg School, Cliff Sharples, Lisa Sharples, and Jamie O'Neill, each in their early 30s, met in the garage of one of their homes. They were all working at Trilogy, a software firm in Austin, but left after only 10 weeks of employment to start a new company. According to a journalist's report, the only problem was that they had no idea what sort of company. "Cliff and I had just gotten married," says Lisa Sharples. "We had moved here, bought a house, and hadn't even made our first mortgage payment yet. My parents thought we were nuts. My grandmother sent me a letter with cash in it because she was worried about us."[50]

Though none of the three founders had any experience in garden retailing, or were themselves knowledgeable gardeners, they picked gardening as the market in which to build an electronic commerce business. It was a large business with no dominant player, and at that point no one was selling gardening products over the Internet. Amazon.com was new, and had made them aware of the potential for online marketing in other sectors of the economy. It seemed like a great idea—there was a $50 billion gardening industry.

One of the three founders became CEO, another, Chief Operating Officer, and the third ran marketing. They called the company Elstrom. The executive team raised its first three-quarters of a million dollars from a venture firm in Austin in December 1995, and opened its Web site for business in March 1996.

The company raised an additional $2 million in 1996, $5.25 million in 1997, $20 million in 1998, and $22.6 million in 1999. The Web site was attracting visits and customers.

Thus over a period of four years, as the dot-com bubble expanded, these three young entrepreneurs, none of whom had a track record as an entrepreneur, and none of whom were previously known to the venture firms which invested in them, raised some $50 million in venture funding.

Soon Garden.com was selling not only garden supplies and plants, but "furniture, candles, lamps, shoes, soap, tea, cookware, perfume, peppermint foot lotion and Christmas tree ornaments."[51]

As Garden.com continued to grow rapidly, investors began seeking an opportunity to put in money. *Texas Monthly Biz* published two glowing articles and in a lengthy profile in *Inc.* magazine in the summer of 1999, just after the company had raised $22.6 million more in private capital, the writer observed that "investors are pounding down the door, coughing up more money than the company knows what to do with." One of the company's directors, Steven Dietz of Global Retail Partners, was quoted as saying, "I kept arguing we didn't need more than twelve million dollars. But there were a lot of good, quality people who wanted in on the deal." ... In spite of more than $50 million in investments, Garden.com had only $5.4 million in revenues to show for it and a loss of $19 million in the fiscal year that ended June 30, 1999.[52]

In September 1999, Garden.com went public. Only a few months later, the dot-com bubble in the financial markets began to pop, and Garden.com, which was spending so much that it again needed to raise money, was left without additional funding. The company now had about 275 employees. Its executives hoped to break even financially in another two years. But without additional investment, the company couldn't continue. In June came the first layoff—24 people. Uncharacteristically for ... a touchy-feely culture, the terminated employees had their computer access shut off and were escorted to the door by fellow employees.

According to *Austin Ventures'* John Thornton, a member of the board who owned 8.6 percent of the company when it went public, "the company's business model was just not viable," he says. "We learned that eventually it's just too damn expensive to get people into your store. That's the whole story." Garden.com had spent 56.7 percent of its IPO proceeds on various forms of advertising and marketing, including hugely expensive glossy catalogs and even a full-scale magazine. "They did not understand what it would cost to attract the traffic," says Thorton.[53]

Not surprisingly, Garden.com's executive team insisted that they did understand customer acquisition costs, and given more time would have driven the costs down to levels at which the firm would have become profitable.

Garden.com went public on September 16, 1999, pricing its shares at $12. They ended the day at $19.06. At its peak, the share price reached more than $24 and the valuation of the company was over $400 million.

Within two years, the firm was gone.

So-called "bricks and mortar," or "old economy," firms in the $50 billion annually garden industry had been astonished at the Garden.com phenomenon. The CEO of White Flower Farms, a moderate sized catalogue retailer, wrote about Garden.com in his fall 2001 catalogue. He marveled at how Garden.com had burned through about $100 million in investors' money. Then he observed that Garden.com forced his own company to look seriously into the Internet and to set up its own Web site. He noted that now White Flower Farms uses the Web continually to supplement what it does via mail, since some things can be done best online.

Gardeners questioned for this book observed that the Garden.com Web site was difficult to use, and offered the opinion that the people running the company seemed to know little or nothing of gardening.

The founders had no background in gardening or garden retailing. They got into the business only because they saw an opportunity and wanted to make a bundle, and they found it easy to find venture capitalists to support them. They had no idea how to go about acquiring gardening customers, and no sense of what the market truly was for their product.

In some circumstances this might have mattered less than it did at Garden.com. There is a long history of people with a knowledge of one industry becoming successful entrepreneurs in another. For example, Howard Head, who invented the metal ski and metal tennis racket, was successful in those industries partly because he came from outside them and wasn't limited by existing prejudices about materials for skis and rackets. But Head was bringing new products to the sports arena, and he required some $50 million in capital to build his initial products.

Garden.com, in contrast, was a marketing ploy only, based on the conviction by its young entrepreneurs that they could change the way people found and purchased garden products. They were trying to lure customers away from existing retail outlets without any real competitive advantage. The revolution Garden.com was trying to bring about wasn't about the product (like Head's revolution), but about how people bought and sold. The Garden.com people didn't understand gardening, or customer behavior about garden products, and they didn't have any new products to bring to the marketplace.

Instead, as in so many areas of the economy during the dot-com boom, bright and energetic opportunists jumped into garden retailing, and without real knowledge or interest in the specific area—and therefore no in-depth understanding of their target customers or products—got venture backing, started a firm, and took it public; then they crashed. A traditional criterion for successful investment is that entrepreneurs should have some expertise in the area in which they are working. Yet it was ignored.

Late investors lost much money on the company. They must wonder why venture firms would back entrepreneurs with no track record and no experience in the garden industry. In their defense, the early investors and underwriters might say they thought the real industry wasn't garden retailing but online retailing, in which case the founders' experience in software might have been said to have had some relevance.

Or did the early investors jettison traditional criteria for investment and finance not a real company, but instead a vehicle that they could sell to the investing public and then sell out? If this was what happened, then the firm's demise was at the expense of entrepreneurs—who had more faith in themselves than venture capitalists placed in them, and so stayed with the companies and the stock—employees of the firm, and late investors—the public.

Boo.com

The period of the bubble was full of instances like that of Garden.com. But some were even more peculiar.

One of the most bizarre choices investors made never made it to the public market, but not for lack of trying. Ernst Malmsten and Kajsa Leander, Swedes in their 20s, had already launched and sold an online bookstore when they went to London and set about raising money for a company to be called Boo.com. They had ambitious plans for Boo.com: Its Web site would feature sophisticated 3D graphics allowing users to spin mannequins and zoom in on merchandise. The animated Miss Boo would pop up to entertain and offer style advice. The site would present a choice of seven languages and 18 currencies, and offer five-day shipping anywhere in Europe or North America. Goods were to be sold at full price, but shipping would be free. Boo.com would be a virtual retailer: Suppliers would hold inventory, then pack and ship customers' orders. Boo itself would avoid these complicated operational requirements.

Malmsten and Leander lacked contacts in the financial world, but he was charming, she was a lovely former model, and they were eloquent about their business idea. They had no background in traditional retailing, only the most limited experience with e-commerce, yet they were able to get meetings with wealthy individuals, and then with top investment banks. In 18 months, they raised $185 million from angels who should have known better, including Bernard Arnault, the French billionaire, and the Benetton family of Italy, Goldman Sachs, and J. P. Morgan.

The greatest strengths of the founders were in raising money and public relations. Running a company was not their forte. The company generated public excitement from the first, but it was also in operational trouble from the start. Boo.com planned to launch its much-ballyhooed Web site—the only means by which it was to do business—in May 1999, but delays forced postponement after postponement.

Software developers struggled not only with the site's innovative graphics, but also with linking Boo.com's software to its suppliers' old (what technologists call "legacy") information systems—yet without effective links, Boo could not manage inventory and shipping.

Meanwhile, anticipating a spring 1999 launch, the company had committed to an aggressive advertising campaign and had scaled up its customer service staff. Unable to cancel all the ads, the company spent roughly $42 million on marketing months before its site went live, wasting most of the money because it had no means to sell anything to potential customers.

While the software development team missed repeated deadlines, staff members sat idle in the company's posh headquarters on London's Carnaby Street, and in satellite offices in New York, Paris, Munich, Amsterdam, and Stockholm. As the company burned through cash, the inexperienced management team seemed nonchalant and distracted by other priorities. For example, Leander, who headed marketing, became obsessed with the appearance of her graphic Miss Boo: Leander flew a hair stylist from New York to London to give Miss Boo a makeover.

In November 1999, Boo.com finally launched its Web site to harsh reviews. Getting around the site was confusing for visitors, and the site crashed frequently. The Web site required the latest browser plug-ins and modem speeds greater than 56K—otherwise, the wait to load graphics was unbearable. Yet most people lacked these technical requirements. Despite all the prelaunch publicity, sales were tepid: Boo.com sold only $680,000 worth of merchandise in its first three months of operation, which included the crucial Christmas season of 1999. Now panicked, management shifted its pricing strategy and offered deep discounts, but to no avail.

In effect, Boo.com had started by keeping most of its target audience off its Web site. Boo advertised how the site's advanced 3D technology allowed users to spin a product around for a full view. But almost 99 percent of European and U.S. homes lacked the high-bandwidth access needed to easily access animations.

Only one in four attempts by customers to make a purchase worked. Customers with Macintosh computers could not log on to the Boo site because Boo.com was incompatible with Apple technology.

Boo.com's hip design confused users with a flurry of orange windows and irrelevant comments from Ms. Boo. Belatedly, Boo.com addressed basic customer needs. But, by the time the site added necessary attributes like privacy protection and persistent product navigation bars, many viewers had already fled.

Nor did Boo have any significant competitive advantage against its competitors. If a person shopped at Boo, that failed to enhance any other shopper's experience in a meaningful way—that is, there were no network effects to tie customers to Boo.com and bring in others. Nor did Boo's costs fall proportionately as sales rose—there were no economies of scale. Finally, customers confronted little in the way of cost barriers to switching to other retailers.

Boo.com was less than a year old, and it was in deep trouble. In December 1999, the company laid off 130 people. By May 2000, Boo.com was reporting less than $1 million per month in sales. But by this time the dot-com bubble was beginning to deflate, and investors refused to commit any more money. The company ceased operations in May 2000, liquidating its assets, including the Web site software and the Boo.com name, for $2 million.

The entire history of Boo.com had consumed hardly more than one year, in which time it had burned through some $185 million, generating virtually no economic or financial value in the process. Its founders had lived high during that time, and attracted much public interest, but they had been completely unable to build a business.

What brought two of the world's best investment banks, and some of its best business people, to put so much money behind such unlikely entrepreneurs? Apparently, it wasn't only venture capitalists who couldn't make proper choices about whom to back and whom not to back.

Did the Venture Firms Make Money from the Bubble?

The investment banks pocketed large fees for taking public Internet companies. This is in the public record. But it's very hard to determine how well or how badly venture firms and angels did. Certainly there were some big winners, but there were also losers. Comprehensive data does not exist to tell us the full story. Neither venture firms nor angels are required to make public their finances.

Some early investors sold out before an IPO, for this can be done with the permission of other investors. These were not sales to the public, but to other individuals or institutions who were acceptable buyers to the other early investors in a company. Unfortunately, the only way to know about this is by looking into a company's records. Some other investors got out at the IPO, and this can be determined from the IPO documents. Other early investors had to hold their shares for a period after the IPO by agreement with the underwriter—a so-called lockup—but sold as soon as they were free to do so. If they were insiders—that is, executives or directors of the firm—the sale would be public record; if they were not insiders, it would not be. A venture firm might have distributed shares to its investors, and they could have sold without record after the IPO (sometimes they were included in a lockup; sometimes not). So it is remarkably difficult to tell if insiders and venture firm investors got out before the collapse of the market. On balance, it appears that venture firms made money over the period of the bubble and its bursting—but this is not certain, and studies are underway which may answer the question.

We might also ask, who got pre-IPO shares? Interestingly, companies sometimes distributed shares to people who made no financial investment in the company. Generally, this is not public information. But in the case of Internet Capital Group (ICG), an incubator of dot-com companies, a quirk in the law allowed a reporter to track the money more completely than is generally possible. Pre-IPO shares went to people with influence in the business world and the business media, and some sold them early at high share prices; others kept them and made nothing. ICG went public on August 4, 1999, at about $10 per share, and peaked in January 2000, at $200 per share.[54] It sells in early 2002 at about $1.12 per share.

There are sometimes glimpses into the money trail at other firms. For example, Idealab Capital Partners distributed much of the stock it had received for an early investment ($2.5 million) in eToys soon after the company had been taken public and while its stock was still hot. Some $358.9 million of value was received by Idealab's investors in this manner, and much of it presumably sold.

But other early investors apparently didn't get out in time. Because of lockup rules and various regulations, many partners weren't able to take their profits in some of their high-flying companies before the Internet bubble burst. Many investors couldn't get out at the high valuations because if they started to sell, they feared it might have depressed the market for the stock. For example, Sequoia Capital Partners, another early investor in eToys, failed to distribute its shares and so its investors presumably went down with the eToys ship when the company declared bankruptcy in the early spring of 2001.

Talking Points

Many start-ups were supported by VCs who had little regard for traditional criteria about who was starting these companies. Previously, a venturer backed not so much an idea, nor a plan, but a person or team. During the bubble, an experienced management team was no longer essential to get funding. As we saw with Garden.com and Boo.com, even the smallest amount of experience was enough.

Some entrepreneurs bought into this new approach completely. Others were made captive by it. Many entrepreneurs were trying to build large and stable businesses, and were willing to take the time necessary, but for too many of them, their venture backers never let them look to the long term, pushing them to do the wrong things.

A summary of how venture criteria for investments had changed during the Internet bubble is given in Table 9–1. The new economy concept had enticed venture firms out of their traditional niche in technology and into the entire range of the economy. After the bubble burst they fled back to their old hunting grounds.

Table 9–1 Change in criteria for venture investments.

Traditional Venture Criteria	Criteria in the Late 1990s
Experienced top executive	An idea
Limited capital exposure	Spend a lot fast
Five to seven years to get it right	Get big fast, 18 to 24 months
The Traditional Business Model	The New Economy Model
Go public when the company is ready	Go public as soon as possible

V   Taking Start-ups to the Public

"As the bubble approached," John Stanton, Chief Executive Officer of a telecom company told us, "there were guys going around Wall Street with freshly printed business cards and business plans for companies they'd just created. Wall Street was raising debt and equity for them at better terms than for companies with existing cash flow, such as my own. For five years, firms didn't have to demonstrate financial capability to Wall Street to raise money. A lot of these not yet ready firms were being funded as early as 1996, and they were time bombs waiting to go off."

10 How Investment Banks Inflated the Bubble

The Banks Bend the Rules

To facilitate the bubble, the investment banks changed their rules, just as the venture firms had done. Because so many dot-coms had no profits, the banks shifted their valuation rules to formulas based on sales, not profits. And since there were no profits, the old Wall Street rule of thumb that said don't take a company public until it had at least three quarters of profits was junked.

The result was that companies were going public so early that Wall Streeters had a hard time differentiating winners and losers.[55]

The abandonment of the old rules caused arguments inside the banks: Should this be happening? Is this how we should be valuing companies? There was nothing to back the valuations, but still the retail investor was willing to pay the high prices. So some bankers said, by way of justifying a higher price, that the retail investor values companies differently from the institutional investor.

This line of argument was thoroughly self-serving. The banking analysts and brokers were helping the retail investors to evaluate companies by pushing momentum, not economic value, as the reason to buy IPO shares. Then the banker made a self-serving assumption that the retail investors' behavior was based on independent judgment, and not influenced by the bank's analysts or salespersons, and justified the bank dumping its old rules. That is, the bank said the retail investor is demanding shares in dot-coms and so we have to provide them to him or her, thus ignoring the bank's role in generating the retail investor's enthusiasm for dot-com shares.

And the retail investor was crazy for dot-com stocks. For example, in Hong Kong where investors' reactions were even more exaggerated than in America or Germany, local real estate magnates brought out Internet company stocks. On one offering, Tom.com, the lines of retail investors preparing to invest their life savings were so long outside banks' offices that police had to be called in to prevent riots.[56] Inside the offices were two stacks of documents—applications to buy shares and prospectuses. At the end of the day all the applications to buy were gone, and all the prospectuses remained.

During the bubble in the United States, the percentage of stock owned by retail investors reached a historic high.

The controversies within the banks probably resulted in underpricing of many of the companies actually offered to the public. This underpricing occurred because the offering price represented a compromise between those who supported taking the companies public, and those who opposed it. This was ironic because during the mania it resulted in very large leaps in the price of the shares the moment they hit the street, providing a valuable commodity for investment bankers to allocate—namely, shares in start-ups.

The gross underpricing had a lot to do with incentives. First, the investment banks, and their mutual fund and hedge fund brokerage clients, profited directly and thus had no incentive to correct the problem. Second, corporate insiders—especially senior management, employees, and directors—received options struck at the IPO price and thus benefited from underpricing. Third, those who had the most to lose from underpricing—large shareholders such as founders and venture capitalists—seemed not to care. Only a small portion of the shares were being offered publicly, which limited the loss due to underpricing, and you could argue that the beneficial effects of keeping employees and others happy offset this cost.

Some also argued that a big pop on the opening day would give the stock valuable momentum by gaining public visibility, which would give the company a marketing advantage for its products[57] and would attract a large potential shareholder base. The base would lead to greater research coverage on Wall Street, which would lead to greater capital market access for follow-on financings and even secondary issues to allow existing holders to liquidate their holdings. A temporary high stock price also allowed the VCs to distribute the shares to their fund investors at high market-to-market prices. The trading price on the day of distribution is used to calculate the VC's carry and so matters a lot. Finally, the IPO price is by definition not a market price. It is simply a notional amount set for contractual and payoff purposes. Thus, underpricing per se is not evidence of market failure, the argument goes. It's perverse, but why not?

The answer is that underpricing took money from the companies that went public and distributed it to investors—some of whom were merely short-term holders who were given privileged access by the banks to shares. The run-up in the price of shares which resulted gave false signals about value to the investing public.

Samuel Hayes, a long-term expert observer of the investment banking industry, commented to the *Wall Street Journal* that at the time of IPOs during the bubble, "the public is taking things at face value, and in the meantime there is a set of under-the-table deals going on that completely distorts the expectations of the individual investor's decision to buy."[58]

The Investment Banks and Institutional Investors

When a mutual fund makes an order, it is supposed to be executed. However, with the bubble, traders for investment banks often found themselves calling a large mutual fund to warn them, "You're offering to pay too much for this stock in an IPO." They couldn't do this for retail investors, as such calls skirted too closely to illegality by providing what might be construed as inside information. Plus, there were too many retail investors to call. Thus, because of their size, mutual funds received many more tips from the investment banks than did individual investors.

In New York at the time of the bubble, the ordinary allocation of shares in an IPO was about 75 percent to institutions, 25 percent to retail investors. The purpose was to give the company doing the IPO, the bank's client, the sort of investor base it wanted. In Internet deals, within a short time after a stock opened, the base shifted the other way—75 percent retail, or even more. The institutional buyers—like corporate pension plans and mutual funds (buying for their own accounts, not their funds)—were flipping the stock, selling to the retail investors, and making lots of money.

Who Brought Those Duds to Market?

In an article entitled "Just Who Brought Those Duds to Market?" *The New York Times* wrote:

> . . . many Wall Street investment banks, from top-tier firms like Goldman Sachs . . . to newer entrants like Thomas Weisel Partners . . . have reason to blush... Of course, investment banks that took these under-performing companies public may not care. They bagged enormous fees, a total of more than $600 million directly related to initial public offerings involving just the companies whose stocks are now under $1.
>
> . . . How did investment banks, paid for their expert advice, pick such lemons?[59]

Part of the answer is that investment banks seem to have assigned dot-coms to analysts who specialized in technology companies. But as we've pointed out before, most dot-coms were not technology companies but marketing companies. The technology analysts didn't understand the dot-com's business models, nor their costs, nor their business prospects. It was as if the investment banks had sent their railway analysts to cover biotechnology companies. If this had happened and investors had known about it, they would have asked themselves, "What do these guys know?" and answered themselves, "Nothing." They'd have panicked and sold the biotech companies' stocks.

But for at least three years, the investment banks had the wrong analysts covering Internet stocks—technology analysts covering marketing companies—and no one seemed to realize this or understand it. During the period at a conference I attended, a professional in the financial markets commented to several people, "The day Amazon.com gets covered by a retail analyst is the day its stock will start to go down."

This question about how investment banks picked lemons to take to the public market became much more commonplace as the bubble burst. "Sudden declines in financial asset prices," wrote Wall Street guru Henry Kaufmann, "often are precipitated by new data that calls into question the original analysis on which the decision to invest was grounded. What investors then do is think probabilistically: If such and such... is in worse shape than we thought when we got in, maybe others... might also be facing similar problems... They set off a chain of selling..."[60]

Privately, some bankers now admit that they took companies public too soon. Most, however, say that they have always been careful with IPOs, and if they're tightening their underwriting standards now, it's because investors insist they do so. Michael Christenson, head of technology investment banking at Salomon Smith Barney, says IPO candidates today need to have at least $10 million in quarterly revenues, and must be no more than two quarters away from profitability. "We've always strived for high quality," he says. "What has clearly changed is that we've adjusted our screen for the market."[61]

So the banks took companies public too quickly. Perhaps the biggest fiasco was pet-food retailer Pets.com, Inc., which took a mere 10 months to go from its $66 million initial public offering to closing its doors. Merrill Lynch took in fees of about $4.6 million for managing the books for the pet-food retailer's stock offering, according to estimates from Thomson Financial. "We had pressure from bankers to go public three months after inception," says Julie L. Wainwright, the former chief executive of Pets.com.[62]

Henry Blodget, 35, of Merrill Lynch, became famous in 1998 when he predicted that Amazon.com's stock price would reach $400 (it was at $240 at that point), which it did. Unfortunately, he also predicted, through reports and television interviews, that companies such as eToys and Pets.com would soar. They never reached profitability, and their stocks never soared. On October 17, 2001,

Blodget lowered his short-term rating on Amazon.com to "neutral" from "accumulate"—meaning he expected it to rise less than 10 percent." It was the beginning of the end, and Blodget left Merrill in November of 2001 to write a book about the Internet bubble. He also left with $2 million that many feel should have been used to compensate some of the investors he misled.[63]

In December 2001, the New York State Attorney General's office announced that Blodget was among a number of Wall Street analysts being investigated for conflicts of interest they may have had while making stock recommendations.[64]

While taking public hundreds of Net companies that have proved to be losers, investment bankers took in $2.1 billion in underwriting fees since 1997, according to Thomson Financial.[65]

Peter Elstrom of *Business Week* asked a representative of Merrill Lynch about the $100 million in fees Merrill had pulled in since 1997 for taking Internet companies public. The representative defended his company's track record. "Investors wanted these stocks," he told Elstrom. "It's tough to tell a CEO, 'We won't take you public' when investors are shouting, 'Bring it on!'"

And Elstrom took the point: "Investment bankers took their cash up front, grabbing a slice of the dough raised in IPOs. If the stock cratered, they already had their money in the bank. Venture capitalists had a similar spot in the food chain. In exchange for footing the early costs of a start-up, they got their stock for as little as pennies a share. Even if shares dove after the offering, they were still ahead. And that's the way it has worked for decades."[66]

Mass Hysteria or Fraud

How did it happen that so much paper of little value was sold to so many investors for such high prices? The banks found themselves trapped, to some extent, by the push from the companies and their backers. So high was the demand from investors that entrepreneurs and their backers—angels and venture firms—were pressing the banks to take them public quickly.

Usually, investment banks are on the look-out for new companies and like to establish a relationship with a potential client as soon as possible. So when entrepreneurs or their backers came to visit the bank to promote their company, it was usually welcomed by the bank. However, during the bubble, potential clients began demanding that the bank underwrite a public offering prematurely, in the bank's thinking, causing a strain on the relationship. If a bank refused an offer to take a potential client public in three months, for example, the client would often find another bank willing to do so. And so competition among the banks for underwriting fees caused banks to abandon their previous criteria for when a company was ready for the public market, and instead took low-quality paper to market.

As the competition for fees among banks grew, bankers increasingly took the initiative to be in touch with potential clients by four methods. First, they reached out to venture firms with whom they'd had relations previously to discover what was in the VCs' inventory of new companies. The banks would press the VCs to urge the entrepreneurs to go to the banks.

Second, the large banks have their own investment managers, and heard about potential deals from the managers and partners in these departments.

Third, banks often manage the investments of people with great wealth who were often angel investors in start-ups themselves, and the bank heard about the start-ups from them.

Finally, bank partners sometimes had business or personal relationships with entrepreneurs, and these provided an entree for the bankers.

Thus the bubble proceeded by bankers initially looking askance at early IPOs and high valuations, then seeing the fee opportunities as some banks took some deals forward to test the market, then proactively seeking out potential clients using the several connections which bankers might find to entrepreneurs. From reluctant participants, the banks became active proponents of the bubble.

Through all this, as the banks grew more and more hungry for the large fees generated by underwriting dot-com offerings, power was shifting. At the beginning of the bubble, banks were gatekeepers, protecting the investing public by rejecting premature applications for public offerings. At the height of the bubble, power had shifted to the entrepreneurs who played bank against bank to get companies taken public at the earliest opportunity and at the highest valuations. The banks had slid from protecting the retail investor to some degree, to competing for a place in the fleecing of the investor.

As the bubble progressed and investment banks sold more shares to the retail public in companies whose futures were uncertain, some partners in investment banks grew concerned that someday they might be held accountable. Debates occurred as to whether or not certain companies should be offered to the public, and if so, at what price.

A goal of banks, imposed by the Security and Exchange Commission, is to protect the retail and institutional investor. If the banks which sold IPOs to the public believed that the businesses were viable, then they were very often badly mistaken; if they believed the companies were not viable but sold them anyway, then they were engaged in fraud. Valuations of many companies were off by a huge amount, and it isn't surprising that some bankers were worried that shareholder lawsuits might result. They protected themselves as best they could, considering that many people in the banks were fully caught up in the mania and were not concerned about possible future legal problems. Those who were concerned tried to prevent the most egregious cases from being taken public, and for those which were offered to the public, they sought to make sure that the prospectuses were replete with cautionary language to investors, and that nothing said by entrepreneurs on road shows was left in the hands of potential investors.

The Blame Game

A key question in the blame game is always: Who knew what, when? This was the question that reporters and Congressional investigators tried to answer during the Watergate scandal, and it's a key question about the Internet bubble. The question is crucial because it's about intent. In the case of the bubble, ignorance and stupidity are not illegal—but pushing stocks intentionally on the retail investor, which a banker knew or believed to be valueless, may certainly be illegal. It is critical to understand what bankers and venture firms really believed about the companies they were taking public.

Intent is also often difficult to establish. This is why trials in investor suits often are lengthy and complicated, and why so many allegations are settled out of court.

Were early investors—angels and venture firms—believers in the possible business success of the dot-coms they funded? Were investment bankers and brokers believers in the possible business success of the firms they sold to the public in IPOs or for whom they raised large sums in junk bond offerings? Since both early investors and bankers were so often wrong about the long-term potential of the companies they backed, is it likely that they knew this at the outset? Were companies sold to the public when the early investors and underwriters knew they were really shells—led by people without the track record to be successful entrepreneurs, with business models which could not provide for financial success without repeated future infusions of capital, and with business strategies that were unsuited to the markets they were in? And if the answer to these questions is yes, was that fact disclosed to potential investors?

This book is not a court; it cannot and does not attempt to establish the legal liability of any individual or any firm.

This topic is unpleasant. It's about potential legal liability, large sums of money are at stake as are potential criminal charges and jail terms. It's a topic full of the bitterness, technicalities, posturing, incompetence, and misrepresentations that characterize American law today. Already financial market professionals have identified two culprits as responsible for the Internet bubble—not surprisingly, neither is a capital market participant. The first is the retail investor—the very person who got taken in the bubble. Blaming the victim is an old device, and is alive and well in the aftermath of the bubble. The second alleged culprit is the entrepreneur, the person who built the dot-coms and telecom companies and brought them to the public market. We'll look at these allegations first, then turn to the question of the responsibility, or lack thereof, of the financial market participants.

Mass Hysteria

The strongest evidence for mass hysteria, not fraud, comes from the participation of professionals—executives and investors—people who should have known better but took baths in the bubble. If these smart people got burned, the argument goes, then it must have been because they truly believed in the financial potential, and it wasn't a fraud.

For example, George Shaheen, Chief Executive Officer at Andersen Consulting (now Accenture), the world's largest consulting firm, left to run Internet start-up Webvan for a compensation package heavy in stock options. Shaheen left Webvan early in 2001, just before it went bankrupt and closed. Shaheen had been a well-compensated executive at Andersen, but had been lured away by the promise of shares of Webvan—his shares and options at one time having been said to have been worth more than $100 million. But he left Webvan with nothing like this kind of money; he had sacrificed both substantial income and status by leaving Andersen. It does not seem to have been a successful move for him, but he was and is a sophisticated businessperson. Other similar examples exist. So it is argued that since smart people made mistakes, the bubble must have been based on more than transparent fraud.

Further, some sophisticated business people suffered serious losses via investments during the bubble. *Newsweek* even compiled a list of 10 large-scale investments by experienced investors in telecom companies which turned out badly.[67]

Because the bubble was a public hysteria, the argument goes, neither investment bankers, venture capitalists, nor entrepreneurs were guilty of anything more than bad judgment. Everyone knew the rules in the game, it is said, and they all knew what they were dealing with. The argument continues by asserting that venture firms were also adding value to the firms in which they'd invested by giving advice and contacts to the companies, and giving them the financial means to get started. The conclusion of the argument is that even though they made some mistakes, the venture firms did want the companies to succeed and did believe that they could do so.

Then the argument goes on to find a villain. It was the banks that misled the public investors and changed the game, it is said, and they also added no value.

But the banks have their defenders as well. It is said that the bank analysts' projections of likely dot-com earnings were based on a premise that the Internet was going to become all-powerful—that all transactions would take place on the Internet, and that the entire economy would change. They were wrong, but they were all wrong—an honest error, the argument continues.

The justification continues to its end as follows: Even if they had concerns and reservations about the new economy notion and about particular firms, it was impossible for banks, and venture firms and entrepreneurs, not to jump on this bandwagon, because there was the fear that they would miss out on a tremendous opportunity. Everyone was in it for the money on the mistaken belief that there were great riches ahead. It was a frenzy, not fraud.

But are these assertions of innocence persuasive? Perhaps not entirely.

What Did the Venture Firms Know?

The strongest evidence that many venture firms knew companies they were pushing into IPOs were not ready for the public market is the change in how venture firms viewed IPOs during the bubble. In essence, the IPO went from a financing event to an exit event (a so-called liquidity event).

It used to be that a venture firm thought of an IPO as one of a sequence of financing events for a company. The purpose of the IPO was to provide money for the continuing growth of the company; it was a critical event in building the company, not the end of building the company. The venture firm hoped to exit its investment profitably after a significant lag from the date of the IPO.

Had the purpose of an IPO been to raise money for the building of the company, then there would have been shouts of rage from the venture community when investment banks systematically underpriced IPOs. In the past, a successful IPO might rise 10 percent to 15 percent in the days after its offering. During the bubble it became common for shares to more than double on the first day of their offering, so that large sums went to speculators and not to the company. Entrepreneurs complained bitterly, as evidenced in some of the cases cited in this book, but venture firms were largely silent. They were looking for a fast exit, and the rise in the value of shares pleased them, while the loss to the company was no longer of concern to them.

During the bubble, the IPO became the desired exit event for many venture investors. The venture firm sought to get out of its investment as quickly as possible after the IPO. There is no better evidence that venture firms knew valuations of IPOs were grossly out of line than that they positioned themselves to get out of their investments via IPOs. There was no point in staying invested, because there was little likelihood of further appreciation of the financial value of the company, even if the company grew and became profitable. Financial value was so far ahead of economic value of the firm at the time of the IPO that the best return for the venture firm was to get out of its investment as quickly as possible. The venture firms saw this clearly. That some didn't get out was the result of one or two factors: Either investment banks had locked them up so that they couldn't sell for a period after the IPO, or some venture firms were so far taken by the momentum of share prices during the bubble that they thought a little more upside could be squeezed out. It appears that there were very few venture firms in the latter category.

Did Wall Street Cross the Line?

There are current regulatory proceedings investigating possible culpability in the financial markets. Did Wall Street cross the line of legality during the bubble?

The issue is primarily one about technical infractions. The regulations that govern financial transactions are detailed and complicated. An investor may get fleeced without any infraction of the rules having occurred. If infractions occurred, there may be no complaints; if complaints are made, there may be no investigations; if investigations are conducted, there may be no charges; if charges are filed, there may be no indictments; if indictments are issued, there may be no trials; if trials are conducted, there may be no convictions. Regulatory enforcement is a long and tortuous process that may result in nothing, even where something is warranted.

Similarly, civil suits by aggrieved investors are likely to take a different but equally tortuous path, with no more likelihood of success, even where the complaints have merit.

It either occurred because of manipulation of the price of shares, or it was an accident of the times. Either way, underpricing led to alleged criminal acts by the banks.

In essence, the suits allege that some investment banks did two things wrong. They went to mutual funds and hedge funds to say, "If you want to get large chunks of IPOs, you need to buy a certain amount in the aftermarket at specific prices." That's likely to be illegal "tying." It's a form of fixing the market. So, when on the first day of an IPO the share price pops up, then part of the reason—besides the general hysteria—is that people had to buy at certain prices if they wanted to receive future allocations. Such an arrangement causes an automatic spike and artificially inflates the price of the stock.

Banks were also allegedly saying, "In order to keep getting shares of IPOs you also need to pay large commissions on your other trades." Arguably, that's illegal tying also.

There's always the possibility that there may have been infractions, but the wrong people get identified and convicted. In fact, so imperfect is the legal system, especially in America, that it cannot really be relied upon to provide honest answers to what happened and who was legally to blame. All that can be learned is which litigants played the games better.

Still, litigation can open doors and provide information, and may in some instances result in legitimate blame being found and restitution made. But this is a long and arduous route.

Frank Quattrone as a banker at Morgan Stanley "brought Netscape public, sowing the seeds of the Internet frenzy," according to an investigation done by *Fortune* magazine.[68] "Later, at Deutsche Bank Morgan Grenfell and even later at Credit Suisse First Boston, Quattrone would become the most visible—and powerful—investment banker in Silicon Valley. The Internet stock run-up of the late 1990s would make Quattrone and his top lieutenants extremely rich."

As a result of how Quattrone's office allocated shares in IPOs, Credit Suisse First Boston (CSFB) ended up as the subject of investigations by the National Association of Securities Dealers, the Securities and Exchange Commission, and the U.S. Attorney's office in New York. In addition, other major banks have been subpoenaed in the IPO probes.

Fate intervened in what was likely to be the major criminal proceeding arising out of the bubble. The Securities and Exchange Commission was engaged in an investigation of the allocation of IPO shares by Credit Suisse First Boston, but the SEC had offices in a building near the World Trade Center. On September 11, 2001, the terrorist attack destroyed many of the records that were central to the case against CSFB. Though the SEC immediately began trying to rebuild the case, it was unable do so and announced that criminal actions would not be brought. On hearing of this, a friend of mine in investment banking responded, "It's better to be lucky than to be good."

> Certainly financial services is a lucky industry. In March 2001, the Securities, Commodity Contracts and Investments industry in the United States employed some 839,000 people at an average weekly wage of $4,644, while the country's economy as a whole employed some 109 million people working at an average weekly wage of $720. This large advantage for financial services occurred in the middle of the postbubble bust. Financial services remains an industry where people make a very good living.
>
> —David R. H. Hiles, "A first look at employment and wages using the NAICS," (the new industrial classification), *Monthly Labor Review*, December 2001, pp. 22-31.

> Perhaps it was the bottle of 1947 Château Pétrus for £12,300 ($17,500). Or maybe it was the 1945 vintage from the same vineyard for £11,600 ($16,500). During dinner at the fashionable restaurant here, six investment bankers lapped up £44,000 ($62,700) in fine wines...
>
> —Suzanne Kapner, "Five Bankers Fired From Barclays Over $62,700 Spent at Meal," *The New York Times*, February 26, 2002, electronic edition.

If You Can't Sue City Hall, Can You Sue Wall Street?

Some lawsuits have been filed on behalf of investors against companies that went public during the bubble. There have not been many, in part because the Private Securities Litigation Reform Act of 1995 has made class action suits more difficult. In general, these suits seek to prove that a company's executives made false and misleading statements about its business prospects and so induced investors to buy the shares. Not only are such suits difficult to prove, but most of the dot-com companies are either out of business or so strapped for cash that they have little to pay successful claimants.

In 2001, more than 1,000 legal suits were filed on behalf of shareholders in some 263 companies that went public during the heyday of high-technology IPOs. "Losses alleged in the suits amounted to between $10 billion and $50 billion," says James Newman, executive director of Securities Class Action Services LLC, a New York research organization, "while securities-fraud cases tend to settle for an amount of between 7 percent to 12 percent of total losses, meaning that settlements could cost Wall Street firms and issuing companies a total of 'between $1 billion to $5 billion for all of these cases.' The allegations generally track regulatory probes into whether brokerage houses broke securities laws by manipulating stock prices. They did so by requiring customers who received shares in an IPO to place so-called aftermarket orders for additional shares at higher prices, a practice known as 'laddering.' Regulators also are examining whether brokerage houses received inflated commissions from investors in exchange for IPO shares, and whether that amounted to kickbacks that violated federal securities law. Some suits allege antitrust violations from the same circumstances."[69]

The people who made money from the bubble are the investment banks and some venture funds. Venture funds are subject to almost no regulation, and play little or no role in the IPO process, so that they are not likely legal targets. But the investment banks play a big role in the IPO process, are highly regulated, and have substantial assets. They would seem a prime target.

An investment bank largely relies for protection from shareholder lawsuits on the language about risk that is included in the prospectus issued when a deal is taken to market. Although the language is very similar in each prospectus, and is often referred to as "boilerplate," it is reviewed carefully by the underwriter's legal counsel to be sure that it is up to date with legal developments in litigation, regulatory actions, and legislation. The underwriter receives from its law firm an opinion that a prospectus is "clean" before it takes a deal to market. But of course, today every prospectus includes 20–30 pages of risk factors that no one reads. Its purpose is not to alert investors, but to protect the underwriters of a share offering.

In addition to the care with which a prospectus is prepared, an investment bank ordinarily goes to great lengths to avoid letting potential evidence get into investors' hands. For example, a common practice is to never allow copies of a management presentation about an offering to be left in the hands of potential investors, lest overly optimistic forecasts come back to haunt the company and perhaps the underwriters. People from the bank are given the responsibility of collecting any copies of a management presentation in the road show which might have been given to prospective investors—copies are generally numbered and retrieved before the end of a meeting.

Also for this reason presentations are generally not sent to potential investors via the Internet, which would leave the potential investor with a copy. But with the advent of Internet conferencing software which allows a document to be seen on computer screens by a variety of people, but which does not involve the downloading of the document onto the hard drives of the potential investors, Internet presentations are becoming more common. The rule has not changed, however: don't leave anything in writing with potential investors except the prospectus.

It seems unlikely that partners in investment banks could have taken so much questionable paper to market without having engaged in some deception of the public. In other words, they knew that either the paper was grossly overpriced, or the company was not viable for more than a year or so ahead. The questions are who knew what about these offerings and when, and who caused the truth to be concealed from investors and by what methods? And finally, was the standard language inserted in each prospectus (to shield the underwriter and its client from responsibility for the financial disasters which were soon to overwhelm investors) sufficient to withstand the consequences of so massive a deception?

The defense of the bankers is straightforward, and consists of three propositions:

1. The retail investor was demanding these stocks and was willing to pay remarkably high prices for them.

2. Other banks were underwriting paper to satisfy the retail demand, so each bank had to keep up with the others, or be denied business.

3. All involved really believed that the Internet was going to make all other companies obsolete, so that the dot-coms had a great future.

When selling themselves to a potential client or to customers: "We are the market." When making excuses for what went wrong: "We are controlled by the market."

Brief responses to these points are:

1. The attitudes of the retail investor are shaped by the sales pitches of investment banks, mutual funds, their analysts with their inflated price targets for dot-com stocks, and by the companies' own inflated ambitions.

2. That competing banks were also engaged in these deceptions may be an explanation, but it is not a defense.

3. Not all investment bankers were drinking the Kool-Aid. Many were perfectly aware that client firms whose paper they were peddling to the retail investor were not ready for IPOs, and that their share prices were grossly overvalued. They expected a collapse at some time in the near future. That some people in the bank were in fact mesmerized by the promise of the Internet did not excuse those who were not, or the banks for whom they worked, from the deceptions practiced to move the paper.

Beware of "Buyer Beware"

The American regulatory agencies, described by Henry Kaufmann as "… less than robust… Understaffed, under-funded, and badly fragmented," have been, in his words, "slow to recognize some of the more serious abuses" in the financial markets.[70]

Among the biggest abuses—now recognized as a result of the bubble—have been those of the analysts who worked in the investment banks. The banks employ two kinds of analysts: Those who issue recommendations about individual firms, and those who try to get investors to buy the stocks. For an investor to have any confidence in a bank's analysts, he or she must believe that an analyst's report is something more than a disguised sales pitch. So banks have ordinarily insisted that analysis and sales were separated by a so-called Chinese wall which left analysts free to make honest appraisals. But during the bubble, it became clear that the Chinese wall was no protection at all for the independence of the analysts. Trying to sell IPOs, analysts gave glowing recommendations to firms which collapsed within months. Trying to support the stocks of firms previously sold to the public, analysts issued buy recommendations as the company's share price plummeted. Trying to justify dozens of mistaken recommendations, analysts insisted that the New Economy was real, and then defended the notion by pointing to analysts at other banks who were making similar erroneous forecasts.

We met Frank Quattrone in a previous section; he was a leading investment banker during the bubble. About him *Forbes* wrote: "…in Quattrone's shop research was expected to serve the bankers' interests. The Internet craze had led analysts at every investment bank to issue glowing reports on Internet companies that were little more than an idea and some PowerPoint slides—a process that Bill Burnham, a former CSFB Internet analyst, calls 'the competitive devaluation of underwriting standards.' But nowhere did the wall between research and banking fall so completely as in Quattrone's group—both at DMG and at CSFB.

"While some analysts insist that Quattrone believed in honest research, others say he tried to bully them. 'I'll have you out of here Monday morning if you say that, one former DMG managing director recalls Quattrone telling an analyst who wanted to issue a less than flattering report about a client. 'Do you want to work in this firm? Do you want to be a team player? When it comes time for bonus review, all this will be remembered.' The managing director says Quattrone would even demand that he raise his earnings estimates. 'I don't think you understand the business,' he recalls Quattrone telling him. 'I've been doing this for 25 years, and I think this company's going to make a shitload of money.'"[71]

It ought to be perfectly clear, and it isn't right now, whether an investment bank has a real interest in a company in some fashion; but this information tends to be buried in very small print in the back of the materials provided by investment bankers rather than up front.

This is a failure of the regulatory system because few people read the prospectuses. Investors rarely do; they get them with the confirmation of a purchase rather than ahead of time. Were there a five-day waiting period before an order could be placed, the current system would perform better. But people want to act quickly, and in markets which are as volatile as today's financial markets, that makes sense. So disclosure is a very important part of a better system, but it has to be more timely and apparent than in the current form of a prospectus.

It was a poor performance by the banks; one that revealed a basic conflict of interest between giving honest advice to buyers and making fees by selling shares. But the banks weren't alone in this conflict of interest—it existed in the mutual funds as well. In the funds, brokerage—the sell side of the financial market, and mutual funds—the buy side of the market, had a potential conflict. Brokerage was trying to sell dot-coms to investors, and for credibility, needed for the mutual funds themselves to load up on Internet stocks. But the funds are supposed to keep away from too speculative investments. In the end, the funds bought the dot-coms and left owners of the funds, investors, with huge losses.

The conflict of interest was only part of a larger problem from the point of view of a potential investor. The regulatory system no longer helps the investor evaluate an IPO candidate. It may still protect against some abuses, even though large ones, like the perversion of the analysts' function slip through untouched, but it doesn't provide investors with confidence in what they hear from investment banks.

The prospectus presents everything legally. It is the document that sets forth the terms of the sale of shares to the investor. It takes precedence over any verbal representations made by the bank or executives of the company going public, except in unusual circumstances.

The prospectus is full of language originally intended to inform an investor, but which now protects the offerers. This is a well-known dynamic of regulation, in which those regulated adapt themselves to the regulations so thoroughly that the regulations become protection for them against legal liability. This occurs in two ways: (1) those actions not proscribed by law are presumably legal, and ways to mislead buyers are continually being developed, and updating of law is slow and uncertain; and (2) boilerplate warnings protect the offerers from liability for failure for all but the most glaring fraud or embezzlement.

The real problems for a potential investor are not those warned of in a prospectus in such general terms as to apply to virtually any company; they are specific matters not revealed in the prospectus. The investor is pitched by bank salespeople, who expect their customers to disregard the boilerplate language of a prospectus. What the salespeople say can be summarized as follows: "All prospectuses say there are potential problems, and we know that many offerings have been huge financial successes, so there's no information in the boilerplate of interest to an investor."

In the end, an investment bank is a sales organization not much different from an auction house that sells used furniture. The bank, like the auction house, prepares sales documents which are intended to do two things: first, to persuade the potential buyer to buy by putting forward positive information while suppressing negative data; and second, to protect the seller from any recourse from the buyer when the item turns out to be junk. Thus, an auction catalogue describes an eighteenth century desk/bookcase without mentioning that the two pieces are thought to be married—not originally together—and includes a page of small print in which the auction house disclaims any responsibility for representations about any item it sells. Similarly, the prospectus for a dot-com described the firm and its promise, without mentioning that there'd been a serious debate in the bank about whether or not the company had any value and should be taken public, without mentioning that it was very likely to need substantial additional financing before ever becoming profitable. But the prospectus certainly included pages of disclaimers, reviewed and approved by a law firm, that were intended to protect the bank from any recourse by a furious investor after the company had collapsed.

In both cases, the principle is "buyer beware." The dynamics of the financial markets are the attempt of the bank to sell to suspicious investors. In bubbles, the professionals in the Financial Value Chain get too successful at fooling the retail investor, and the balance needs to be restored. One way it gets restored is for the investor to quit buying—but that puts the brakes on both corporate investment and technological innovation for an extended period. A better method is to update regulation to restore a modicum of honesty to the relationship between investors and banks.

Talking Points

The venture firms were joined by investment banks in changing their own rules about when to take a company public in order to take advantage of a developing public mania for Internet investments. Because so many dot-coms had no profits, the banks shifted their valuation rules to formulas based on sales. And since there were no profits, the time constraints on when to take a company public based on profits were no longer in effect. All this suggests that not only were the venture firms and banks in a hurry, but that they suspected or knew that many of the companies going public were unlikely to be viable entities. In addition, there was significant underpricing of IPOs, possibly due to disputes within the banks about how to price these nonprofitable companies, resulting in very large leaps in the price of the shares the moment they hit the street, and providing a valuable commodity for investment bankers to allocate—namely, shares in start-ups.

Traditional Rule for IPOs	Rule during the bubble
Three quarters of profitability	Possibility of sales in the future

11 The Retail Investor: Victim or Fool?

Perhaps it's not too surprising that mutual fund companies bought dot-com IPOs on their own account and flipped them to retail investors for a handsome profit—mutual funds are in business for profit themselves. But what surprised many people was that mutual funds loaded up on shares of companies that many fund managers and fund executives, like other professionals, knew to be very speculative paper. To a significant degree, they were buying these stocks for the public's pension plans. When the market crashed, so did the pensions of many people.

How should we interpret this: Was the small investor a victim of fund managers who were speculating without the retail investor's knowledge, or was the small investor a fool who didn't do his or her homework and got what she or he deserved?

The Buyers' Side of the Capital Market

Mutual fund managers represent the buyer's side of the market for stock in companies—not the sellers' side (which are companies and investment banks). Mutual fund managers are paid to help their buyers purchase valuable stocks. If an investor buys a security or a mutual fund in a brokerage account, his broker has a "suitability" requirement. That is, the broker has a legal obligation to be sure that the investment is a suitable one for the client—a form of qualification of the client for the purchase. But if an investor buys a mutual fund directly from the fund advisor, the advisor has only disclosure responsibilities, not suitability ones.

Because mutual funds are buyers' side agents, buying shares in companies not trying to sell them (as investment banks, companies, and brokerage houses do), mutual fund managers shouldn't be tempted to exaggerate the value of IPO shares like the analysts and salespeople at investment banks are. But in the midst of the bubble, one could hardly tell the difference between the two because many mutual fund companies have their own brokerages that sell individual stocks (not only mutual funds) to the public and thus hyped dot-com shares right along with the banks, VCs, and the press.

For many of the most flamboyant of the dot-com IPOs, the underwriter's book was filled with orders from Fidelity, Putnam, Janus and other mutual fund companies. By the presence of these large-scale buyers, the underwriters came to know that a dot-com or telecom stock would pop when it hit the street—and sure enough, most doubled on the first day. These quintessential bubble companies— eToys for example, which collapsed not much more than a year after going public—were launched with huge buy support from the big mutual funds. The mutual fund companies were buying on their own account to flip the stocks for big profits—but also buying for the portfolio of mutual funds sold to people saving for retirement.

Mutual funds also helped to push the shift toward early IPOs and therefore to the get-big-fast strategy that lay behind them. Mutual funds agreed to buy stock in the new companies, even when the companies weren't really ready for an IPO, in order to boost their portfolios in the short term by virtue of the IPO excitement.

Why Mutual Funds Got on the Bandwagon

During the bubble, Americans began to invest in mutual funds in unprecedented numbers. By 2000, more than 50 percent of American households owned shares in mutual funds, the percentage having almost doubled during four years that saw the start and growth of the Internet bubble. Great sums went into the mutual funds, rose in value during the bubble, and then crashed. How did this happen and why did mutual funds get into the business of speculating in Internet stocks?

Mutual funds compete for investors' dollars largely on the basis of the return shown by the fund, and investors' money can be very hot—that is, investors can jump from fund to fund seeking the highest recently reported return. Mutual fund returns are publicized by Morningstar and other rating services so that investors can compare them. When some mutual funds went into the bubble and showed substantial percentage returns, investors moved their money to those funds. Other fund managers then felt obligated to raise their returns by investing in dot-com stocks. Otherwise, they feared they wouldn't be able to compete for investors' money.

Fund managers became speculators when others did successfully for a while. This wasn't irrational, nor even herd behavior, but rather the economics of the system.

Further, the incentives of fund managers had been changed in the period immediately preceding the bubble. In the past, fund managers had been paid primarily on the basis of the absolute return to the fund—the mutual fund company itself is paid by investors via a percentage fee based on the total assets in the fund. But more recently, fund managers had been compensated on the basis of the relative performance of the fund—that is, how their fund's performance compared to similar funds at their own or other mutual fund companies. Thus both the fund itself—paid on the basis of total assets under management, and fund managers—paid on the basis of the relative performance of their fund—are paid whether the fund is going up or down.

The mutual funds have created what are perverse incentives for fund managers in the long term. The managers are rewarded for beating each other, not for beating the market. As long as they are doing better than their peers, even when losing money, they are rewarded. They are rarely fired, even for terrible showings.

They thus have an incentive to ignore individual company research. If they follow research, identify stocks which are very much overvalued but are currently rising in a bubble, and avoid those stocks, then they will not be making as much money as their peers who are following the momentum of the market. Instead, they need to guess what the rest of their peer group will be doing, and do that too, thus adding to the momentum of the bubble.

In retrospect, fund managers should have said no collectively to most dot-com stocks, but collective action was not possible, since each was trying to outperform the other rather than act in the direct interest of mutual fund investors. In effect, fund managers bought dot-coms that they could and should have known to be overvalued stocks in order to keep up short-term rates of return, and must have hoped to be able to sense a market downturn coming and to sell out at that time. They had become speculators in weak stocks trying to time a market turn. Most missed it.

Mutual fund managers and mutual fund executives were not bamboozled by Mary Meeker of Morgan Stanley. They were fully informed, and were surely aware of the conflict of interest at the investment banks between analysts and the sales forces, even if retail investors were not. As agents for retail investors, mutual fund managers should have rejected the bank analysts' glowing reports on dot-coms, and should have paid attention to their own analysts, who were more objective. It was a case of buyer beware, and the mutual funds were sophisticated buyers.

But the mutual funds rushed into the bubble anyway. There even emerged specialized mutual funds, including, for example, Munder's Net Fund and Internet Index Fund, Merrill Lynch's Internet Strategy Fund, and PBHG's Technology and Communications Fund which allowed investors to put their money in funds directly specializing in Internet stocks.

In itself, this cannot be objected to. Retail investors could buy into these funds and know exactly what they were doing—that they were buying stocks that were said by some observers to be very speculative. But many people who bought these funds did not know how speculative they were, and therein lay a problem.

Speculating with Pension Money

It's hard to justify the appearance of Internet shares in mutual funds offered explicitly to people who were saving for retirement. Yet as the bubble grew, this became common. In the limited group of mutual funds offered by fund companies to annuity buyers there appeared growth funds, technology funds, and small cap funds, which were loaded with dot-com and telecom stocks. In fact, some of the funds offered to purchasers of annuities were among the most heavily loaded with dot-coms and telecoms of all mutual funds.

When a fund is purchased in a 401(k) account, the choice of funds available to the employee is actually the responsibility of the employer. The actual distribution of investment among the allowed funds is entirely up to the employee.

Much of the money from retail investors flowing into mutual funds came from their private pension accounts, 401(k)s under American tax laws. Approximately 2/3 of 401(k) pension plan assets were in the stock market in 1996—about 75 percent by 2000. More than half of 401(k) pension investments of people in their 60s were in the stock market at the peak of the bubble.[72] Since most people have little more than their pensions, Social Security, and the equity in their homes to draw on for retirement, the bursting of the bubble was a financial and all-too-human disaster for a great many.

Many young people in particular chose aggressive growth funds for their investment because they wouldn't be touching the money for so long (the several decades before they retired). It must be cold comfort for young investors who got caught in the bubble's bursting and saw their retirement accounts deflate like balloons that reporters say that the "401(k) stock slide was easier on the young... since their accounts generally are smaller, so losses were less."[73]

Older people also bought into the mutual funds with higher returns because they were trying to build assets for an increasingly long retirement. The 401(k) plans of older workers suffered the most in the bursting of the bubble because one year's contributions couldn't counterbalance the effect of the market slump on a substantial portfolio built up over the years.

This has been one of the great problems of retirement funding in America. What people have received as a pension fund—for defined contribution, not defined benefit, plans—is not sufficient for the rapidly increasing expected life span. So people leaving work now have relatively small retirement accounts relative to the length and cost of their remaining life times. Since this is the situation, people were looking for high return funds to build their asset base for retirement. But they weren't looking for wildly speculative investments, and they trusted—naively, it turned out—the large mutual funds who advertise safety, and supposedly felt some responsibility for their customers' financial well-being, to keep them out of too speculative investments.

In fact, the preponderance of private tax-sheltered retirement savings, 401(k)s, is invested in equities—about equally split between retail mutual funds and the stock of the company for which a person works. In 2000, there were some 42 million investors with 401(k) accounts, and there was some $1.7 trillion in these plans (out of a total of approximately $8.3 trillion in all pension plans), and the average private tax-sheltered retirement savings plan is reported to have lost about 10 percent because of declining stock market prices.[74] Investors and their employers continued to contribute to funds, and new contributions largely offset portfolio losses.[75]

Shaky markets since the bursting of the bubble did not seem to drive investors toward safer investment products. Instead, listening to advice to buy and hold for the long term, investors stayed in the mutual funds they'd purchased, and saw their assets decline dramatically.

Momentum Investors in Disguise

Why didn't the large mutual funds use their buying power with the investment banks to protect, rather than endanger, retail customers? They certainly have the power. Single large mutual funds can shut down the trading floor of a major investment bank by ceasing to buy for a time. But there is no evidence that mutual funds used their power to defend investors—they used it only to increase the fund's allocation of hot IPO shares.

In effect, mutual funds mimicked the behavior of venture firms. They recognized that investment banks, pushed by venture firms, were taking companies public at a very early stage. Companies were coming to market with no track record, no profitability, and mutual fund managers knew this—they're professionals, with experience assessing just these things—yet they decided to buy the stock. When stocks like these entered the portfolio of a mutual fund, and were not merely flipped, then the fund manager was essentially becoming a venture fund—investing in companies at an early stage of their development. Many mutual fund managers seemed to think, "Being a venture capitalist is easy, and has great returns. I want to do it too." So mutual fund managers took their often unsuspecting investors into venture capital with all its risks and uncertainties.

Mutual funds are on the buy side of the new issues market. They represent retail investors, and should protect them from the investment banks, whose job is to sell, however they can. Instead, many mutual fund managers ignored their own companies' research in fear that other funds might show higher short-term returns, and became venture capitalists of a sort.

Investors are entitled to be greedy, but mutual fund managers are paid to help investors be selective, to do the research investors don't have time or expertise for. Why then did the mutual fund managers go along with the high valuations for which dot-com companies were trading? The answer is that their own incentives and personal interests drove them to become momentum investors in disguise just as the venture funds were doing. Mutual funds claimed in their prospectuses that they made decisions based on fundamental analysis. In fact, they were playing the momentum game like others.[76]

Blaming the Investor—She's a Pig

Challenged to explain the losses taken by small investors in the aftermath of the bubble, investment professionals point to the investors themselves.

Writing at the height of the market, and with commendable recognition that the market was overvalued and in danger of decline, Robert Shiller commented, "The market is high because of the combined effect of indifferent thinking by millions of people, very few of whom feel the need to perform careful research… and who are motivated substantially by their own emotions, random attentions and perceptions of conventional wisdom."[77]

Writing after the market had collapsed, a major business magazine reported, "Experienced money managers say the lesson to draw from the Net bust is that investors need to do their own homework and not just rely on the experts."[78]

Business magazines also blame investors. 'We think most of the shareholder class actions against technology firms amount to nothing more than a desperate attempt by investors to recoup money they mismanaged."[79]

An old stock market adage has been brought out, dusted off, and offered as a profound judgment: "Bulls make money, bears make money, but pigs get slaughtered." In a sense this is unobjectionable, but when it's cited about the bubble, it suggests that the retail investor who got slaughtered in the market did so because she or he was a pig.

This is financial market Darwinism—survival of the fittest. Taken to its logical conclusion, it holds that professionals can take advantage of nonprofessionals in various ways, including by not giving them honest information. As such, it's a point of view that has been rejected by several decades of bringing greater transparency to financial markets and thereby increasing public participation in the market. Finally, by blaming the small investor for being taken advantage of, market Darwinism is also grossly unfair.

In fact, financial professionals urge small investors not to try to out-trade the market. An ad placed in magazines directed at the general reader (including

Natural History, November 2001) by one of the larger mutual fund companies (TIAA/CREF) exemplifies the position taken by the financial services industry. Under a photo of Albert Einstein is text reading "...when it came to things like money he never wasted time thinking about it. That's where we came in, the people with over eighty years of experience..." This advertisement makes explicit what is implicit in almost every relationship between a financial services company and a small investor—that the retail investor entrusts his or her money to the company to manage it so that the retail investor can benefit from the full-time attention, experience, and know-how that the professional possesses and the retail investor does not. The only exception to this arrangement involves the active investors, including day-traders. But such people are a small minority of retail investors. For financial service firms to then assert, or accept the assertion when it's made by others—including some academicians—that retail investors' losses are because they failed to more actively manage their investments is disingenuous.

Investment professionals who advise retail investors to not trust investment professionals but to themselves study potential investments in detail are disingenuous. In reality, only a professional can do what a professional calls careful research—too much critical information is obscured or hidden in the accounts of firms, too little information about prospective business is available, and too little time and expertise is available to the average investor. This is why an industry of professionals exists to support the nonprofessional investor. Unfortunately, this industry is too often predatory regarding its clients. In the dot-com and telecom bubble, major investment banks had huge conflicts of interest by which stock analysts, giving advice to investors, were in fact being paid for making recommendations helpful, not to investors, but to the companies and banks involved.

Nor could the public rely on so-called experts in the new economy. For example, the era spawned a new sort of firm allegedly expert in the development of businesses that developed and applied the new technology—the incubators. The executives of the incubators were supposedly experts about business in the new economy. Stock in the incubators themselves was sometimes sold to the public, including David Wetherell's CMGI, Internet Capital Group, and Bill Gross's Idealab. In fact, the fingerprints of the men who led the largest incubators are all over the dot-com bubble.

Wetherell got his early experience as the head of the College Marketing Group, a marketer of college courses and faculty information. In the mid-1990s, he remade the company into the country's first major incubator for start-ups. During the Internet boom, seven CMGI companies went public, raising $647.2 million. CMGI scored early hits, including its investment in search engine Lycos. With the collapse of the bubble, both CMGI and most of its public companies were of little value. Thus, the very people who were supposedly the experts on the new economy turned out to be merely another group of people building and exploiting the mania, and in the end the shares of the incubators collapsed as fully as those of the dot-coms they nurtured.

Nor are those who blame the public for the bubble entirely candid about the hysteria, which they suggest somehow emerged from retail investors like fire from spontaneous combustion. In fact, years of hype participated in by venture firms, entrepreneurs, angel investors, investment banks, brokerage houses, and much of the media set the fire of hysteria in the investing public.

Another investment professional wrote in *The New York Times* that Americans are demanding to know what happened to them in the bubble, and he gave an answer—they were fools who wanted to be deceived and they got what they deserved. Here are his exact words, "The truth is simple: there was a boom... Booms begin in reality and rise to fantasy... Were investors out of their minds?... Investors are right to resent Wall Street for its conflicts of interest and to upbraid Alan Greenspan for his wide-eyed embrace of the so-called productivity miracle. But the underlying source of recurring cycles in any economy is the average human being... The world wants to be deceived, therefore let it be deceived."[80]

To me, blaming investors for the bubble is like blaming a patient for not diagnosing his own illness and prescribing his own medicine. Instead, when we go to a doctor, we pay him or her for expert advice. Should we second-guess the doctor? Maybe occasionally, on serious issues, when we might seek a second opinion, but if three doctors tell us the same thing and they are the experts, it really shouldn't be necessary for us to go on our own to read medical texts and figure out whether they are right. In fact, in our society, if the doctors are wrong, and we are injured as a result, we can sue them, and be compensated.

Similarly, financial markets are full of well-compensated professionals who purport to advise the retail investor, and some of whom have legal obligations toward their retail clients. It's not reasonable to blame the retail investor for not acting as if she were the professional herself.

How Important Is the Freedom to Speculate?

Some people associate speculation with freedom, saying that the opportunity to be a winner or a loser is a key element of freedom. To them, it follows that financial speculation is worth preserving for everyone in society, no matter how ill-prepared or lacking in financial assets.[81] But surely this is not the case for people who didn't know they were speculating in the financial markets, but thought instead that they were in prudent, though hopefully lucrative, investments.

Did small investors in America transfer savings and pension money into mutual funds knowing they were speculating? Was this disclosed to them? Did they understand the dynamics by which mutual funds competed for investment dollars and so abandoned prudence; or by which mutual fund managers were paid for beating competitors' performance, and so abandoned prudence for speculation, to keep up with the others?

To ask these questions is to answer them. The small investor did not know these things, and had no way of knowing them. He or she did not have the freedom to speculate, but a license granted to professionals to misallocate his assets.

What most people want, and what the government should do its best to provide them, is that they be able to be comfortable in their jobs and homes, free to pursue their interests, hoping that others are doing well also, and without the risk that the financial markets will bring the whole thing crashing down on all our heads in a speculative frenzy.

Talking Points

With venture funds and investment banks providing fuel in the form of IPOs to the Internet mania, mutual funds became unlikely speculators. In order to keep up with high returns being reported by the most speculative funds, others moved heavily into Internet stocks. The result was that many small investors who placed their savings and pension money in annuities with major mutual fund houses suddenly discovered, after the bubble burst, that beneath high returns lay wild speculation by the fund managers, and the investors lost large amounts.

In effect, with Wall Street taking start-ups public at a stage which in the past would have been a venture investment, and mutual funds loading up on such stocks, mutual funds became like venture capitalists—with sometimes high returns but also high risks. Without realizing it, small investors had moved via their mutual fund investments into one of the fastest, most risky games in the financial markets.

Much, perhaps the majority, of money flowing into mutual funds in the United States came from 401(k)s, a form of self-managed pension plan. More than half of 401(k) pension investments of people in their 60s were in the stock market at the peak of the bubble. This meant tremendous losses when the bubble burst for many unsuspecting investors who did not realize their money was being used for speculation.

Many blame the individual investors for making foolish investments, and yet, not only were they unaware that they were speculating, they were paying the mutual funds to act as the experts in the investment of their money. Having not the time, money, nor resources to do the research, they chose experts to do this for them. Unfortunately, the experts took such large risks that their clients ended up losing much of their money.

12 Influencing Factors: Where Does Responsibility Lie?

Accountants, the media, and government regulators all have a role in the Financial Value Chain and all contributed to the bubble—substantially.

What the Accountants Should Have Done and Didn't

Dot-coms were desperate for sales to sustain their high valuations, and found a way to get some. They engaged in creative accounting. Unfortunately, the accountants permitted it.

"The only way most Internet companies were showing any money on the books," a close observer commented, "was by doing deals with one another. The business development heads would meet for lunch. They wouldn't have any idea what the outcome of the meeting would be, but they'd work it out at lunch, and then they'd both show some revenue. But it wasn't real revenue."[82]

So the income statements of dot-coms filled up not with real sales, but with exchanges of services from each other, which each company booked as sales. Accountants approved to these deals on the dot-coms' financial reports. They didn't have to give unqualified approvals; they could have cited qualifications— essentially that a firm will need to raise more capital to be successful—that it's not likely to be "pay as it goes." This would have tipped off investors to be careful in buying the shares of these firms; it might have kept the bubble from forming as quickly and going as far as it did. But the accountants failed to do this.[83]

Further, the accountants permitted companies to exclude from their balance sheets large quantities of debt which were laid off instead on so-called off-balance-sheet vehicles, such as partnerships. The result was to have the company appear financially stronger than it was and to allow it to report higher levels of profit than otherwise possible. Off-balance-sheet accounting was a key to the Enron financial scandal.

Would it have mattered had accountants done their job properly? Did the IPO buyers really think they were getting companies that had economic value? Probably the day-traders didn't think so, at least—they were speculating on the direction of stock price movements—that is, betting that the upward momentum would continue. And many other retail investors were at least basically aware of the inflated prices of Internet stocks. But the magnitude of the deceptions permitted by American accounting during recent years was concealed from investors, professional and novice. "Creative accounting," in which the traditional measures of a firm's financial position were sacrificed to clever devices that concealed rather than exposed the true financial condition of a firm, became a norm in the new economy.

Signals by accountants to the financial value chain and to retail investors might have helped to keep the bubble's momentum from building if those signals had come during the bubble's two-year gestation period. They would have saved Enron investors from disaster had they come even after the bubble had burst.

The Hype Machine

The press leapt onto the Internet bandwagon with an abandon that is astonishing only a few years later. Without the media hype machine, it's hard to imagine the bubble getting so large.

"Follow the personal computer and you can reach the pot of gold," said George Gilder. "Follow anything else and you will end up in a backwater. What the Model T was to the industrial era . . . the PC is to the information age. Just as people who rode the wave of automobile technology—from tire makers to fast food franchisers—prevailed in the industrial era, so the firms that prey on the passion and feed on the force of the computer community will predominate in the information era."[84]

"The easy availability of smart capital," wrote *The Wall Street Journal*, "the ability of entrepreneurs to launch potentially world-beating companies on a shoestring, and of investors to intelligently spread risk—may be the new economy's most devastating innovation. At the same time, onrushing technological change requires lumbering dinosaurs to turn themselves into clever mammals overnight. Some will. But for many others, the only thing left to talk about is the terms of surrender."[85]

What more could be said? The old economy was dying; the new economy was triumphant. What more would a retail investor want to hear? The only question left for her or him was how to get shares in the clever mammals—and with that the investment banks were preparing to help.

The Fed Was Also at Fault

The Federal Reserve System had much to do with the Internet bubble, and should not be as permissive the next time.

At the end of this chapter appear excerpts from the speeches and Congressional testimony of Federal Reserve Chairman Alan Greenspan given during the years of the bubble. In 1996 Greenspan saw the danger of a bubble and gave it a name, "irrational exuberance," but the Federal Reserve (the "Fed") did nothing. As the bubble grew, Greenspan pointed to it as a danger, and simultaneously justified it—as if he were debating the matter in his own mind and giving the debate public utterance. It seemed he couldn't make up his mind.

On the negative side, he recognized the threat to the economy from an unrestrained bubble that must someday burst. But on the positive side, he argued that the bubble was justified by the improving performance of the U.S. economy; that the bubble was itself a constructive force that was causing consumers to spend more and thereby increasing economic growth; and finally that the bubble was of limited scope and if it burst, was not likely to damage the economy as a whole. In fact, as we revisit Greenspan's testimony, we realize that no one else gave stronger support to the notion of the new economy—of a new high level of productivity improvement based on the dissemination of information technology in the economy—than Alan Greenspan. As we've seen previously, it was the assumption of a new high level of productivity, and of more rapid economic growth, that was used on Wall Street to justify the very high valuations of Internet companies. Greenspan gave the assumptions of the analysts credibility, and he continues to do so today, even after almost everyone else has given up the mirage of the economic miracle.

In fact, it was a miracle that didn't occur—or at least if it did occur, it was a very small miracle, not the big one the Fed's chairman repeatedly endorsed. Recent revisions in economic data for the United States and Europe show that the growth of labor productivity in the domestic American economy from 1996 to 2000 was only 1.75 percent per year, near our long-term average rate, and was only .25 percentage point ahead of the rate of productivity growth in Europe.

Further, economic growth itself had been overestimated by the government. In 2000, for example, industrial production had grown not at three percent as originally reported, but at less than two percent.

Overestimation of productivity and economic growth rates meant that the economic miracle of the 1990s on which the stock market inflation was based never really happened. The Fed had based its policies and its glowing endorsement of the new economy on illusions.

Further, some say the real Internet bubble was started in late 1999 by the actions of the Fed with respect to the nation's money supply. The bubble emerged from the crisis in Long Term Capital Management when the Fed flooded the markets with liquidity.[86] Already the story about an economic miracle had primed the pump with investors—the Fed's immense credit creation combined with margin borrowing by investors to inflate the market.

Fed Chairman Alan Greenspan's few attempts to deflate the bubble with words—criticizing the market for "irrational exuberance" being one—were not matched by actions. Instead, the Fed ran a largely expansive money policy for years, while excess liquidity was permitted to be poured into stock market speculation.

The Fed's incapacity was noted before it was too late. "My concern about the bubbling of American financial markets," wrote Henry Kaufmann, "was heightened in August, 1999, as I sat in the audience listening to Alan Greenspan... and... [realized] that the Fed did not know how to deal with a bubble."[87]

The bubble was the Fed's business because the Fed was partly responsible for it. It was also the Fed's business because a bubble in financial markets can get transferred by wealth effect into real economy. When the bubble was inflating and the wealth effect was increasing economic growth, the Fed looked on it as benign. When the bubble burst and the wealth effect worked the other way, threatening a recession, the Fed looked the other way. The Fed both contributed to the growth of the bubble and then let it crash.

In fact, the sequence and timing of Fed policy in late 1999 and early 2000 couldn't have been worse. When the bubble was expanding in 1999, the Fed poured liquidity into the economy as a result of both the Long Term Capital Management debacle and the Y2K fright. Then, when people in early 2000 were beginning to perceive the lack of foundation for the Internet bubble, the Fed cut liquidity and drove asset values down so fast that the economy fell into a recession.

The Fed should have intervened to dampen the bubble far sooner than the year 2000, and it would have been perfectly proper for the Fed to do so. The Fed plays an important role in regulating financial markets. For example, in order to stop a bubble in the price of silver in 1979–80, "Paul Volcker, chairman of the Fed, ... warned American banks... not to supply loans for speculation...." wrote a historian of the period. "[Yet] the Hunts' [Texas billionaires who tried to corner the silver market] borrowing for speculative losses during February and March [1980] accounted for 12.9 percent of all business loans in the United States..." In this period, the historian continued, "federal officials... [took] a series of increasingly strong actions... to ensure that the price decline was orderly and a spiral of bankruptcies was avoided. This direct government intervention insured the survival of banks, brokerage houses and exchanges."[88]

But during the Internet bubble, the financial institutions remained strong. It was only investors who were being mauled. So the Fed remained largely inactive.

Perhaps the Fed should have taken a wider view of its responsibility to the American people, and acted on their behalf—but it did not. "I believe the primary objective of a central bank," wrote Henry Kaufmann, "should be to maintain the financial well-being of society in the broadest sense. That means establishing stable financial conditions by exercising careful oversight over financial markets, institutions, and trading practices; anticipating potential problems; and taking remedial action *before* those problems can do widespread damage." In retrospect, as the bubble was inflating, the Fed should have increased borrowing margins for investors and reduced liquidity.

The Fed chose not to intervene to protect small investors, or even the economy, from the bubble and its consequences, until a recession loomed on the economic horizon and the Fed belatedly began to cut interest rates.

The Fed bears a dual responsibility for the bubble and its consequences—one via its actions to encourage the financial excesses and provide liquidity for them; and one via its inaction as a regulator to stop the excesses. "[The NY Fed] ... wants to hear about anything that might upset markets or. . . the financial system," wrote a historian of the Long Term Capital Management crisis, quoting an officer of the New York Fed.[89] What more "upset" could the Fed have desired in order to take action against the bubble? The financial markets were generating instability in world economy, and interfering with economic growth.

There was too much speculation, noticed and remarked upon, but nonetheless tolerated too generously by regulators, especially the Fed. Following are excerpts from Chairman Greenspan's speeches and testimony before Congressional committees during the period before, during, and after the bubble. The total volume of the Chairman's speeches and testimony is quite large, so that it cannot be provided here in its entirety. But these are representative comments, and their full context would not, we think, change their interpretation by the reader. The Chairman's views were important for three reasons: First, his favorable views of the new economy helped influence investor opinion favorably toward investing in new economy businesses; second, Greenspan's views were continually cited by Wall Street professionals as evidence of the value of Internet companies; third, his views help explain why the Fed chose not to act for the explicit purpose of avoiding or deflating the bubble.

Alan Greenspan and the Great Bubble

Excerpts from Federal Reserve Chairman Greenspan's
Speeches and Congressional Testimony 1996–2001

1996

Chairman Greenspan recognized early on the danger a financial asset bubble posed to the economy.

...How do we know when irrational exuberance has unduly escalated asset values, which then become subject to unexpected and prolonged contractions as they have in Japan over the past decade? And how do we factor that assessment into monetary policy? We as central bankers need not be concerned if a collapsing financial asset bubble does not threaten to impair the real economy, its production, jobs, and price stability. Indeed, the sharp stock market break of 1987 had few negative consequences for the economy. But we should not underestimate or become complacent about the complexity of the interactions of asset markets and the economy. Thus, evaluating shifts in balance sheets generally, and in asset prices particularly, must be an integral part of the development of monetary policy.

Remarks by Chairman Alan Greenspan
"The Challenge of Central Banking in a Democratic Society"
At the Annual Dinner and Francis Boyer Lecture of The American Enterprise Institute for Public Policy Research, Washington, D.C. December 5, 1996

1999

But he became a proponent of the new economy.

...it has been the ability of our flexible and innovative businesses and work force that has enabled the United States to take full advantage of emerging technologies to produce greater growth and higher asset values...

As I have testified before the Congress many times, I believe, at root, the remarkable generation of capital gains of recent years has resulted from the dramatic fall in inflation expectations and associated risk premiums, and broad advances in a wide variety of technologies that produced critical synergies in the 1990s.

...the rate of return on capital facilities put in place during recent years has, in fact, moved up markedly. While discussions of consumer spending often continue to emphasize current income from labor and capital as the prime sources of funds, during the 1990s, capital gains, which reflect the valuation of expected future incomes, have taken on a more prominent role in driving our economy.

He asserted that the bubble was helping people save for retirement.

...the net worth of the average household has increased by nearly 50 percent since the end of 1992, well in excess of the gains of the previous six years. Households have been accumulating resources for retirement or for a rainy day, despite very low measured saving rates.

Yet he recognized that the bubble might not be sustainable.

The recent behavior of profits also underlines the unusual nature of the rebound in equity prices and the possibility that the recent performance of the equity markets will have difficulty in being sustained. The level of equity prices would appear to envision substantially greater growth of profits than has been experienced of late.

Testimony of Chairman Alan Greenspan
State of the Economy
Before the Committee on Ways and Means, U.S. House of Representatives
January 20, 1999

Again he endorsed the notion of the new economy.

Can this favorable performance be sustained? In many respects the fundamental underpinnings of the recent U.S. economic performance are strong. Flexible markets and the shift to surplus on the books of the federal government are facilitating the build-up in cutting-edge capital stock. That build-up in turn is spawning rapid advances in productivity that are helping to keep inflation well behaved. The new technologies and the optimism of consumers and investors are supporting asset prices and sustaining spending.

But he expressed concern about overvalued equities.

Equity prices are high enough to raise questions about whether shares are overvalued.

Testimony of Chairman Alan Greenspan
The Federal Reserve's semiannual report on monetary policy
Before the Committee on Banking, Housing, and Urban Affairs,
U.S. Senate
February 23, 1999

Greenspan remained one of the strongest proponents of the new economy.

Something special has happened to the American economy in recent years. An economy that twenty years ago seemed to have seen its better days, is displaying a remarkable run of economic growth that appears to have its roots in ongoing advances in technology.

I have hypothesized on a number of occasions that the synergies that have developed, especially among the microprocessor, the laser, fiber-optics, and satellite technologies, have dramatically raised the potential rates of return on all types of equipment that embody or utilize these newer technologies. But beyond that, innovations in information technology—so-called IT—have begun to alter the manner in which we do business and create value, often in ways that were not readily foreseeable even five years ago.

...the recent years' remarkable surge in the availability of real-time information has enabled business management to remove large swaths of inventory safety stocks and worker redundancies, and has armed firms with detailed data to fine-tune product specifications to most individual customer needs. Intermediate production and distribution processes, so essential when information and quality control were poor, are being bypassed and eventually eliminated. The increasing ubiquitousness of Internet Web sites is promising to significantly alter the way large parts of our distribution system are managed.

Still he expressed some reservations.

The rate of growth of productivity cannot increase indefinitely. While there appears to be considerable expectation in the business community, and possibly Wall Street, that the productivity acceleration has not yet peaked, experience advises caution.

Testimony of Chairman Alan Greenspan
High-Tech Industry in the U.S. Economy
Before the Joint Economic Committee, U.S. Congress
June 14, 1999

He advised caution about the bubble.

As recent experience attests, a prolonged period of price stability does help to foster economic prosperity. But, as we have also observed over recent years, as have others in times past, such a benign economic environment can induce investors to take on more risk and drive asset prices to unsustainable levels. This can occur when investors implicitly project rising prosperity further into the future than can reasonably be supported.

But he insisted that asset inflation is good for the economy.

The rise in equity and home prices, which our analysis suggests can account for at least one percentage point of GDP growth over the past three years.

Then he returned to the danger of a bubble and its bursting—he saw it coming.

One of the important issues for the Federal Open Market Committee as it has made such judgments in recent years has been the weight to place on asset prices. As I have already noted, history suggests that owing to the growing optimism that may develop with extended periods of economic expansion, asset price values can climb to unsustainable levels even if product prices are relatively stable.

The 1990s have witnessed one of the great bull stock markets in American history. Whether that means an unstable bubble has developed in its wake is difficult to assess. A large number of analysts have judged the level of equity prices to be excessive, even taking into account the rise in "fair value" resulting from the acceleration of productivity and the associated long-term corporate earnings outlook.

But he refused to place confidence in his own judgment.
...bubbles generally are perceptible only after the fact. To spot a bubble in advance requires a judgment that hundreds of thousands of informed investors have it all wrong. Betting against markets is usually precarious at best.

And he insisted there was not much danger.
While bubbles that burst are scarcely benign, the consequences need not be catastrophic for the economy.

Testimony of Chairman Alan Greenspan
Monetary Policy and the Economic Outlook
Before the Joint Economic Committee, U.S. Congress
June 17, 1999

Greenspan continued to praise the new economy.
At the root of this impressive expansion of economic activity has been a marked acceleration in the productivity of our nation's workforce. This productivity growth has allowed further healthy advances in real wages and has permitted activity to expand at a robust clip while helping to foster price stability.

Testimony of Chairman Alan Greenspan
The Federal Reserve's Semiannual Report on Monetary Policy
Before the Committee on Banking and Financial Services,
U.S. House of Representatives
July 22, 1999

2000

Near the height of the bubble, Chairman Greenspan saw the danger it posed to the economy but called it only a "remote possibility."
The Federal Reserve... must... foster the fundamental soundness of our financial system and put in place safeguards to protect against the remote possibility that unsound behavior in the financial sector is transmitted beyond the firms involved to the economy more generally.

Testimony of Chairman Alan Greenspan
On nomination to fourth term as Chairman
Before the Committee on Banking, Housing, and Urban Affairs,
U.S. Senate
January 26, 2000

Just as the bubble was about to break, Greenspan expressed no concern.

There is little evidence that the American economy, which grew more than 4 percent in 1999 and surged forward at an even faster pace in the second half of the year, is slowing appreciably.

He remained an advocate of the new economy.

Underlying this performance [of strong economic growth], unprecedented in my half-century of observing the American economy, is a continuing acceleration in productivity.

He declared the bubble to be good for the economy.

Outlays prompted by capital gains in excess of increases in income, as best we can judge, have added about 1 percentage point to annual growth of gross domestic purchases, on average, over the past five years.

Yet he saw the problem coming in the economy and connected it to the wealth effect of asset inflation.

With foreign economies strengthening and labor markets already tight, how the current wealth effect is finally contained will determine whether the extraordinary expansion that it has helped foster can slow to a sustainable pace, without destabilizing the economy in the process.

But decided there was no significant danger.

Although the outlook is clouded by a number of uncertainties, the central tendencies of the projections of the Board members and Reserve Bank presidents imply continued good economic performance in the United States.

**The Federal Reserve's Semiannual Report on the Economy
and Monetary Policy
Before the Committee on Banking and Financial Services,
U.S. House of Representatives
February 17, 2000**

2001

Even as the economy prepared to enter a recession and the federal budget surpluses were about to disappear, Chairman Greenspan continued to applaud the new economy.

The key factor driving the cumulative upward revisions in the budget picture in recent years has been the extraordinary pickup in the growth of labor productivity experienced in this country since the mid-1990s... The most recent indications have added to the accumulating evidence that the apparent increases in the growth of output per hour are more than transitory... It is these observations that appear to be causing economists, including those who contributed to the OMB and the CBO budget projections, to raise their forecasts of the economy's long-term growth rates and budget surpluses...

And insisted that the bubble was good for the economy and appropriate.

Had the innovations of recent decades, especially in information technologies, not come to fruition, productivity growth during the past five to seven years, arguably, would have continued to languish at the rate of the preceding twenty years. The sharp increase in prospective long-term rates of return on high-tech investments would not have emerged as it did in the early 1990s, and the associated surge in stock prices would surely have been largely absent. The accompanying wealth effect, so evidently critical to the growth of economic activity since the mid 1990s, would never have materialized.

Testimony of Chairman Alan Greenspan
Outlook for the Federal Budget and Implications for Fiscal Policy
Before the Committee on the Budget, U.S. Senate
January 25, 2001

The U.S. economy entered a recession in March 2001, and the great productivity advances of previous years were revised out of the nation's economic statistics, but Chairman Greenspan remained a proponent for the new economy.

The prospects for sustaining strong advances in productivity in the years ahead remain favorable... Even consumer spending decisions have become increasingly responsive to changes in the perceived profitability of firms through their effects on the value of households' holdings of equities. Stock market wealth has risen substantially relative to income in recent years—itself a reflection of the extraordinary surge of innovation. As a consequence, changes in stock market wealth have become a more important determinant of shifts in consumer spending relative to changes in current household income than was the case just five to seven years ago.

Testimony of Chairman Alan Greenspan
Federal Reserve Board's semiannual monetary policy report to the Congress
Before the Committee on Banking, Housing, and Urban Affairs, U.S. Senate
February 13, 2001

Taken as a whole, including his frequent qualifications, Chairman Greenspan's public comments endorsed the notion of a favorable new era in the American economy driven by new technology and the Internet. Further, his views helped investors believe that there was no great danger of an economic downturn or of a market collapse, even at times encouraging them to believe that the investments they were making with their pension money in new economy stocks would in fact increase their retirement nest eggs. Greenspan's comments were widely reported in the press and were heeded by many Americans, including small investors.

Talking Points

There were several players other than venture firms, investment banks and mutual funds that contributed to the bubble. Accountants permitted Internet firms to engage in creative accounting that inflated sales. The media hyped the bubble almost without reservation. The Fed not only did almost nothing to prevent the bubble—other than a timely warning by Fed Chairman Alan Greenspan, which was not followed by action—but provided the credit which made it possible.

VI The Road Kill of Capitalism

"A jumbled pile of broken computer components sits peacefully in a park. Deep within the pile a recording of a strangled voice yells, 'Sell, sell, sell!'"

—Proposal for a monument to the dot-com bubble[90]

13 Sell, Sell, Sell!

In this chapter we briefly summarize the major elements of damage done by the bubble. Those who believe that financial market excesses such as we've just experienced are an acceptable price of capitalism accept the costs below as the road kill of capitalism. To people who think this way, the financial and human casualties identified below are the necessary cost of economic progress, just as the carcasses of animals left beside the nation's highways are the necessary cost of automobile travel.

That these are human victims does not disturb those who believe financial manias serve a useful purpose. Whether or not it disturbs the majority of our society remains to be seen.

We begin by recounting the story of theglobe.com—one of the most publicized of the dot-coms. This is a tale that neatly encapsules many of the topics we've addressed previously, and shows their consequences. The entrepreneurs were young and inexperienced, but angels and venture backers gave them money because they had imagination and energy—which in this event were not enough to make the company successful. Venture capitalists pressed on the skeptical managers of the company too much money. At the IPO, the bankers grotesquely undervalued the issue, leaving the company with far less money than it could have used, the entrepreneurs with paper—not real—wealth, and speculators, including some favored by the banks with otherwise hard to obtain IPO shares—with riches. Finally, after the company was public, Wall Street analysts threatened to withdraw support if the company didn't lose more and more money in the attempt to gain sales and market share. When the bubble burst and the shares tumbled, the analysts turned away and left the company to its fate.

theglobe.com

This is the story of two young men who were among the first to perceive the Internet opportunity. They started a company, became multimillionaires, and then saw much of it slip away. In this book such stories are beginning to sound familiar, and yet remain surprising and even fantastic.

Starting from Cornell   Todd Krizelman, a biology major from San Francisco, and Stephan Paternot, a computer sciences major from Switzerland, discovered chat rooms while undergraduates at Cornell University in 1994. They believed these chat rooms had many uses and would become popular. In their junior year of college they borrowed $15,000 from friends and family, and designed a Web site that had all the available tools for building Web "communities," but let users decide how to use the tools. theglobe.com, Inc. became, as the company Web site described it, "a virtual community." The company later grew into the emerging video game industry, publishing game information online and in print magazines.

Good fortune was on their side. They met fellow Cornell alumnus Michael Egan from Dancing Bear Investments who invested $20 million in 1997 and became chairman of the firm. "I had no reservations about investing so much in a company run by kids," Egan told a reporter.[91] The company also received smaller investments from David Horowitz (former MTV CEO), Bob Halperin (former Raychem vice chairman), and David Duffield (chairman and CEO of PeopleSoft).

Seeking capital from venture firms, theglobe.com endured an extensive process of due diligence, something which later in the Internet bubble would be much abbreviated. Todd Krizelman described the venture firm's due diligence process: "It was *so* substantial. For people on the outside, it's probably hard to imagine. A team of accountants went back to inception to see that every last thing we had said was true, and that we had accounted for everything. A group of lawyers worked to make sure that all the contracts we had written with our advertising clients as well as our subscription agreements, everything, were alright. The venture firm brought in a very top tier consulting firm to come in to do more diligence. They did a valuation model and said 'hey, this is right, these guys are right, these guys are on to something'—giving us an outside seal of approval. And then finally, the venture firm had one or two people from its office quite literally live in our office for about two months to really go over all the nuts and bolts of how we marketed the product, where we thought we'd build the product, and how we might spend additional cash."

Diligence coming to a successful end, the entrepreneurs and the venture capitalists began to discuss financing—not just the terms, but how much. "In the beginning," Krizelman reports, "the venture guys had to convince us that we needed more capital. So there was a lot of time spent saying, "Hey, I bet if we put more money into this we could really grow this thing much larger." We were very concerned with this idea of dilution and giving up control. We really didn't start this to become millionaires. This was our company. We spent a lot of time negotiating over control rights over the company as we accepted the investment. And ultimately it's a main reason we ultimately did retain control of the company."

Going public The company was incorporated in 1995 and went public three years later on November 13, 1998. It was the 48th company to go public in the Internet space. The decision to go public was not a simple one, but there were good reasons. As Krizelman says, "For a salesperson to go out and say 'The company is doing so well we can go public, you can look us up on the NASDAQ,' was immensely powerful. Even from the time we filed, sales ramped. In the year we went public we did $6 million in sales, and I think something like a third to half of it happened in the last four months."

The company made stock market history by appreciating over 900%, from $9 to $97 in its first day of trading, leaving Krizelman, then 25, with a stake of $73 million, and Paternot, then 24, with $78 million.

The bankers left too much on the table But this was not as good a fortune as it then appeared to be. Krizelman says, "When we went public and the stock went straight up we were very upset. It meant that our bank had left a lot of money on the table for us and had not serviced us well. It did not mean that we had personally capitalized, because management is locked up. This created a public relations problem immediately. The next morning you saw in the *New York Post* and others that I was worth this much, when in fact you're not worth anything. We were locked up for about a year."

Stock analysts demand more losses from the company The pressure to spend the company's money quickly was great. "You really would go into a meeting with stock analysts and one would say, 'You're not losing enough money,' and you would say, 'I think we're losing plenty.' And they would say, 'Your peers in the space, your competitors, are willing to lose twice as much as you. What are you going to do about it?' and you'd say, 'Nothing, I'd rather have the money.' And they'd say, 'Then we'll downgrade you.'"

Much of the money the company did spend went into advertising. Theglobe.com's strategy was to start building its brand name in second tier markets, such Miami, Atlanta and Chicago—rather than New York and Los Angeles. They put a lot of money into branding early on, because the rate of return was great. However, in 1999 and 2000, the rate of return on investment in branding weakened, because of fierce competition. Thus, theglobe.com started to limit its advertising in the second half of 1999.

The business press drives the business   Theglobe.com also took advantage of public relations created by the financial press. "You learn that the great news is that you can get so much press that you can drive your business. We had upwards of twenty million people visiting our site monthly, and it was mostly generated by just a few people in our PR department. Conversely, when the press was negative you had 10 negative articles a day coming out on the company," says Krizleman.

"In early 2000, the company enjoyed four million viewers a month and was counted by Jupiter Media Metrix as one of the 100 most-visited sites. But audiences and advertising dollars came in far more slowly than predicted, and acquisitions were difficult to absorb. By the end of the year, with its shares trading well below $1 each, theglobe.com reported a loss of $103.9 million and revenue of $29.9 million." ("After Soaring IPO and Fleeting Fame, What Comes Next?— theglobe.com's Founders Hit Midlife Crises at Age of 26," by Ianthe Jeanne Dugan and Aaron Lucchetti, *The Wall Street Journal*, Europe, May 3, 2001)

The end of the story   The end of this story is now familiar. In 2000, Krizelman and Paternot handed control of their company to Chuck Peck, former senior vice-president of the American Institute of Certified Public Accountants. In April 2001, the staff was reduced to approximately 100 employees. While smaller, the company is now close to cash-flow break even. The stock was taken off the market on August 3, 2001, at $.15 a share.

Contribution: theglobe.com

**Highlights of an interview with Todd Krizelman,
Co-founder, former co-CEO of theglobe.com
October 30, 2001**

Many believe venture capitalists and investment bankers somehow caused the Internet mania of the late 1990s. While they certainly played a part, it was only a supporting role. Financiers are in the business of trying to find returns for their investors. In this context, they were not acting irrationally or immorally by pursuing investments in the Internet; they were simply doing their job. All financiers will pursue the highest returns and the Internet provided that. Venture capitalists, investment banks, and fund managers probably didn't act too differently in the Internet bubble than they have acted in the past. The biotech craze of the 80's comes to mind.

What did change dramatically was the public's perception of how easy running a company might be. The press glamorized Internet companies, made them look fun and created idyllic representations. Of all perceptions, it became common for people to believe they could create substantial wealth instantly. As a result, thousands of people actively left their jobs to take a chance being an entrepreneur. What they did not know were the difficulties running or working within a start-up.

Start-ups are high risk, even in the best of situations—and the role of the entrepreneur is equally as exhilarating as it is terrifying. It's as if disbelief was suspended in this time. During 1998 and 1999, many people with low appetites for risk, without good ideas and without experience, established new firms and raised capital. The result was a substantial decline in quality of new companies and a saturation of competition. This is a stark contrast to the earliest Internet companies. In the beginning, start-ups were mostly run by management teams with smart capital behind them. More importantly, there was limited competition, and the growth rate in Internet usage was rising sharply (making it cheaper and faster to find customers). This made it possible for companies to grow quickly and allowed room for mistakes along the way. Conversely, by the end of the century, usage growth was diminishing, user loyalties were already established, and the substantial competition caused the market to suffocate (think Thomas Malthus on population). This made it difficult for both bad companies and good companies to survive.

What made people forget about risk?

I think they looked at the press and saw time after time the press talking about some star that made tons of money, or how Jim Barksdale's secretary made a couple million. Those stories become pervasive. It is the American story. It's very Americana. Rags to Riches. And there was enough of that in the press that people said "You know what? I can be in any field and I can just jump into this Internet thing." And I think this idea of low barrier to entry is a huge difference between the high tech and the Internet. In high tech in the past, like hardware and real software development, as well as in bio tech, as well as most of the fields you associate venture capitalists with, there's a real barrier to entry. If you didn't have experience in engineering you weren't going to understand it. You're never going to start Genetech unless you're a biologist with four years of undergraduate work and a Ph.D. So suddenly this new field comes along, where you can, by 1999, buy off-the shelf software to set up your own site. You have tons of companies trying to sell bandwidth, so it's easy to set up your business. And so because there aren't these barriers, a lot of people thought, "I can do this," and I think a lot of people were probably very surprised.

Didn't giving stock options to employees imply get-rich-quick?

In the beginning that's what I thought. But you want to tell people that it's going to be bad. I liked to sensitize people before they were hired by saying, "I don't want to dress this up. This is going to be hard." We were building a company that was going to be a long-term investment of their time. It was a very quick way to self-select in the hiring process. We were very selfish with the options—or I'm sure that's how it would have been perceived. But it was more than that. It was to enforce that we were building a culture that wasn't falling all over itself to get rich.

For us there was this fear of failure. When you start hiring 100 people, and they have kids and families and health care, this is your family. You don't want to screw over someone in your family. We wouldn't so much say, "We're going to fail," but we would certainly tell them a lot about how the job actually would be. When you came to our offices you did not see fancy chairs. It wasn't highly decorated. Our first administrative person came in our fourth year. We really went a long way to say, even when we didn't have to be that way, even when we had a lot of money, "Let's still be paranoid and frugal."

One of your early investors, David Duffield [founder and CEO of PeopleSoft], said "I can't honestly say I understand their products"— this was some time after he wrote a $2M check. This is someone early on who didn't understand the risks. What do you think led him to invest?

The article in which David was quoted was written in 1997. The company had been in business for three years at this point.

Most venture capitalists, especially with very early investments—some look at specific products—but most look at people—the quality of people, the team of people. That's our relationship with David and some of the other early investors. When you are dealing with very new technology and you have a passive investor, you want to be able to evaluate the integrity of the management team: Are they in a position to evaluate and see trends before they hit the mainstream? And that was consistent with our relationship with him. That was not a negative comment, especially in 1997 when the Internet was new enough that people didn't know in general how it was going to change society. They didn't know that the Internet was going to shift Dell's whole model online. You didn't know all these variables.

If you go back in 1999 and read *The Wall Street Journal* or *The New York Times*, you would believe that 50% of the U.S. GDP was being produced by start-up companies, based upon the amount of space they were allocated in *The New York Times* or *The Wall Street Journal*. That was the predominant topic. In the case of *The Times*, they actually added a new section, "Circuits," just to accommodate it, in addition to still seeing it all over the paper. So I think a lot of people really did jump in during those years and, as a result. the price to run your company escalated, both to retain employees, to attract employees, and to purchase insurance. All the costs that are cost components into your business rose dramatically.

How did you go about selecting bankers?

As an entrepreneur, especially when you're doing an IPO, the prestige of your bank doesn't matter as much. When you're looking to raise $30–$50 million, you go to people who are going to get you public first, and who are going to charge least to do it. Those are the qualifications.

Some people say, "If you go with Merrill or Goldman this makes a big difference." But in fact it doesn't make a big difference.

For those who believe that Merrill or Goldman are going to support your stock in the aftermarket, you're going to have a rude awakening. You're only important so long as you are the current client. As soon as you are the former client, it just doesn't matter.

What was the nature of their questions?

Research analysts egg you on to increase your numbers, but they don't tell you to change your model.

Did the institutional investors ask the right questions, knowing what you knew about the business and what your worries were? Did they serve their clients well?

I think for us, they did. I wonder if that was true for other companies. We went public in 1998, early in the bubble, so there was still a sense that there weren't companies going public every day. It was not a free-for-all at the time we went public. Some people spent a lot of time with us. Bankers were pretty thorough with us. Some invested. Some didn't invest. It was the way I would have imagined it being.

People would argue that these mutual fund guys just rubber-stamped a whole bunch of companies and got screwed afterwards. I didn't have that feeling at all. They were doing models on us, research on us. Certainly, at each mutual fund there were some about whom you said, "That guy was a great analyst," and others, "This is just an average analyst." But this kind of inconsistency is going to be in any environment.

Is there a fault anywhere among the key players?

I would certainly take the financial press and say, "These guys played a much larger role than I bet they believe." This idea of the Fourth Estate was very powerful, as I'm sure you can imagine. For years we had about 10 articles a day coming out on our company. We thought long and hard about PR. It wasn't something we took lightly. We hired some good people.

We used the press because we thought it would be cheaper than using cash dollars in marketing. I assign financial press a different blame than just press. Press is under no obligation to be accurate or right, whereas the financial press does have some obligation to its readership to be accurate. We were spared the brunt of this inaccuracy. You saw a huge number of errors in the financial press. As well, you had the financial press taking an opinion that was consistent with this idea of, "How much is right?" judging for themselves what is right and wrong for companies. If the financial press didn't like your product, then you didn't have a company.

So I do assign some blame there. I also say that because there are some times when the financial press in the early days would say, "This is a great business. Got to buy in! Got to buy in!" and people would do it. One of the scariest things is that you have CNBC, who has investment fund managers to talk about what they like, and of course those fund managers are buying that stock, and they stand to gain by hyping.

It's interesting to compare and contrast Todd Krizelman's comments in this interview with what we've described in the previous chapters of this book. Krizelman believes the venture funds hadn't changed their modes of behavior for the bubble, but they had. He views the mutual funds as carefully analyzing his firm, but little of this analysis seems to have made its way to mutual fund investors. And he sees a significant role played in the bubble by the business press, as we do.

Not a Smart Thing to Do

Entrepreneurs were not the only ones who ended up holding the small end of the stick. The other big losers were small investors who bought shares at valuations that made no sense.

In a previous chapter we discussed how the bubble was funded largely by retirement plans. When the bubble burst, many people were left without savings. For example, two middle-aged women working in clerical positions at a New York financial services firm placed their entire 401(k) retirement savings in annuities with a major mutual fund, believing that because it was a large, well-known firm, their savings were secure. But much of the fund in which they were invested had been placed in Internet stocks. When the bubble burst and the value of their fund began to decline, they did what they'd been told to do—stay invested for the long term. After 12 months their savings were almost gone, and still they held on, saying that they would sell when the technology companies in which they'd been invested regained their share prices of the past. Finally their employer told them that this would never happen, and they began to realize that their nest eggs were gone for good. These working people, and millions like them, had become the road kill of capitalism.

It's important to be clear about the financial losses imposed by the bubble. To some degree, the losses were only paper losses. An entrepreneur had little or no net worth one day, and a huge amount the next, and nothing the third. Had he or she really lost money? It had always been on paper, and in a sense he had not. So when it is mentioned that some trillions of dollars were created by the Internet bubble and then disappeared in the bust, the loss was funny money.

But there were real losses to some people, and real gains to others. Managers and employees at dot-coms worked for low pay and in the hope of gains on stock options, and when the companies crashed, they got nothing on the stock and had contributed much of their effort to the company for nothing. They took a real loss.

Many small investors bought into the bubble near or at its height—they were the last people to be allowed in—and when the bubble burst, they lost real money—money they had saved or salted away in pension accounts, and which was gone. These were real, not imaginary losses.

And some people made real, not paper gains—people who invested early and got out early, and bankers and brokers who handled transactions for fees.

As pointed out earlier in this book, there was a substantial transfer of wealth from employees of Internet companies, and from small investors, to professionals in the Financial Value Chain which was a primary economic result of the bubble. The total wealth in the economy went up by some $4 trillion in the bubble and came down by the same amount in the bust, but during the process, other billions of dollars changed hands, and this is where the significant losses occurred.

Whether by virtue of investments in their own company's stock, or by virtue of investments in mutual funds, or by speculating in the shares of dot-coms and telecoms, many small investors, using their pension money, were virtually wiped out by the bubble's bursting.

During the bubble, many companies induced employees to invest in the companies for whom they worked by using a variety of means: 1) buying shares directly through employee stock purchase plans; 2) investing via 401(k) retirement plans; and 3) through incentives and pay in stock options. And many companies, including Gilette, Coca-Cola, Procter & Gamble Co., and Qwest Communications International, Inc., continue to do so. "Benefits consultants Hewitt Associates found in a recent study that nearly half of 215 firms offering company stock in their 401(k) plans only contribute their own shares to employee accounts [that is, they match employee contributions to the retirement plans but only in shares of the company's stock, not in cash], and that 85% of those companies restrict sales of stock." In many companies, employees can't sell the stock the company has invested in their 401(k) until they are in their 50s.[92]

Lucent was one of these companies, and a major player in the telecom bubble. At Lucent, some employees "had their [401(k)] plans entirely invested in Lucent," reported *The New York Times*.[93] As Lucent's share price declined, employees' pension savings went down with it.

The Lucent story is bad enough, but is dwarfed by the disaster that overwhelmed employees in the collapse of Enron. At one time Enron was among the 10 largest American companies, and it was a darling of the dot-com era because of its online trading of electricity and natural gas. Because the company was so large, and its success was believed to be so substantial, Enron share prices weathered the first stages of the collapse of the bubble very well. It wasn't until fall 2001 that apparent misrepresentations in the company's financial reports got wide attention and precipitated a sudden fall in the company's share price.

Many of Enron's 30,000 or so employees had most or all of their retirement savings in Enron's stock. The company made its contributions to their plans only in its own stock, and in fall 2001, the plan administrators in the company had restricted sale of Enron shares by plan holders. In consequence, when the company's share price went to almost zero, so did the value of employees' savings plans.

A sobering contrast can be drawn between the experience of Enron's employees in the company's defined contribution plans—which was a disaster—and the very different experience of the employees of another large company that had a defined benefit plan. At the very time Enron's employees were losing their pensions, Unilever was successfully suing Merrill Lynch (though the matter was settled without trial) because Merrill had not made enough money for Unilever's pension plan—not lost money, but not made as much as the contract for management of pension money by Merrill had provided.[94] It's hard to imagine a clearer example showing why the clout of a large investor (Unilever) is valuable to people saving for a pension with a member of the Financial Value Chain (Merrill Lynch). The employees of Enron, each managing his or her own pension money under a 401(k) plan, had no clout with either the company or its plan managers, and they got killed financially. Unilever, acting to support its pension obligations to its employees, was able to make a performance contract with a major financial services firm, and largely to hold the firm to its commits as to performance of the investment. Unilever's employees were much better protected than Enron's.

Probably what would best have protected the investing public generally from the Enron disaster would be a requirement that every five years or so, the audit committee of a publicly held company must change its public accounting firm. New accountants put more resources into constructing a view of the entire business process of a company. As the complexity of some businesses grows, this is a necessary thing.

A fresh look doesn't ordinarily occur with existing accountants because of the current dynamic between corporate audit committees and accounting firms. Basically, audit committees (which include the chief financial officer of a firm) beat down over the years the audit fee, and often tell the accounting firm that it will make up the lost audit fee in consulting fees from the company. So the accounting firm devotes less time and resources to the audit. This is exactly the wrong set of incentives and directions from the point of view of investors in public companies. If accountants were changed on a five-year basis, there would be more actual accounting business, and far better accounting of the complexities of modern business. The Enron disaster might not have occurred as it did.

Young People Succeeding Early

There is yet another category—besides entrepreneurs and small investors—who became road kill after the Internet bubble: young people who'd gone to work for the dot-coms.

During the Internet bubble young professionals had a lot of fun, and some of them made a lot of money—at least for a while. Both of these accomplishments were deeply resented by others.

Among those most unhappy about it were, ironically, the banks and venture firms which were creating the bubble. During its peak, firms that ordinarily employ lots of young professionals—banks, venture firms, and consulting companies—found themselves losing these people to the dot-coms. In fact, it was during their daily interactions with the professional service companies, getting ready for an IPO, reviewing the progress of a venture investment, or assisting a dot-com with its business model, that the young professionals made the contacts that led to their dot-com jobs.

The young professionals found a very attractive situation at the dot-coms. The dot-com people were also young, fun to be with, doing things that had never been done before, and seemingly making big money via stock options. The dot-com companies were exciting, relaxed, often with a few seasoned executives at the head to give the company balance and a feeling of security. So young professionals left the banks, venture firms, and consultancies, and leapt to the dot-coms.

The professional service firms raised salaries, accepted casual attire for work, paid big bonuses, and where possible, granted stock, in an attempt to hold onto them. But there was resentment, especially among higher level executives who had worked their way to influential and high paying positions over many years, and with many sacrifices and little fun. Now they saw young people succeeding early, and it didn't seem right.

It didn't last long. When the bubble began to deflate, most people in the Internet companies held on, thinking the stock markets would soon turn about and resume their upward climb. But except for a few false rallies, the market tumbled at an increasing pace. Soon the dot-coms began letting people go; then the entire staffs of companies were laid off as the firms floundered.

In one well-publicized example, the CEO of a telecom company sent the following email to his employees: "Right now we are all out of jobs. It's time to pack up your personal items and move on in life."[95]

During the bubble, one of the large consulting firms told me that it was having 50 percent turnover annually in the information technology area, with the people going to dot-coms. Soon after the bubble burst, the firm found itself with no turnover at all among its Information Technology employees.

Displaced, refugees from the dot-coms and telecoms boomeranged back to the banks, venture funds, and consulting companies that they'd left, when there were places for them and a willingness to forgive their earlier departures. For others, there were no jobs readily to be found. Some took off traveling abroad for extended periods or tried to go back to school, others kept looking for jobs, slowly adjusting their expectations.

But often employers didn't want them. They are, a management consultant wrote a reporter, "Young, ambitious and currently flooding the job market... former dot-com CEOs, CFOs, and vice presidents..." A management consultant told the reporter the following about these refugees from the dot-com bust, "The Internet economy produced a sense of entitlement... a sense that people shouldn't just have a job, but a really cool job... I don't know if these people can fit in anywhere."[96] Long periods passed and people like this failed to find new jobs.

The Return of Big Company Values

Finally, people weren't the only road kill of the bubble. An incipient social revolution was a casualty as well. At the inception of the new economy, many people saw it as an opportunity to shake off the strict behavioral norms of large companies for a much more casual company culture. As new companies emerged, the search for a different kind of corporate culture became almost a crusade, but one which was dealt a perhaps fatal blow by the collapse of the bubble.

In the aftermath of the bubble, as the economy turned down and unemployment rose, old economy employers were not going to accept refugees from the dot-coms on any but the terms the employers found agreeable. "The young people coming to us now have a higher respect for big company values," the senior vice president of one of America's largest firms told me in the summer of 2001. At the banks, casual attire began to be restricted, stock was less available, bonuses went down. At the great manufacturing and retail companies, young professionals were suddenly again seeking jobs in often hierarchical social structures in which they were expected to serve time-in-grade in order to slowly progress up a ladder of promotion.

There was more lost in the bubble than the personal careers of many young people—and more lost than a great deal of money; a social revolution had been attempted, failed, and now a reaction was beginning. A revolution in the social mores of business had accompanied the Internet boom. Some leaders of dot-coms had explicitly sponsored it. John Doerr of Kleiner Perkins, a venture firm, was said to be fond of giving a slide show to potential investors as the bubble grew.[97] In the show he contrasted the old and new economies, in part as in Table 13-1.

Table 13–1 Old economy versus new economy.

Old Economy	New Economy
a skill	lifelong learning
labor versus management	teams
business versus the environment	growth
security	risk taking
monopolies	competition
standardization versus customized	choice
standing still	moving ahead
top-down	distributed
wages	ownership, options

Similarly, James Kenefick of Net-tel had a list as in Table 13–2:[98]

Table 13–2 The old way versus the new way.

The Old Way	The New Way
Security	Opportunity
Steady advancement. Wealth is a reward after a lifetime of work.	Everyone's an entrepreneur. Success means being able to retire at 35.
Detachment	Total Commitment
You get a paycheck. Someone else worries about the company.	You get equity, so you strive to make the company better.
Hierarchy	We're All Equal
There are workers and there's management. They know who they are.	The parking lot is first-come, first-serve. You call the chairman "Jerry."
Work and Fun Don't Mix	Pamper Me
Lunch is from 12 to 1. You can dress casually on Fridays.	"Sorry about that deadline. I've got a massage at 2."
It's Just a Job	It's So Much More
The search for meaning takes place elsewhere, if at all.	You're making the world a better place—or you call in sick.

To some of us these lists likely read as bad against good. Who can object, for example, to lifelong learning, to teamwork, to opportunity, and so forth? But in fact these are hard-won reforms which are still strongly contested by the bureaucratic procedures in many companies and government agencies. For example, lifelong learning means that people must have an opportunity to take courses and bring new ideas to the workplace. In some companies that's welcomed (including some old economy firms), but in many others people are expected to do their assigned tasks without showing interest in learning, except through required training for new methods or machinery, and without opportunity to advance. In fact, the workplace remains largely in the old economy tradition.

The advocates of the new economy claimed without justification that they were the originators of many major advances that had been made in American economic society in the past two decades. But even if they didn't create them, new economy spokespersons certainly both exaggerated and championed many of these changes.

Thus, when the bubble burst, it potentially endangered useful social advances as well as the financial situation of many people. There immediately began a return to large company, old economy values. More was and is at stake, that is, than money.

Talking Points

Entrepreneurs were both beneficiaries and victims of the bubble and the other players in the financial value chain. Excited by the prospect of great wealth, they eagerly took their companies public; but usually they were unable to sell out quickly, and in the bubble's burst, many lost all their wealth and their companies as well.

Entrepreneurs generally started with an idea and hard work; were pushed to make their companies get-big-fast; saw their companies taken public to the great profit of many, but rarely themselves; and then when the market crashed, lost most of both their paper wealth and their companies. What had been lost by a young entrepreneur? The answer is years of intense effort, and a business which might have, in a different context, survived to prosper to the benefit of its founders, employees, and customers. What had been gained? Some bitter experience.

Not only the entrepreneurs and late stage investors lost in the bubble. Many people worked for Internet companies, and many lost their jobs after the bubble burst. Those who were able to get hired by old economy firms found that they were returning to a more authoritarian and formal workplace than they had enjoyed in the new economy. More than economics had been at stake; a cultural revolution in the workplace was also set back when the bubble crashed.

14 Dire Consequences

Creating a New Business Cycle

The bursting of the Internet bubble has now played a major role in tipping the world economy into recession, and there is the danger that this is merely the first of a new series of such recessions. The world is building a new business cycle via financial market instability. The business cycle cannot be considered tamed until the financial manias that now regularly threaten the world economy are reined in.

We have tamed the old business cycle, driven as it was by inflation, overheated labor markets, excessive investments in certain sectors, inventory overbuilding, and extreme variability in housing finance. The business cycle then caused swings in capital markets. The 1929 stock market crash, for example, followed the descent of the world economy into recession.

Inflation is more or less moderated.

Macro economic policy plus increased productivity and increased immigration have kept labor markets at a balance between too loose and too tight, and thereby have kept wage-cost-driven inflation in bounds.

Business has moderated investment behavior: The competition-driven investment booms of the past (as, for example, in oil refineries and nuclear power plants) have largely disappeared.

Inventory overbuilding has been moderated by just-in-time management of inventories.

The old housing cycle has been extinguished. It was driven by sudden shifts in mortgage availability (including lack of availability at any price) which were a consequence of dedicated lending institutions (for example, savings banks, and savings and loan institutions). Today, mortgage financing is provided by the capital markets generally, and rates move within a more narrow range, without credit sometimes becoming completely unavailable, so that housing is less given to sudden and extreme swings of building activity.

All these changes are significant advances and have essentially abolished the old business cycle that was caused by dramatic swings in the business economy.

But today causality has reversed itself. We have a new business cycle worldwide that is being caused by the financial market downturns which follow speculative excesses. For example, from 1994 to 2000, the ratio of capital spending by business to personal consumption in the United States rose from 14 percent to 23 percent, the classic pattern of an investment boom which is virtually certain to end in a bust. Why? Because of the telecom bubble in which investors shoveled money at telecom companies to be spent on expansion.

Previously a barometer of business activity, the financial markets are now becoming causes of major instability. Every two years there is a crisis that sends some or all of the world economy teetering toward recession:

1995   Mexican financial crisis

1997   Asian financial crisis

1999   Long-Term Capital Management crisis

2001   dot-com and telecom bubbles

In each case government financial authorities had to rescue the world from the risk of recession following the collapse of a speculative orgy in the financial markets.

The situation may be getting worse. The United States today is in the grip of a recession caused in large part by the collapse of the Internet bubble. To get the economy growing again, the Fed is supplying money to the economy at a rapid rate. The increased availability of credit is threatening to set off another asset bubble. In effect, we are going from boom to bust to boom in asset values at a quicker and quicker pace. A dynamic new instability is being built into the world economy originating in the financial markets.

Economic Losses Caused by the Bubbles

Henry Kaufmann concluded, even before the bubble burst, that "...the tilt toward unbridled...financial entrepreneurship has exacted economic costs that often far outweigh their economic benefits."[99] He is speaking of entrepreneurship in the financial value chain—that is, abandoning old rules of thumb and bringing new types of financial products to retail investors—and pointing to its serious economic consequences.

What was the real economic impact of the bubble? The bursting of the bubble was a contributor to the sharp drop in consumer confidence that took place in late 2000, and 2001. In addition, the actual decrease in wealth dampened consumer spending. Business investment was set back directly by the collapse of the bubble and indirectly by its impact on consumer spending. The result of falling consumer expenditures and weak business investment was a recession that began in the United States and spread abroad.

During the bubble there was much speculative building of office building space in the expectation that venture-financed dot-coms would take the space. There was a steady rise from 1992 through 2000. Then, in the first quarter of 2001, leasing fell off a cliff—from a strong positive rate in the fourth quarter of 2000 to as strong a negative rate in the first quarter of 2001. Although new office buildings which were already under construction were being finished in 2001, as the year progressed, things were finished and almost nothing new was started. So the dot-com burst shut down construction just as it did advertising and new technology investment.

There was a vast waste of financial capital. Junk bonds were used to finance building of excessive fiber optic networks, to the degree that some one-half trillion dollars of high yield debt was burned through. Some of this capital came out of junk bond mutual funds and therefore was the 401(k) pension savings of individual investors; but much more of it was provided, and lost, by large institutional investors (again often pension funds) that took the debt because it was liquid and came in very large amounts. Apparently the investment committee of each institution thought they could dispose of the debt to other institutions, and when the bubble burst, no one wanted it.

The world—especially the United States—was left with excess capacity in fiber optic communication cables, but this capacity will ultimately find its own demand, as happened with overbuilt railways in the 19th century. That the cable will ultimately find a use does not mean that overbuilding was not a serious misallocation of the world's investment resources, however.

To summarize thus far, the largest financial loss and the greatest misallocation of physical investment occurred in the telecom sector, via the telecom bubble. Telecoms involved a huge amount of money, and a small number of people.

The opposite was the case in the dot-com sector. The great wastage of the dot-com sector was not financial capital (only a small portion of the investment which went into telecoms, primarily via bonds, was made in the dot-coms, primarily via equity), but the misallocation of people's lives.

For years people, especially young people, worked to build companies that ultimately failed, to build new social mores at work which ultimately were abandoned, and to build a start toward retirement funding which was ultimately lost.

The dot-com bubble, and the broader telecom and computer technology boom of the 1990s, disguised in America what was evident in Europe and Japan: the dismal prospects for young people in the labor force. In the United States, the technology boom created many thousands of jobs for young engineers and business graduates, and the dot-com bubble created an image of instant wealth. Meanwhile, abroad, there was a glut of the young on the labor market, with resulting high unemployment rates, relatively poor compensation, and social tensions. In the United States, the redistributive aspects of the bubble were especially subtle. In effect, savings of mature workers and retirees, in the form of their pension funds or direct savings, were invested in dot-coms, providing high paying jobs for young people, and the opportunity for instant wealth for them as well. With the collapse of the bubble, the job market for young people immediately darkened, and a long-term problem of careers—like that already being experienced in Europe and Japan—began to show itself.

Starving Entrepreneurs of Capital

A real danger is that a number of potentially important start-ups are being starved of capital in the aftermath of the bubble. The post-bubble world is in many respects indiscriminating with regard to who gets dragged down. Venture firms are not taking the time and effort to separate the good from the bad. This is unfortunate because good companies and bad suffer alike. CEOs of new firms are spending unreasonable amounts of time trying to raise funds, and valuations are so low that the incentive to be an entrepreneur is limited.

Innovation is the engine of the U.S. economy, and it runs on money. Heavy tech investments have enabled the productivity gains that have helped the economy in recent years. If investors lose faith in the experts that are supposed to be guiding them to the most promising businesses, they may shy away from investing in start-ups, good and bad. Already, the number of initial public offerings for tech companies has slowed to a trickle. "This is totally unprecedented," says Garrett Van Wagoner, president of the mutual fund firm Van Wagoner Capital Management. "People got so badly burned that they may never be back."

Never is a long time, but the impending money drought may seem that long. The last protracted plunge in the NASDAQ index was the 31 percent drop over 13 months in 1983 and 1984. That slowed the flow of offerings through 1985.

This time, though, the index has fallen twice as much, and it may not have hit bottom yet. "It took about three years after 1983 [to coax investors back to tech offerings] and I think we have hurt investors even worse this time," says Dennis. "I think it'll be at least three years this time." Worse, the closing of the IPO market is scaring off venture firms, which will further dampen innovation.[100]

Wilfried Beeck is a seasoned hand in the software business. Intershop was a start-up of his that got caught in the bubble. From the point of view of this one company, was the bubble good for technology or bad?

After its IPO, Intershop experienced a rapid upturn in its performance in the stock market. Beginning with a price of 3.41 Euros (adjusted for splits) in July 1998, the share price rose to over 140 in March 2000, a capitalization equivalent to 14 billion Euros. Afterward, it became clear to investors that Intershop's share price performance, like that of many other technology firms, was not based on sober economic appraisals. Share prices collapsed.

At the height of the bubble, many companies were being traded at unrealistically high prices, but today, many companies are confronted with a market valuation that does not reflect their true worth. Several players in the so-called new economy today, including Intershop, have possessed liquid capital in excess of their market valuation, reflecting the extremes of the stock market in the last three years.

To what extent did the existence of the Internet bubble hurt or help Intershop? Wilfried Beeck, co-founder and COO of Intershop, analyzed the situation in the following terms:

Contribution: Intershop

Wilfried Beeck, Co-founder and COO Intershop

Corporate Image and Human Capital; the Effects of the Internet Bubble on Technology Companies

As with many things, the implications of the Internet bubble cannot be seen in terms of black and white: decisive factors and arguments are gray. Therefore it makes sense to inspect the so-called trade-off—the good things and the bad with which technology firms were often confronted during the Internet bubble and are still today. From the perspective of a participant, two areas should be observed closely: corporate image and employees.

Corporate Image

As a sailor might view it, during the bubble, Intershop raced along with a tailwind of force 10. Today, with the hype over, the company has encountered a headwind. While in the beginning, a consistent upward trend in the stock market regularly provided the media with good news for PR, which helped build brand awareness, Intershop is now confronted with just the opposite. New customers are now asking whether Intershop will still exist in a year. The question of the actual quality of Intershop's technology, and with it the question of the real strength of the company, unfortunately often remain in the background. Hence, with regard to corporate image, the Internet Bubble led to a gamble for Intershop. In the good times, Intershop profited more than was its due as a consequence of positive attention from the media; and in the bad times, the company was hurt more than it deserved.

The Employees

Qualified and motivated employees are one of the most important keys to enduring success in business. During the expansion of the Internet Bubble, many New Economy firms were successful in luring employees away from Old Economy companies. For some people, motivation lay in the promise of instant wealth via stock options. For others it was simply exciting to be in the midst of something revolutionary and to work in an atmosphere known for flattened hierarchies and individual freedom. Media attention added its inciting effect to the exodus of talent to IT start-ups. By 1998, it appeared that the "talent war" was clearly being won by New Economy businesses.

In the aftermath of the bursting of the Internet Bubble, many technology companies lost their most important people. Knowledge, which had been carefully nurtured in the previous two to three years, was partially lost. Especially important were the exorbitant stock prices which characterized this period, allowing some key employees to sell their stocks and leave their respective companies. At the same time, other successful firms, with more attractive compensation packages, drew off high achievers. Many companies spun out of control in trying to top offers from the competition because of accelerating personnel costs. When the bubble burst, labor costs normalized and the temptation to hire away top talent was reduced to a more recognizable level.

Thus, the bubble itself was a negative. Start-ups did not need the bubble to attract people, and they lost key ones because of high share prices. Finally, the bubble caused compensation costs to spin out of control. From the people side, the bubble was a disaster for young companies like Intershop.

The experience of Intershop was replicated by many other technology firms during the bubble. At first the public excitement and investor interest seemed to help the company. But when the bubble burst and investors fled the technology sector, the bubble was seen to have been a damaging experience for the company. For Intershop, the inflating phase of the bubble was not necessary to its early stage growth, while the deflating stage of the bubble set back its prospects.

Setting Back Technological Innovation

One of the most significant consequences of the bubble was that in the rush for riches, many entrepreneurs were bypassed for funding who would have done a better job than those who were funded.

One significant example involves the laying of fiber optic cable under the oceans of the world. Global Crossing, a firm created by Gary Winnick, a Wall Street insider and a former associate of Michael Milkin, the junk bond king, crowded out firms with greater capability and promise. In the mid-1990s, as a need for more bandwidth to carry the Internet became evident, he hatched a scheme to lay fiber optic cable under the world's oceans. He had no experience in anything like this, but Wall Street quickly financed his company, and placed billions of debt for it. He took his company, Global Crossing, public in August 1998, at $9.50 a share, and a few months later it peaked at more than $60 a share.

Meanwhile, an entrepreneur, Suneil Tagore, who had actually worked with the phone companies to build undersea cables and now sought to do so on his own was denied funding by the venture and investment banking community because Global Crossing had pre-empted the domain. His company, Oxygen, soon ran out of angel funding and disappeared. This is not merely to say that Oxygen was denied access to capital in a general way but instead it was pre-empted in a very specific way. Both Global Crossing and Oxygen sought financing from Chase (now Morgan) Bank. In the end, Morgan decided to back Global Crossing with very substantial loans. As described in *The Wall Street Journal*, the head of Morgan's investment banking unit introduced Winnick to David Rockefeller Jr., former chairman of Morgan, allowing Winnick thereafter to refer to Rockefeller as his "new best friend."[101]

Morgan made the decision to back Global Crossing and reject Oxygen presumably for many reasons but knowing full well Winnick's background. In part, Morgan presumably wanted a deal large enough to put to work a lot of its capital. The leader will recall that a similar dynamic now operates in the venture world. Both banks and venture firms have become so large with so much money to invest (although even the largest venture funds are dwarfed by the large money center banks), that often the large size of an investment dictates its selection rather than the likely success of the business activity. When large size dictates investment instead of business prospects or leadership quality, then the tail is definitely wagging the dog.

The preference of the larger venture firms and investment banks during the bubble for large deals rather than good deals suggests that bigness was itself a high-priority criterion for choosing which deals to support. This makes very little sense from the point of view of the quality of the enterprises backed and therefore of the interests of investments—whatever sense it might make from the perspective of the venture firms and the banks. An economy with more and smaller venture firms and banks than the large institutions which now dominate our financial markets might do a better job of selecting entrepreneurs, new business ideas, and business models to finance.

In the outcome, Morgan is now seeking to recover some $95 million from Global Crossing, which went bankrupt early in 2002. It is possible, however, that Morgan generated enough fee income from Global Crossing for various services it provided to have covered the bank's likely losses from loans to or investments in Global Crossing.

Regardless of the bank's position, Global Crossing—essentially a built-for-the-bubble company—crowded out of the market smaller but more-likely-to-be successful firms, and this happened on a large scale in many businesses during the bubble.

Global Crossing also made very large political contributions and paid large fees to politically well-connected individuals for professional services. Newspaper reporters have written that they find few favors for the contributions. But because Global Crossing was believed to be well-connected politically, and was rumored to be making large contributions to politicians, key banks and other investors preferred to deal with Global Crossing, believing it to have an inside track to the business via connections to regulators of the telecom industries. This is where the company benefited most from its political largess—in denying support to competitors who were believed at a disadvantage because of Global Crossing's political connections.

Global Crossing overextended itself enormously, and by September 2001, its share price had collapsed. Meanwhile, the investment banks had pocketed large fees for the IPOs and the junk bond deals, and Winnick is reported to have cashed out some $600 million while the stock was high.[102]

This was a classic example of damage done by the players in the Financial Value Chain during the bubble—people from the financial community working with others in that community to set up companies which were poorly managed and virtually certain to fail, but which pre-empted by the size of their fundings other companies led by people who could have succeeded. The results were great losses for later stage investors, and massive capital misallocation for the national economy.

What Happened in e-learning

e-learning offers an example of how the U.S. bubble set the U.S. back in a key space—one that is critical both to productivity enhancement and to increasing employment. e-learning is about increasing what economists call human capital.

The United States took an early lead internationally in applying the Internet to learning. In 1999, says a study of e-learning in the United States, "Almost weekly, new learning portals opened—some for consumers, others for businesses, and still others for specific industries or trade associations. By October 1999... consultant Elliott Masie predicted more than 150 such portals would emerge before the end of the year."[103]

During the late 1990s, online higher education was subject to the same kind of extravagant predictions of a magnificent future as other industries. John Chambers of Cisco and Peter Drucker both predicted that the current system of college campuses would soon be displaced by large online universities. Many states tried to add to their public systems of higher education online classes.

Hearing all this, and seeing the prospects for themselves, numerous entrepreneurs sought venture funding for software and services designed to facilitate online education. Some $150 million of venture funding was poured into companies trying to exploit opportunities in this space.

But while the promise of online education is undoubtedly great, it has been slower to materialize than hoped by those who advanced and those who spent so much money in its development.

An industry of start-ups quickly grew in higher education. Among the companies were some which offered software for putting courses on line; some which offered online courses to colleges to supplement their own classroom offerings; some which offered retail sites at which students could locate the online courses they wanted; some which offered an e-commerce capability by which students could buy courses at Web sites; some which did other things. Yet none of the companies were able to make much money. Only a handful of already established colleges, with campuses of their own, which offered online courses in addition to their classroom courses, were able to make any money from online education, and many others which tried were unsuccessful.

In large part the difficulty was that no start-up had found a successful business model in the online education space. Yet many were pressing ahead with the get-big-fast strategies which were favored by venture investors and bankers. Companies spent large sums on staff and marketing; expenditure levels (so-called "burn-rates") required either substantial sales or continuing rounds of investment. Revenues were slow to materialize, and with the collapse of the bubble, investment dollars all but disappeared. Companies began to cut back on expenses and ration cash very carefully as the day when money would run out got closer and closer.

During this time, a few companies resisted the urge to go to venture firms for large investments, fearing to embark on a get-big-fast strategy when a successful business model was not yet evident. In effect these careful firms were the get-it-right strategists of the online education industry. They watched other firms which had taken venture money pour it into business models which could be modified only at the margins, since a redo of the total model would have undercut a get-big-fast strategy.

The careful watchers—surviving on shoestring financing—learned a great deal from the expensive experience of well-funded firms, and in time developed novel business models in which they had confidence. But when they took these models to the venture community for funding, they were told that the industry was already dominated by well-established firms. It didn't matter that the leading firms had little revenue, high costs, and no profits, for at that time the bubble was expanding and investors sought none of these.

Promises were enough. In the early spring 2000, I accompanied the CEO of a get-it-right company in the online education industry to meetings with a series of venture firms. He was seeking only a few million dollars to begin to implement his business model. In each instance, the venture firm representatives listened politely but briefly—they were very busy people—then declared that the space was already dominated by a major player, well-financed by venture firms, and with a top management team. Further, the company had good software, said the venture people, and important corporate clients, and sufficient financing to be successful. The already-existing company to which the venture people were referring was Edupoint, a California-based firm which over about seven months spanning late 1999 and early 2000 had secured some $20 million in venture funding. Representatives of two venture firms sat on its board. In March 2000, Edupoint had been named one of San Diego's top 25 emerging companies. There was no point, the entrepreneur was told, in any venture firm investing even a small amount in a rival when Edupoint was the clear winner in the space.

In fact Edupoint wasn't a winner at all, and neither were any of the well-financed firms then in the space. All were following less-than-ideal business models and trying to raise more money from investors, or use what invested funds they already had, to acquire companies in related markets and migrate there.

Edupoint was trying to sell college online courses to large corporations. It had a good Web site designed for e-commerce, a large staff including many salespeople, executives with little experience in the world of education, a grab bag of course offerings limited by its weak relations with its supplier colleges (which are ordinarily not-for-profits and are often difficult for a profit-seeking firm to deal with), and a high burn rate. Early in 2001, Edupoint had some 88 employees and a burn rate of almost $1 million per month.

After several years of effort, and some $20 million of investors' money spent, Edupoint had to show for its efforts one paying client.

The business model was not working—at least not at that time, and no one knew how much longer and how much investment would be required to make it work—and the get-big-fast business strategy was burning cash very fast.

In the summer of 2001, Edupoint was collapsing. It couldn't acquire further investment, and couldn't find buyers at decent prices for its software—its only significant asset.

Jeff Creighton, founder and chairman of the company, told a reporter, "We spent the first nine months growing as fast as we could and then the market literally flip-flopped.... At that time we should have cut down on our burn rate to give us more time for this model to take shape."[104]

The company offered itself for sale to its small get-it-right rival at a tiny fraction of the amount of capital which had been invested in Edupoint, but was refused. It then sold what assets it could at very low prices and ceased business.

Meanwhile, the get-it-right firm was still seeking funding for its different strategy and business plan, but venture funding, which had been closed to it previously due to Edupoint's perceived success, was now closed to it because of Edupoint's evident failure. When approached, venture capitalists no longer said that an investment in the start-up was not warranted due to Edupoint's being the winner in the space, but instead an investment was not warranted due to Edupoint's failure. Evidently, if Edupoint couldn't make it work, the venture firms had concluded, then there was no opportunity in the space, so no one should be funded.

It was by this peculiar logic that mistakes in whom to fund, what strategy to press upon entrepreneurs, and in building pancake companies, became the cause of failing to fund better conceived and led start-ups at lower costs and better prices for investors.

It's very hard for a dispassionate observer to conclude anything other than that in most, though not all, instances, the venture firms and investment banks had no notion of what was likely to be a successful business and what wasn't, and after funding so many mistakes were afraid that fresher ideas would be no better and so were afraid to fund them as well.

Meanwhile, in Germany...

Starting later than in the United States, small companies emerged in Germany in the e-learning space trying to mimic the American efforts, but didn't get e-learning started because for these start-ups there was:

- No brand recognition,
- No network of support,
- No funding,
- No competitive advantage since there were none of the above.

But after the bubble burst large firms like Bertlesmann, which has the factors mentioned previously, stepped in to grow the space and was successful.

The U.S. venture firms, in contrast, had put a lot of investment in e-learning companies in the beginning, which they had pressed too far, too fast. When the bubble broke and e-learning stocks fell, the investors held back, believing e-learning was a money sink-hole, and so e-learning in the United States was set back. In the beginning, at the start of the bubble, the United States was about 18 months ahead of Germany in e-learning. In the aftermath of the bubble, Germany was poised to catch up and move ahead of the United States.

The following contribution describes the life cycle of a German start-up company, DATACOM.net, which operated in the e-learning market. The article starts with the development of the idea, follows the financing process, the start of the operating business and the end of the company.

Contribution: DATACOM.net

Dr. Juergen Kohr, Managing Director, DATACOM.net

The Start

In August 1999, our idea to found an e-learning company emerged. The company would be able to employ the already-existing assets of DATACOM Academy, a small but well-known training company in the area of data communication. These assets included existing content, brand identity, and customer relationships. At the time, e-learning was considered an innovation in the training industry in Germany, while in the U.S. some companies were already planning their IPOs (e.g., SABA, Digital Think). In the e-learning timeframe, the U.S. market was considered to be 12 to 18 months ahead of the European market.

The management team of DATACOM.net consisted of three partners with different professional backgrounds, skills, and networks. The combination of the founders was seen as one of the key strengths by prospect investors. After finishing the business plan, in November 1999, the team started to contact venture capital firms and strategic investors.

The business plan pointed out the following four success factors:

A. High Quality Content in the Area of Network Training

DATACOM Academy's knowledge of and experience in more than 1,000 completed presence-based training courses over the last 11 years comprised the online training content of Datacom.net. The wide selection of training courses included, for example, the introduction and techniques of data communications, corporate networks, LAN technology, network security, protocols (TCP/IP, ISDN; ATM), Internet/intranet, as well as telecommunication. All subjects were independent from hardware and software vendors. In other words, no product training of Microsoft, Novell, or Cisco was offered.

B. Existing Brand and Customer Base

In the IT professional domain, DATACOM Academy was already an established brand name for network training of first-rate quality and competence. This brand and image was assumed to be very useful in approaching potential customers and the existing customer base.

C. Growing Demand for IT Professionals and IT Training

The need for IT experts and the respective demand for training and development have been expanding steadily for years. In 1999, IDC estimated that in Germany, by 2002, in the area of data communications alone, there would be a deficiency of about 200,000 experts. As a result, 42% of the job vacancies in data communication were expected not to be filled.

D. Growing Demand for Localized High Quality e-learning Content

Due to the fact that e-learning is a low-cost alternative, more and more large companies were expected to implement Learning Management Systems (LMS), so that they could control their internal training and development processes more efficiently. With each new LMS, an increased demand of localized e-learning content was assumed. At this point, virtually no provider offered high quality content in the German-speaking region.

The business plan emphasized the combination of existing skills and proficiencies of DATACOM Academy with the advantages the Internet provides as a learning tool. The team looked upon DATACOM.net as the logical reaction to the large demand of IT experts and the vast opportunities in the expanding market of Web-based training.

Our vision was to become the leading provider of Web-based training for IT professionals in the German language. Based on the competence in information technology, DATACOM.net was intended to be positioned in other e-learning fields, e.g., in management, soft skills, and customized solutions, over the next years.

In March 2000, DATACOM.net was officially established as a limited liability company with the objective to position the firm in the content segment of the fast-growing e-learning market.

The team never considered building an e-learning portal because in the U.S. the first venture capital funded learning portals were already in financial dire straits in the autumn of 1999. The second reason the team chose not to follow a portal strategy was that these companies normally concentrate on small- and mid-sized customers, or individual learners on the Internet. At the time, the customer base of DATACOM Academy consisted of large corporations.

The Offer

By December 1999, however, a slow-down in the venture capital market had begun. After the insolvency of Boo.com, the investment market grew skeptical towards every business plan built on an idea starting with an "e." In May 2000, DATACOM.net received a first letter of intent (LOI) after having contacted numerous prospective investors and made over 30 presentations. In the LOI, the company was valued at DM 15.05 million post-investment. Given a capital need of DM 6 million, the three founders were supposed to give away 38 percent of their shares.

After intensive discussions the team decided not to sign the LOI and to withdraw from further negotiations with the venture firm. A further reason was that the team had begun negotiations with a U.S. publishing and event company, 101communications, which had been founded in 1998 and was itself backed by venture capital.

The team accepted terms stipulated in the offer from 101communications and took over the management function in a company created by a merger with 101communications' existing German entities. Through the merger, a company with a revenue of 9.5m DM in 2000 emerged. The contracts with 101communications were signed in September 2000, and went into effect on January 1, 2001.

The End

After moving the three companies into one office in February 2001, the management team started to adapt its business plan to a new scenario and to contact prospective investors in order to raise an additional 4.5m DM for the e-learning unit. The initial idea was to sell parts of the shares of the whole organization to a venture capitalist. But with each new week following the burst of the dot-com bubble, the climate in the capital market worsened. The venture capitalists, especially, were reluctant to negotiate over new investments. As a result, the team intensified talks with strategic investors, e.g., German publishing groups and large training providers. With an ongoing general slowdown in the German economy by spring 2001, however, the situation did not improve. The publishing houses and training companies are usually the first sectors to face falling revenues. Thus, representing the most variable cost in the company, the advertising and training budgets are suffering from the cuts.

After numerous, at times seemingly endless, meetings with third parties, and in some cases, dramatically differing assessments of the company's value, there were virtually no openings to discuss the sale of shares in the merged company.

Beginning in mid-July 2001, the team started the last attempt to offer DATACOM.net, again as a single entity for the symbolic price of DM 1. For the DM 1, the buyer would receive the following assets:

- A highly motivated and efficient team of developers, who had produced five e-learning courses totaling 19 learning hours.

- A working, customized, and AICC-certified Learning Management System.

- A sales team of two employees with a qualified sales pipeline.

Unfortunately, this offer could not convince prospective investors because these companies were afraid to invest another DM 3 million to reach the break-even with DATACOM.net. In mid-August the initial investment of 1.5m DM was used and neither the German holding nor the U.S. company were in a position to continue to finance DATACOM.net due to the dramatic slowdown in the IT industry. In the end, DATACOM.net had to file for insolvency on August 24, 2001, when the last prospective investor ended negotiations with the company.

Conclusion

The question to ask in this matter is, how can it be that the value of a company can rise from DM 0 to DM 15.05 million when the company is only a piece of paper, and then drop to a negative valuation although by now the company has created an infrastructure and a product portfolio? To our mind there are three possible reasons:

A. The Economic Climate

There was a suspicion that something was wrong with the economy during the dot-com bubble but nobody really wanted to face it. Thus, the Internet crash and the fall of the whole IT industry had, and still has, a deeper impact on the economy than most of the experts dreamt.

B. Operational Mistakes

At an early stage of the business, the management team put too much emphasis on negotiating with Learning Management System providers. It was a waste of both time and resources because the ongoing negotiations and the stringent focus on LMS led to a delay in the launch of the first content courses.

Further, the team completely underestimated the timeline of the sales process in an immature market.

C. The Development of e-learning Market Lagged Behind Expectations

e-learning is not the "next big thing" in the Internet, as once predicted. It is an important new type of training medium, not more, not less. And it needs time to gain acceptance by the learner. The manifold assumptions of the analysts were wrong: the market has not exploded the way some so-called prophets once forecasted.

Most likely, companies will succeed in the content segment only if they have a strong financial background obtained via an affiliation with a large media group or training company. They will also require access to content provided by a well-established company or an investor.

Dr. Kohr asks an intriguing question from his experience at DATACOM: "How can it be that the value of a company can rise from DM 0 to DM 15.05 million when the company is only a piece of paper, and then drop to a negative valuation although by now the company has created an infrastructure and a product portfolio?" The entire story of the negative consequences of the financial bubble can be summarized in the circumstances which gave rise to this question. When the company was economically worthless, it had a huge financial valuation; and when it was worth something in economic terms, it was without financial value.

Dr. Kohr makes an admirable attempt to explain and rationalize the paradox, but there is no good answer other than that the operation of financial markets today is decoupling economic from financial value in a way that is damaging to companies and national economies.

Another Wave of Internet Companies Is Coming

A second wave of Internet companies—labeled by the business press "Internet II"—is now taking shape, and the sophisticated products and services of these newcomers will make the Net a much more powerful platform for business. Smart navigation systems, like those being developed by Endeca, will permit customers to find what they're looking for without wading through the long lists today's search engines generate. Tools for consolidating and dynamically updating educational and other service offerings, like those being built by SCT and MindEdge, will let customers get exactly what they need without having to bounce from site to site.

To fulfill their promise, these companies will need substantial funding. But the bursting of the dot-com bubble has spooked the markets, and nervous investors may turn their backs on the new round of opportunities. That wouldn't just be bad news for the start-ups. It would be a blow to the entire economy, as it would stifle innovation at a crucial period of technological progress.

How did we arrive at this dangerous juncture? The whole notion of a second round of Internet firms is a result of the dot-com bubble. Had there not been the excessive speculation that caused the bubble, we'd have had a steady development of Internet business with successive rounds, not of businesses, but of technology. The fact that we'll have another round, and perhaps another after that, of Internet business is not a consequence of business logic, or of technological logic, but of financial market logic, or illogic.

A List of the Economic Consequences of the Bubble

- The world economy has been tipped into recession.

- The aftermath of the financial bubble is that high technology is starved for capital today. The Fed's August 2001 survey of senior bank loan officers found that banks have limited exposure to high tech and are tightening lending standards to high tech firms more than to other companies.[105]

- Nor is much venture money available—new early stage commitments to entrepreneurial firms by venture funds are about one-tenth what they were during the bubble. The bad crowded out much that was good—start-ups following the tried and true path of get-it-right-first are now denied capital as a result of the fiascos brought on by the get-big-fast strategies championed during the bubble by the venture firms and investment banks. Think, for example, of what better entrepreneurs could have done to build viable companies with the $100 million squandered by Garden.com, with the $30 or so million wasted on Edupoint, with the almost billion dollars consumed by Webvan, or with the multibillions spent by Global Crossing. Further, because of the rapidity of the downturn, some good technologies are likely to be orphaned forever. The capital markets have abandoned promising innovations as the financial markets overshot on the down side. First round venture funding for entrepreneurs in the second quarter of 2001 was only $1 billion, down 87 percent from a year ago.[106]

- The capital markets wasted vast amounts of investment dollars, lessening, not increasing, intelligent business investment. This was especially true in the telecom arena, in which much more money, largely in the form of junk bonds and coming from large institutional investors, was wasted.

- The markets often picked the wrong companies to finance, and starved better companies of capital. The Internet companies used valuable resources that could have been more efficiently allocated elsewhere in the economy. The people who worked at failed Internet firms could have spent their time and energy creating lasting value in other endeavors, and the capital that funded the dot-coms and telecoms could have been ploughed into viable, lasting companies that would have benefited the overall economy.

- The bubble undermined incentives to save. People who watched their savings fly out the window are reluctant to have the same thing happen again.

- The bubble undermined good management because the volatility of share prices drove option values under water and undermined incentives. Yet Wall Street and academics strongly support incentive stock options as a key tool of motivation for employees.

Insuring Public Confidence

During the bubble, many financial market professionals violated public trust and their responsibility to the economy, thus damaging both the economy and individual investors. This was particularly the case in America where, for example, we had four years of investment banks doing the wrong research, with the wrong analysts covering the wrong companies and making the wrong recommendations, and selling the wrong companies to the public in IPOs.

Recent years have seen flush times for the financial community under regulation that pretends that transparency is enough to justify public confidence. For example, the former Chairman of the SEC: "The Commission's mission is to preserve market integrity by promoting fair, orderly and transparent markets, and to protect investors. An essential component of market integrity is investor confidence. Investors lose confidence when misleading information and exaggerated claims are allowed to go unchecked."[107]

The dot-com bubble has confirmed this statement. Currently transparency—that is, the amount of information provided by a firm and its underwriters in the IPO process—is insufficient to convince the public that the system is fair. In undermining public confidence, financial institutions are playing with fire. If the investing public cannot trust the system, the capital markets will be dead.

In large part as a result of their recent terrible financial experience, American investors are less accepting of the process by which new firms are brought to investors than they used to be. We are now in a tearing-down phase of the financial value cycle in which companies which have been funded in the building-up phase and which fail are destroyed. Given the uncritical character of what got funded in the building-up phase, a tearing-down phase is inevitable and useful. But as one financial market professional has recently told us, "Less and less… are we bold and irrepressible Americans willing to suffer the tearing-down phase of the cycle. After all, it has seemed increasingly unnecessary. With a rising incidence of federal intervention in financial markets, expansions have become longer and contractions shorter."[108]

We are seeing mixed reactions from individual investors. Many are wary to reinvest their money, as they no longer trust brokers and mutual funds. Alternatively, a *Wall Street Journal* report shows that it is the small investors who have been holding on, especially when the situation looks dim.[109] Soon after the September 11 terrorist attack, it was the small investors who maintained their confidence. However, this could be a temporary situation, with individual investors being slower to react than institutional investors. For example, after the 1987 crash, "some small investors hesitated initially, and then bit by bit withdrew money from stocks, selling as their shares returned to prior levels and then got 'even' again."[110]

Regulation is necessary to restore confidence in the capital markets and their institutions. The weakness of the stock market has contributed to economic recession.

Talking Points

We've seen in previous chapters how the financial value chain divorced financial value from economic value on a systematic basis for hundreds of Internet companies, selling their shares at inflated values to the public, and that the result was financial disaster for many and badly damaging our economy. If this is to be pre-vented in the future, financial markets need more effective regulation. The key reasons for this are:

1. It's necessary to protect the least-sophisticated investors, both for ethi-cal and economic reasons. This is a key role of government, and it has been done particularly poorly in recent years.

2. Successful financial markets are vitally important to national economies and are best promoted by preserving public trust in them.

3. Without reforms in regulation, the world economy is going to be sub-ject to a continuing series of economic crises that reduce economic progress and increase human misery.

4. Since financial markets are already highly regulated, needed reforms can be made without undue disruption of the current functioning of markets. In fact, most of what is needed in the way of regulation to avoid another significant bubble is to reestablish effective regulations which have been eroded by changes in the markets.

VII A Troubled System

"The dot-com bubble cost investors trillions. It's time to get serious about the lessons it taught us."

—Joe Berardino, CEO of Arthur Andersen,
Testimony to Congress, December 4, 2001

15 Can America Lead?

The Internet bubble points to significant problems that now trouble our financial markets. In particular, protections for retail investors have eroded far too much. The bubble has made it clear that by using modern communication methods, the hype machine of the professionals in the financial markets can cause the retail investor to make illogical and irresponsible decisions against his or her own interest. Such behavior is part of human nature, but that doesn't mean it should be sanctioned; financial market players should not be permitted to cause at will their customers to lose their savings and pensions, and this is what happened on a very large scale in the bubble. Such a manipulated squandering of assets by the population is not good for the economy; it's not fair for the society; it's not in the best long-term interests of the financial markets themselves (though at the time, certainly some of the companies which are major players currently in the financial markets profited very much for themselves).

Scale matters. During the Internet bubble, what had been a limited problem became an enormous one. It isn't that this or that person was defrauded directly by this or that broker. It's that the system as a whole, functioning as its major institutions chose for it to function, had a general result that was not tolerable to a large portion of our society. This is a system problem and requires a large-scale solution.

It's now apparent that there is no longer sufficient protection in the system to stop the large-scale victimization of small-scale investors during a bubble fostered by financial market players. Fiduciary responsibility has declined to a minimum; professionals and institutions have gotten very sophisticated in justifying their actions based on false assumptions and the behavior of their peers. In effect, every professional offers one of three excuses for what happened in recent years to the small investor:

- All of us were thinking the same things, so it's okay that we misled people with false assumptions.

- All of us were saying the same things, so it's okay that we enticed people with false expectations.

- All of us were doing the same things, so it's okay that we sold people what quickly became valueless investments.

Because they were thinking and saying and doing the same thing, the financial industry says, it was okay for them to profit greatly at the extreme expense of the small investor. This isn't a result which society should accept. Nor can the society simply accept that a critical part of our financial market, the IPO market, should be largely shut down—as it has been since the bursting of the bubble—until investors forget how they've been fleeced and return again to the IPO market. A key reason for wanting to avoid this result of the hangover of the bubble is that while the IPO market is down, the progress of innovation is much reduced.

Instead, the system needs a new level of protection for the average investor—a safety net—in order for investors to have confidence in the system.

The United States as the World's Financial Leader

The United States prides itself on being the financial leader of the world. By far the largest economy, it wields tremendous influence over, and bears responsibility to, the financial markets of other nations. There are two areas recognized as key to its economic leadership: its financial markets, and its high technology industry.

The United States capital market is generally thought to be the best in the world at allocating capital. It is highly developed, effective, and transparent. About America's financial markets, Fed Chairman Alan Greenspan told a Senate Committee in April 2000, "Participants in our equity markets have succeeded in concentrating a great depth of liquidity that is the envy of other nations and a symbol of the United States as the world's preeminent financial power..."[111]

Similarly, America's high technology sector is the largest, the most advanced, and the best funded in the world, and essential to our advanced defense systems.

So it is ironic that over the past several years, the U.S. economy experienced a largely dysfunctional interaction between these two key sectors. The Internet bubble occurred when the capital markets funded the technology companies in a careless and seriously damaging manner. This, in turn, wreaked havoc on the technology companies themselves, the investors, the U.S. economy, and ultimately, the world economy.

The consequences of the dot-com bubble are much more than that a group of young people (thought by many to be undeserving, if media commentary on the subject is to be believed) got rich, and then got poor again. The consequences include a serious weakening of our economy.

The American economy was seriously damaged in the short run because the collapse of the bubble has helped drive it into recession. The bubble blinded the United States to the weakness of the world economy. By mid-2001, the media was recognizing that the major economies of the world were slowing and recession was in danger of spreading worldwide. "The world is experiencing economic whiplash," wrote Joseph Kahn and Edmund L. Andrews of *The New York Times*, "with growth rates retreating more quickly and in more of the leading economies than at any time since the oil shock of 1973.[112]

Should American Leadership Be Followed?

America is like Germany and other developed economies in having a substantial financial sector of its economy with specialized firms such as investment banks, mutual funds, brokerage houses, accountancy firms, and so forth.

In other ways, the American economy is unusual, including three ways which are very important to our economic success:

1. It has an unusually large and important entrepreneurial sector built largely around technology;

2. It has institutions specialized to facilitate innovation, especially venture capital companies; and

3. It gives a great deal of responsibility to individuals to manage their own savings and pension assets.

It's significant that each of these three elements is emulated in Europe today. The American entrepreneurial sector is envied because it provides military strength, economic growth, and exports. Venture firms are being copied in Europe because they've had high financial returns and contribute to the growth of high technology innovation. Finally, there is a movement now to give greater responsibility to individuals for managing their own assets, much as America has done.

But the United States has just had a very serious experience that calls into question its leadership in each of these three areas. The financial bubble and its aftermath have:

1. Damaged America's methods of financing technological innovation;

2. Helped throw the American economy, and maybe the world's, into recession; and

3. Wiped out the savings and pension assets of many people.

During the bubble, many small investors bought stocks at greatly inflated prices without understanding the factors creating these prices. This brings into question the transparency and basic fairness of the capital markets. It appears that many entrepreneurs, venture firms, and investment banks failed to provide the honest disclosure which underlies all transactions between buyers and sellers; for without confidence in each other's representations, trade soon dries up.

It's important not to adopt the position of damning the entire capital-raising mechanism because securities were in some cases sold to the wrong people. But more was involved than that. The system as it has operated in recent years is full of deception instead of transparency, of conflicts of interest which persist even when publicly acknowledged, and of unethical practices, of which selling to the wrong people was a significant, but not the only, one. The Enron case shows that the rot in the American capital-raising system went far beyond selling some securities (highly speculative IPOs) to the wrong people (small investors). Instead, it is pervasive and has involved the largest players in the Financial Value Chain, and both Congress and the executive offices of our government. Unless the corruption in the system is eliminated or much reduced by the sort of reforms proposed in the final chapters of this book, then the American capital-raising system cannot be a valid model for the rest of the world.

Further, there remains abroad in the world the notion that America is a favorable, even easy, environment for an entrepreneur because of supposed ease of raising capital. But think of the experience of a representative entrepreneur in the past five years. An entrepreneur approaching venture firms would have received bad advice about strategy, more money than he or she needed, and pressure to take the company public when it wasn't ready. There would have been, except in a few situations, no concern for the long-run viability of the business. After the IPO, the entrepreneur would have been rich on paper, but in less than a year would have lost virtually all his paper wealth, possibly be in deepest debt to the tax authorities, and his company would be either dead or dying, with his venture allies providing no assistance. As for entrepreneurs seeking to start businesses during the bust, they would receive no funding.

Even if entrepreneurs and investors were to be smarter for the next few years and better able to protect themselves from the excesses of the capital market, the current system remains an ineffective way to run the world's largest economy, and one that can't be offered as a model to other nations.

In the aftermath of the bubble, with the defects of the American model evident, German authorities are reconsidering their interest in emulating America. The bubble is particularly damning of the American approach because it occurred in the financial links between the entrepreneur and the average investor, who is the eventual source of capital for his/her company. It is the entrepreneur and the average investor who, from an economic point of view, are the key players—the entrepreneur because he is the engine of innovation in the economy; the average investor because his or her money is the ultimate source of capital for the economy. The Financial Value Chain which links the two is of less importance because it is merely a connection.

The problem in America now lies in the linkage. As we have seen before, professionals who are part of the linkage say something different. Quietly they suggest that the entrepreneur is dumb and doesn't know how to run a successful business. They say the average investor is greedy, lazy, and emotional, and doesn't know how to find the right companies to back. But as we've seen in previous chapters of this book, neither of these criticisms is on the mark, nor holds up under careful scrutiny.

The bubble was like a few professional guides taking a group of outdoor novices on a hike. The group got into trouble and some of the novices were badly hurt. Whom do we blame? The guides, of course, largely regardless of what the novices did. The guides were experienced and should have been in charge, and are responsible for the outcome.

Professionals in the financial markets are like guides in this fable, and retail investors like novices. When there is a disaster, it is the professionals who must accept the responsibility, and whose behavior demands investigation and change.

Dare We Privatize Social Security?

The Bush Administration is proposing a partial privatization of Social Security by diverting a portion of payroll taxes into individual accounts. A bipartisan presidential commission has backed private accounts as a way of improving Social Security and boosting the private savings rate of Americans. The basic notion is that invested accounts would, over time, give a larger pension than Social Security as presently provided (via the general revenues of the government) can do. Proposals offered by House members would permit small accounts to be invested in stock and bond index funds selected by the government; larger accounts could be placed in private brokerage and mutual fund accounts of the individual's choosing. Benefits would generally be paid via annuities.

The experience of the dot-com/telecom bubble doesn't provide much confidence that putting the Social Security pension money of individuals into corporate equities via the stock market is sensible when financial manias are happening. Nor can the public have much confidence in the proposal. The reforms proposed previously in this book would help to make privatization of Social Security advisable.

A possible model for the privatization of Social Security is provided by Chile. Part of the national pension plan can be invested by individuals in state-chartered mutual funds that operate under strict guidelines about diversification. The individual pensioner is expected not to make intelligent stock picks, but intelligent choices about professional investment managers who will diversify and choose stocks.

If the public gets scared and loses confidence in financial firms, then the capital markets can't perform their services for the economy, and financial firms and their employees can't make a living. Effective regulation is key to public confidence. The form that regulation takes, and how extensive it is, is of great importance.

Why Current Regulation Isn't Working Well Enough

The capital markets have a special significance to the economy and aren't treated like other markets. They are more regulated, for the good of all, and they need better regulation now if faith isn't to be lost and the economy further damaged.

Although capital markets in Germany and the United States are highly regulated, financial firms can get away with things not permitted in other industries. In the capital markets, a company can sell a product to the public which completely fails to produce its benefits within a short time, and yet the public has virtually no protection against the seller. In fact, the seller is allowed to stand behind boilerplate language in the selling documents which absolve the seller of all responsibility if the product doesn't work, but which is belied by the selling pitch of the sellers' agents. In no other area of the economy, with the possible exception of homeopathic medicine, is this the case. For example, cigarette companies are no longer protected from legal liability to the injured by the boilerplate language on packages of cigarettes: WARNING—THIS PRODUCT MAY BE HAZARDOUS TO YOUR HEALTH. But underwriters still claim protection based on the boilerplate language of offering documents.

It's a particularly interesting situation because organizations in the capital markets—banks, stock brokerages, and publicly held business firms, among others—are among the businesses most highly regulated by the government, in part to protect the investing public, and in part to keep the economy working and progressing successfully.

It seems that the regulators sometimes get priorities confused. For example, asked by a scholar about how the American Federal Reserve System dealt with possible conflicts between its two roles: one to keep the economy as a whole functioning well, and the other to preserve the financial health of the nation's banks, an official of the Fed replied, "Oh, but only one is important."

He meant, of course, that only the health of the banks was really significant. And if pressed, he might have justified that priority with the notion that the role of the Fed is to protect the nation's financial system from disorder, because banking crises were, certainly in the 19th Century, the cause of most major contractions in the economy as a whole.

In some of his presentations to Congress, Fed Chairman Alan Greenspan seems to suggest certain priorities of the Fed. For example, on April 13, 2000, he told a Senate committee, "Today, equities constitute a substantial portion of the net worth of households, both direct holdings of shares and indirect holdings through mutual and pension funds. In addition, U.S. equity markets are a significant factor in the international competitiveness of our finance industry. For these reasons it is vital that our public policies foster equity markets that remain efficient, innovative, and competitive."[113] But where, one asks, is fairness? It's not in this list—efficient, innovation, competitive, yes—but not fair, not honest, not reasonably safe for retail investors. Is Greenspan's list limited to these qualities because fairness, honesty, and safety are responsibilities of other regulators?

Perhaps, but the Fed's Chairman has also recognized that regulations are necessary to protect participants of different levels of sophistication and resources in financial markets. For example, discussing derivatives, he commented, "...the professional counterparties that use OTC derivatives simply do not require the protections that CEA provides for retail investors. If professional counterparties are victimized, they can obtain redress under the laws applicable to contracts generally."[114]

It would seem appropriate, therefore, for government to protect retail investors. Unfortunately, the regulations we have in place showed themselves seriously inadequate during the bubble. The bubble revealed that much of the regulation of financial markets was off the mark. In the United States in particular, the wrong things are regulated, the wrong way. This isn't surprising; the principal players—companies and regulatory bodies—have been in place for decades and slowly have become locked in controversy over the details of the regulations with little concern for its overall suitability.

What is needed now is a return to first principals, not merely a tweaking of the current system—a new start, with fewer technicalities and more real protection for the retail investor.

It would seem that early stage attempts to provide greater protection to small investors are underway in Germany. The key case in point involves Infomatec.

Contribution: Infomatec

**Christiane Sommer, Journalist at *Brand Eins*,
a German Management and Marketing Journal**

At first glance, Infomatec is not distinguishable from many other new issues on the Neuer Markt. This company specializes in software, as do many. Moreover, its management underestimated the demands of doing business being a publicly held company, which is also not unusual. Investors, analysts, and even employees themselves have become tangled in the demands they have placed on the company. Even that is nothing new. Why, then, is the story of Infomatec told in this book? Because it exemplifies a further dimension of the Internet bubble.

Infomatec was for a time a darling of the market; then suddenly it crashed. Its share price went into the basement when its founders, Gerhard Harlos and Alexander Haefele, came under the scrutiny of a district attorney's office and were arrested shortly thereafter. The two are the first board members of a Neuer Markt company to be detained for questioning because of alleged insider trading.

The story isn't yet over; the end remains unclear. Let us look back to the beginning.

Infomatec's story begins in 1988, in the spare bedroom of an entirely normal single family residence, in a little town near Augsburg, Germany.

Gerhard Harlos, having just finished his mathematics degree, puts together a business idea with his friend Alexander Haefele. They write software for, among other things, databases. They find their first client, and then another, and then another. The business goes well after a few years, but they dream of bigger things. They want to develop complex solutions for retailing: inventory control systems that are tied into supermarket cash registers. By the mid-1990s, they have become authorized SAP R3 consultants. In addition to Internet-Standard software for e-business and chain stores, Harlos and Haefele have added another business line to their firm, but the founders need more capital, primarily for software development. Their accountant, a renowned firm, advises taking the company public in 1997. Harlos and Haefele give the idea consideration and decide it's a good one.

Under the stewardship of the West German State Bank, Infomatec makes its IPO early in July of 1998. The new issue is oversubscribed by a factor of 37. Volume is 50 million DM with a price of 53 DM per share. Nearly 100 employees held stock at the time of the IPO, the majority of whom were software developers. In 1997, Infomatec had revenues of 8.7 million DM where it had 4.9 million DM in 1996. For the year of the IPO, 20 million were planned. Profit was supposed to rise from 0.8 million DM (1997) to 1.6 million DM (1998).

The market wants to see growth and therefore Infomatec begins buying other firms. Soon, again, their means are too meager. In November 1998, four months after going public, the board announces a cash call. Business is clearly going well: Infomatec makes ad hoc announcements, including the mention of a large contract.

On the stock market, Infomatec is celebrated: with a gain of 560 percent, it is the best new issue of the year. Infomatec continues to grow, buying up other companies. In February 1999, another cash call brings 123 million DM net into Infomatec's coffers, with which it intends to finance its rapid growth. Shortly thereafter, the board sells a block of shares: 62,500 per board member.

The market seems not concerned that many new businesses are not meeting their goals for 1998. In April 1999, Infomatec presents its first financial results since going public. The company ends 1998 with a shortfall of 4.8 million DM. The board justifies negative numbers by citing eight successful acquisitions of other companies and the costs associated with taking the company public.

The disappointing numbers are not challenged by the analysts. Not only the syndicator, the West German National Bank, but also the analysts of Bankhaus Delbrueck continue to recommend the stock for purchase.

Alexander Haefele reports that Infomatec will grow to be one of the largest IT companies worldwide in the coming five years. On May 20, 1999, Infomatec actually appears to come a large step nearer its ambitious goal. In an ad hoc announcement, the company makes public the largest deal in its history. Infomatec has negotiated a framework with Mobilcom for the sale of 100,000 Surfstations. The revenue for this transaction alone stands by 55 million DM.

The Surfstations are devices which allow a combination of television and Internet surfing. At last, the arrangement with Mobilcom will allow the set-top boxes, based on Infomatec's Java Network Technology, to meet expectations. The technology appears to have finally been sufficiently developed. That gives reason for hope.

At the shareholders' meeting on June 24, 1999, Infomatec presents its promising new product to the stockholders: the audience is thrilled, all the more so as the board announces further large customer contracts.

Everything appears to be on track. In the course of the year, several more contracts are made public. Expansion into Asia also looks to be slowly taking shape, promises the board. Everyone is pleased.

Then, in spite of all of the announcements, in 1999 Infomatec again fails to reach its own targets. Nonetheless, the great vision is still being feverishly pursued. One does not want to become discouraged. And yet, there is a bitter disappointment. In the summer, Infomatec drastically revises its projections for 2000 to more conservative estimates. Revenues of 100 million Euro, for which it was striving, would not be reached. At best, Infomatec hopes to achieve half of that. In addition, management reveals a loss, before taxes, interest, and write-offs (EBITDA), of 26 million Euro.

The results are disappointing; it gets worse. An article in the trade journal *Computerwoche* appearing on August 18, 2000, alarms the public and brings Infomatec severe distress. The magazine reports on substandard management, the possibility of nonexistent customers, and that Mobilcom has purchased only 14,000 instead of the advertised 100,000 Surfstations.

This is strong stuff. The market responds immediately: The stock takes a nosedive. Suddenly the shareholders are asking questions. They want to know exactly what is happening. Rumors are circulating. All at once, there is talk of price manipulation and insider trading. Not only the stockholders but the partners as well become nervous and fear they personally will be drawn into the affair. The banks cancel lines of credit and call their loans.

The consortium banks, WGNB, on the Neuer Markt, and Sal. Oppenheim terminate their collaboration. WGNB manager Volker Mueller-Scheessel resigns his position on Infomatec's board.

For a while it appears that no one could be found to supervise the company's presence in the market. That would be the end for the firm on the Neuer Markt. Then Lang & Schwarz Financial Services and Future Securities jump in as designated sponsors.

It doesn't look good for the one-time shooting star. At a press conference, Harlos and Haefel go on the offensive. They want to rescue what can be salvaged and make clear to the public that the previous week's accusations are unfounded.

Accusations of insider trading and price manipulation are groundless, says Harlos at the conference. The firm's solicitor explains that both founders had sold 62,500 shares through WGLB after the cash call in February 1999 once the restriction on doing so expired. The date had been arranged with the bank in advance, says Harlos, precisely because one would not want to come under suspicion of insider trading.

The accusation of making misleading statements is denied as well. At the time they were made public, it was taken for granted that the agreement for the delivery of Surfstations to Mobilcom, Global Well, and World Wide Database would in fact be executed. Infomatec was even considering a suit against Mobilcom, because they did not want to honor the contract.

Furthermore, Infomatec was also in negotiations with a protective association of small investors who had filed a complaint for price rigging and insider trading. The partners acknowledge the critical situation in which the company finds itself. Infomatec has a loss of 15.5 million Euro before taxes, interest, and write-offs on revenues of 28.5 Euros in the first two quarters of 2000. For the second half of 2000, management is anticipating revenues of 21.5 million Euros and a loss of 11 million Euros. Through staff reductions and a decrease in office space, around 1.3 million should be saved. For 2001, the company is projecting revenues of 65 million and breaking even. To achieve this goal, the organization must be restructured. In the end, Harlos and Haefele even announce that they will leave the company by year's end at the latest to make way for a new beginning. Shortly after the press conference, the district attorney conducts a search at the offices of the company and at the homes of the founders. At the beginning of November 2000 the company announces a new strategy: In the future, it will concentrate its business exclusively on interactive television. For all other business lines, partners or buyers are being sought.

On November 16, Haefele and Harlos are arrested. Never had anything like this happened before in the Neuer Markt. The public is as astonished as those personally affected. Harlos is taken into custody at his house; Haefele in the street. Both are held for questioning. They are charged with suspicion of price rigging (because of the ad hoc announcement of the Mobilcom deal, among other things), insider trading (because of the sale of stock after the cash call in January 1999), and violation of Corporation Law. Both partners maintain their innocence. Their attorneys appeal their arrest and hold all accusations to be groundless. The DA remains unimpressed. For half a year, Harlos and Haefele sit separated from one another in prison. Only their attorneys are allowed to visit. Friends and family are permitted to see them every two weeks. Their mail is meticulously controlled.

All of Harlos' and Haefele's property is impounded, including files. According to the company records, the two hold more than half of all Infomatec stock, valued at around 60 million DM. Meanwhile, things continue to go downhill for the company itself. After the arrests, the stock price slips more than 9 percent to 2.27 Euro. In February, 2000, it had reached its high point of 52 Euros. In December, the price has fallen to 1.20 Euros.

The new chairman Helmut Schiner, who took office in January, tries his best, but the firm's reputation is tarnished. In any event, the company achieves its target numbers for the first time since going public. The price rises to 2.36 Euro.

While the company is struggling for its life, the accused are struggling to attain their freedom. In May 2001, almost exactly six months after being imprisoned, both are let out on bail of 750,000 DM each.

The state court in Munich defends its decision to parole the suspects, saying that there is no danger of the suspects fleeing. Harlos and Haefele must hand over their passports and may not leave the country without permission. Unmoved by the proceedings in Munich, the court in Augsburg continues its investigation.

A few days later, on May 9, the management of Infomatec files for bankruptcy. Thereby it becomes the fifth case of insolvency on the Neuer Markt. One hundred fourteen jobs are threatened. Since the accusations were leveled in the summer of 2000, the company has had to fire 580 employees.

The stock reaches its lowest point up to that time: 0.76 Euro. On the same day, the company lets it be known that it has signed a large contract which will at least cover the operating expenses of the firm. In addition, there is talk in the industry that a well-heeled investor wants to rescue the company.

None of this gives solace to the investors. Many are seeking to sue Infomatec for damages, and Harlos and Haefele as well. The shareholders maintain they were tricked into buying stock by the false ad hoc announcements. In particular, the reported volume of the Mobilcom deal had created confusion.

This is new in the Neuer Markt. In Munich and Augsburg, the courts and the attorneys prepare for a process that represents a new legal frontier in Germany.

The suits lead to very different results: While the court in Munich decides unfavorably for the stockholders, the court in Augsburg decides otherwise. It awards private investors damages of around 90,000 DM plus interest. For this amount, Harlos and Haefele are to be held personally responsible.

This is the first time a court has awarded small investors in the Neuer Markt damages. In contrast to the judges in Munich, the court in Augsburg arrives at the conclusion that the investors have convincingly shown that they based their purchase on the ad hoc announcement of the Mobilcom deal. The Augsburg court rests its decision on paragraph 88 of the stock exchange legislation, whereby the organs of a corporation, i.e., the board and its management, can be prosecuted if they distribute false information about the financial situation of the company. In the court's opinion, investors also enjoy the protection of this clause. Furthermore, the court was convinced that Harlos and Haefele were personally responsible for the questionable reports. Harlos and Haefele's lawyers saw it differently, and entered an appeal.

The court in Munich decided in favor of Harlos and Haefele because they were of the opinion that securities regulations only oblige companies to make ad hoc announcements to the so-called trading public. This is understood to include professional investors, but not private ones.

How these two different judgments will influence German jurisprudence in the future is not yet clear. Bernd Jochem, counsel to the plaintiff in Augsburg, is cautious too. It is a precedent-setting case, but whether or not it will be applicable to other jurisdictions remains to be seen.

At Infomatec, work continues for the time being. Gerhard Harlos is again chairman of the company; again it has but a handful of employees. He and his fellow board member Alexander Haefele struggle on: for the survival of Infomatec and their reputations.

Ms. Sommer has provided a fascinating account of a new phenomenon in German law: an attempt in the courts to hold entrepreneurs criminally liable for the financial harm done to small investors and to regain for small investors some of what they lost in the bubble. Provisions of law in Germany and America both overlap and are different, so exactly what happens in Germany will be different from what happens in the United States. But perhaps German legal innovation will spread to America, so that America, which led in creating the bubble, will now follow in rectifying its consequences.

Talking Points

Disorders in financial markets, especially the Internet bubble, are a source of a new and damaging business cycle in the world economy.

The American economy is envied abroad for its entrepreneurial sector that contributes to our military strength, economic growth, and exports. Yet the bubble damaged technological innovation, threw the economy into a recession, and wiped out many peoples' savings. This isn't a model that deserves emulation abroad in its present state.

16 Reforms to Protect Small Investors

What is needed in the United States is regulatory reform of financial markets that will increase public confidence by setting higher ethical standards for the behavior of the players in the Financial Value Chain. In part, this involves maintaining more transparency not only of financial data about firms—a favorite reform of professionals in the Financial Value Chain —but also of the transactions among financial institutions.

But more than increased transparency is needed today to protect the small investor.

The German Experience

Germany went through an Internet bubble, just as did America, but with considerably less damage to the small investor. In Germany, small investors didn't get sucked into the speculative frenzy to the degree that in America destroyed the savings and pensions of many people. There were several reasons for this.

First, in Germany the individual has far less control of her or his pension money than in America. Germany has a state-run pension plan which has little room for corporate-managed defined benefit pension funds of the older American type, and none at all for pension plans managed by the individual. Hence, Germany has no 401(k) plans or Individual Retirement Accounts which leave to the individual the direction of his or her pension assets. During the bubble, this looked like a shortcoming of the German system, for American investors were showing much more rapid appreciation in their portfolios. Then the bubble broke, and today the German system looks better.

Second, a system that qualifies both investors and investments prevented individual savings from being invested in very speculative shares (whether in companies or mutual funds). In Germany, banks play a much larger role in savings and investments than in America—providing savings and investment products and advice to people. According to the German Securities Trading Act, formulated on September 9, 1998, investment services enterprises must follow specific rules of conduct. They must demand from their customers the particulars of their experience or knowledge of transactions in order to protect their customers' interest with regard to the type and scope of the intended transactions. They classify each of the customers into one of five risk categories, based on their experience:

- **Category 1:** Bonds with very good financial rating, Euro real estate funds, short-term DM pension funds.

- **Category 2:** DM and Euro Pension funds in Euro, German pension funds, bonds with very good financial rating.

- **Category 3:** Euro blue chips, mutual funds with international portfolio, convertible bonds, option bonds.

- **Category 4:** German and European shares (other than blue chips), emerging market mutual funds, regional and sector mutual funds, international blue chips.

- **Category 5:** International shares (other than blue chips), highly risky mutual funds, options, and futures.

Each investor must be counseled by his or her bank as to what are the risks of a certain category of investment. Further, an investor must have qualified in a number of ways, including net worth and experience over time, to buy investments of higher risk.

Working together, these elements of the German system caused there to be far less damage to the average investor in Germany during the bubble than in the United States. There was no American wild ride in which markets went up 300 percent, then down 300 percent, leaving people disillusioned and bitter. Instead, in Germany there was a slow but steady appreciation of investments even though a bubble was occurring in Internet stocks which involved mainly large investors.

Every Investor a Qualified Investor

The United States is good at what we may call *microregulation*—prohibiting insider trading and certain types of misrepresentation and fraud perpetrated against investors. Germany has less regulation of this type, and could benefit from borrowing from the American example.

But Germany is far better than the United States at what might be called *macroregulation*—protecting investors from adverse consequences—not just prohibiting certain kinds of self-interested dealings by those offering securities for sale. The United States could benefit from following Germany's example in this area.

The United States already has a mechanism at hand. For early stage investments, including investing in start-ups and venture funds, a person must fill out a lengthy statement which insures that he or she is a qualified investor—one who knows the risks involved and has enough financial assets to be able to make a very risky investment. It's the purveyor—the seller—of the investment who must obtain the qualification documents and file them with the appropriate authorities. A person who lacks the experience to understand the risks involved in an investment, and has too few assets to risk so much, is not permitted to make the investment. Similarly, when a person signs up as a customer for a brokerage firm, he or she is required to fill out forms. It is commonly asserted that customers regularly lie. Many brokerage houses have forms that ask "Are you an aggressive investor? A conservative investor?" A customer is asked to put down income, assets, and liabilities. Yet people seem often to inflate their assets, deflate their liabilities, and lie about their sophistication. Further, it often appears that brokers pay little attention to what is revealed about their customers. Somewhat similar things occur in Germany.

It follows that if qualification is to play an important role in securities market regulation, it must be taken more seriously. It's not hard to verify financial information—every bank lender asks account numbers from applicants for loans to verify assets claimed by aspiring borrowers—and often brokers, like bankers and venture capitalists, have a very good sense for when a potential investor is falsifying his or her financial situation and sophistication. It's not, therefore, difficult to give more value to qualification if regulators insist on it.

Because the qualified investor system was applied in only part of our financial markets during the Internet bubble (NASDAQ regulates the sales practices by securities dealers), it sometimes had a perverse and ironic impact on the average investor. He or she was denied an opportunity to participate directly in venture funds, but was allowed to buy shares in the same companies backed by venture funds when they went public. Since the companies went public far before they should have, then failed, the retail investor lost his investment; the venture firms made money on the same companies because they'd been allowed to invest at an earlier stage, but the retail investor had been excluded from that opportunity. In effect the current system, supposedly designed to protect the small investor, operated to destroy him or her. It kept the small investor out of the profit-making early stages of Internet investments, and allowed him or her to buy into the late stages during which the companies collapsed.

It's time to rectify this situation. America needs to take a leaf from the German book. All investment professionals should be required to qualify their customers for the sorts of investments being offered to them.

Further, America should add an extension to the German system—one that Germany should adopt as well, because of a problem illuminated by the Internet bubble. Investment professionals should be required to requalify their clients as conditions change materially. For example, when the mutual funds offered as part of annuity packages became much more highly speculative, as they did during the Internet bubble—both because of the inflation in the price of stocks and because of the types of stocks being incorporated into the portfolios of mutual funds offered for pension backing—then professionals should be required to requalify their clients for these investment products.

Extending Fiduciary Responsibility

At the core of the system that generated the bubble and the massive losses that the general public sustained was a collapse of fiduciary responsibility in America. The fiduciary principal had been an important protection for investors from the rapacity of the financial markets, but had largely disappeared by the late 1990s. Under the fiduciary principal, banks and mutual funds did not sell to retail investors and pension funds the type of shares that were taken public and placed in mutual funds during the bubble.

The essence of the fiduciary principal is that a professional must subordinate his or her self-interest to that of the client or customer. It includes a duty of loyalty from professional to client that prohibits self-dealing by the professional. It includes a duty of care, which prohibits negligence, recklessness, and/or intentional misconduct by the professional. Further, it imposes on the professional a duty of disclosure, so that the client knows what is being done by the professional.

Fiduciary responsibility is a higher order of relationship between a professional and a client, than is, for example, a contractual relationship. In a contractual relationship the duty of each side is to perform all material obligations in the contract. But a fiduciary responsibility goes further and imposes obligations on the professional—the "fiduciary"—that go beyond any explicit contract.

Fiduciary responsibility is especially appropriate when the client or customer is at significant personal or financial risk, and lacks the sophistication to watch out for himself. This is certainly the situation in our capital markets. In fact, many investors, knowing their vulnerability, assume that professionals with whom they deal have a moral and legal fiduciary responsibility toward them—how could the system function otherwise, they think. The answer is that the system functions to fleece them, which they learn the hard way.

What is the situation now in the capital markets? Howard Stevenson, a professor at Harvard Business School, repeated the following remark by an investment banker when he was asked about the bank's relation to retail investors, "They go in the door and out the door and I take their ticket both ways."

In recent years we have been seeing the disappearance of the fiduciary notion in many parts of our society. In construction, the architect or the general contractor used to take full responsibility for a project on behalf of a customer. Now the architect, general contractor, and construction manager accept responsibility for only a set of specialized services, leaving the owner to alone have responsibility for the whole. Of course, the owner is ordinarily the least prepared to assume this responsibility. The result is that an increasing proportion of construction jobs in America now end in litigation.

We see the disappearance of the notion of fiduciary responsibility in the family court system in which attorneys now routinely file multiple motions, stretching out litigation to the advantage of no one but themselves via increased fees. Judges rarely resist the practice.

The capital markets are no different. In the past, employers provided defined-benefit programs by which a company assumed a legal responsibility to pay a retired person a pension of a certain amount monthly. In effect, the company makes you a promise and has a legal responsibility to deliver. But during the late 1980s, so many large companies got into financial trouble that they found ways to avoid their pension liabilities, and faced with this reality, we moved to a defined contribution system for pensions. The shift from defined benefit to defined contribution plans for pensions was largely achieved via bankruptcies, recapitalizations, the sale of companies, and renegotiation of labor agreements under threat of shutdown or major layoffs, though in some important instances defined contribution plans are better suited to a mobile or professional work force than are defined benefit plans. But then who is responsible to see that the contributions are invested in a prudent way that will in the end provide a secure pension?

Is it the money manager? No, the professional insists that he or she is only executing the specific instructions of the owner of the assets.

Is it the company that made the defined contributions? Not at all. It has largely washed its hands of the retiree's financial security. The company does choose investment vehicles that are made accessible to employees who save for retirement via the plans, but it is rarely concerned with whether or not an employee successfully funds his or her retirement, and it appears to have little or no legal liability when an investment vehicle turns out to be a loser.

Even where the pension remains a defined benefit, the consultant to the plan denies responsibility for the return. The professionals are all specialists, and none is responsible for overall performance of the assets. The result is that there is no fiduciary obligated to protect the pensioner. The individual saver who is not a professional is the least knowledgeable of all those involved and the person least able to protect his or her interests. It's a system in which the individual is a sheep being led to the shearer.

Had fiduciary responsibility continued to live in our country, bankers, brokers, and mutual funds could not have so enriched themselves at the expense of retail investors.

Improving Disclosure and Governance at Mutual Funds

Mutual funds have grown enormously in recent years, and have become a major investment vehicle for small investors. In fact, the retail investor buying individual stocks is a less and less important factor in the market. Instead, small investors put their money in mutual funds, and because of professional management and greater diversification, that's where it ought to go.

But there are both disclosure and governance issues. The boilerplate of mutual funds is virtually useless to investors, and many funds tend to drift away from whatever principles are stated in their prospectuses.

If the profile of a fund's investments is being changed, then that information ought to be disclosed both in an amendment to a prospectus and in a notice to fund investors.

Governance in mutual funds seems a bit confused today because the managers of the fund seem to be legally the same people as the investors in the fund. It's the responsibility of the board of directors of the fund to act in the interests of investors; it's their responsibility to remove fund managers if the fund is performing poorly.

Mutual fund directors are fiduciaries, like corporate directors. Their responsibility is to look after the best interests of those investing in the mutual fund. This is proper. But mutual fund directors seem to lack the realization to which corporate directors have come regarding what corporate governance means. Mutual fund directors haven't come as far as corporate directors in looking after shareholders.

There have been several cases in which fund directors have tried to dismiss investment advisors on the grounds that the investment advisor is doing a poor job, and fund directors have sought to get another investment advisor. But the investment advisors then ran proxy contests, and the boards lost. In consequence, the structure of mutual fund boards is not yet at a point that they can take decisions on behalf of investors with any confidence that they will eventually win. Today the dominant machinery is in the hands of the investment advisor. The situation is not like that in a corporation, where the board of directors can fire the chief executive officer of the firm, and if necessary, people all the way down the line. In a mutual fund, all the board can do is terminate the contract with the investment advisor, but the investment advisor as an institution stays in place. It's fully mobilized, with lawyers and accountants and all the rest. In contrast, the board of the fund has very little.

To rectify the situation, we might require that all directors of funds be hired by outsiders independent of the investment advisor, and that the board hire independent counsel and accountants.

A Return to a More Restrictive Prudent Person Rule

During the bubble, pension plans in the United States became, in effect, venture investors. This was absurd, and it was the U.S. government that allowed it to occur. The government permitted corporate and public employee pension plans to be invested in venture funds, and thereby fueled the bubble and ultimately led so many people to financial slaughter.

Yet to many people the logic of this development seems unassailable. It is that large corporate pension funds are big enough and well-managed enough to benefit from diversification of investments—including the opportunity to reap the supposedly high rewards of venture capital investment.

Responding to such arguments, in the mid-1970s, the Department of Labor changed the rules under ERISA on pension investments. Prior to that time, each investment of a pension plan had been separately subject to a standard called the "prudent man rule." With this standard, venture investments were rarely justifiable—they were too risky. But when the Department of Labor relaxed the rule to look at a portfolio as a whole, then a portion of pension funds could be allocated to venture activities. So suddenly in flowed pension money to the VCs, and soon it was the most important part—and it caused the amount of venture capital to swell greatly.

Venture investing via funds and specialized managers began in the 1960s. Possibly the first success was Arthur Rock's sale of Scientific Data Systems—which had been funded by a venture partnership—to Xerox for about $1 billion in the mid-1960s. Xerox wrote off the whole purchase a short time later.

Wealthy private individuals were the first investors in venture funds. Then came college endowments. Then corporate pension plans. Finally, the pension plans of public employees—who swelled venture coffers just in time for the bubble and its collapse.

There had been, of course, a venture industry for many years. But in the 1980s and 1990s, the pension funds and the insurance companies were able to allocate more capital toward private equity because of changes in the rules and restrictions which applied to them. Pension fund money started flooding into the venture industry.

In the late 1980s and early 1990s, venture returns weren't good. They started getting good in 1994 and 1995, and it hit pension fund managers like an addictive drug. The pension funds and the insurance companies were able to enhance their financial returns by allocating not two or three percent to private equity, but five to ten percent. The more they pushed into venture funds, the more they seemed to like it. They flooded the venture industry with money. There was so much money that many venture guys left their jobs at established venture firms to start their own firms.

By putting pension plans into venture activities, the government appeared to approve all the 401(k) money invested in mutual funds that went into bubble investments. And during this time, the number of 401(k) plans had grown substantially. In 1985, employers in the United States had some 168,000 defined contribution plans; there were 461,000 single-employer defined contribution plans. By 1999, there were some 40,000 defined contribution plans and some 700,000 defined benefit plans. In 1975, about 15 percent of the American privately-employed workforce (that is, not public employees) was covered by defined contribution pension plans of some form; about 39 percent were covered by defined benefit plans. By 1995 (the most recent data available), about 39 percent of our workforce were covered by defined contribution plans, and 23 percent by defined benefit plans.[115] Thus, as more and more people were taking over management of their own pensions, the government was permitting pension plans to move into more risky investments. Corporate pension plans were permitted to invest in venture funds, and while 401(k) participants were not, they did so indirectly by buying mutual funds which invested in IPOs taken public at so early a stage that the 401(k) investor was effectively invested in venture funds.

The last 18 months have seen very poor venture returns.[116] Over the last 20 years, venture returns have averaged about 20 percent per annum, above the public equity market that averages about 15 percent. This is the reason that pension fund managers have been pouring money into venture funds, with the result as we saw in a previous chapter, that the venture funds had and have so much money that during the bubble they changed their standards for investment and sometimes poured money on entrepreneurs. Yet there has always been something unconvincing about the estimates of annual return which show venture capital leading other types of investments.

The core of the matter is that venture firms rarely mark their investments to market price; instead, an investment is carried on their books at cost until it is disposed of. Thereby, losing investments are often concealed for years, while successes are rushed to market. The result is that risk is underestimated and performance overstated.

Because venture firms do this, word got out among pension fund managers that venture capital had both low risk and high return—which is, in any decently functioning financial market, an oxymoron. No investment category over more than a short time can have both low risk and high return, because so much money would pour in that the returns would be cut down very much. Pension fund managers should have known this, and tempered the amounts shifted to venture capital, but they did not. The result was just what theory would suggest—too much capital poured in, resulting in poor quality investments which drove the return to venture capital down, even given venture firm's favorable financial reporting.

In the aftermath of the bubble, venture returns are down substantially and the latest investors in venture funds—including, especially, public employee pension funds that came in after corporate funds—got killed.

The argument for diversification that permits large pension funds to invest in venture capital has some merit, but it must be qualified so that too much pension money doesn't flow into venture funds. There is not enough legitimate investment opportunity in start-ups to justify the recent inflows of capital. The result is counterproductive—a bubble in asset values and a collapse of support for the innovation. It's the opposite of what is supposed to happen and it's a result of trying to feed the baby—entrepreneurial start-ups—with a fire hose. In effect, the baby drowned.

Preventing Another Enron

In the aftermath of the Enron scandal a debate is underway in American financial and political circles over how to strengthen the nation's regulations to prevent another such occurrence. President Bush has advanced proposals, as have the Democrats; and the elements of the Financial Value Chain have entered with their suggestions. Much needs to be done, and in addition to more detailed suggestions made in this chapter, additional legislation or regulation should include the following:

1. Placing more direct liability on corporate executives—in part outside of directors' and officers' liability insurance—when investors are misled by corporate financial accounting;

2. Revising accounting standards to increase transparency to investors, especially with respect to

   a. Conflicts of interest for corporate executives, their bankers, and accountants,

   b. Off-balance sheet financing, and

   c. Recognition (that is, counting) of nontraditional revenue;

3. Regulating accounting firm practices, including especially separating consulting from accounting services;

4. Permitting 401(k) and other defined contribution pension plans to

    a. Provide expert financial advice to participants,

    b. Require reasonable diversification in investment portfolios of participants,

    c. Prevent trading freezes that are unreasonable in terms of timing or length of time, and

    d. Provide for outside directors on the administrative boards of large plans.

New Regulations to Protect Investors in IPOs

At the heart of the bubble and all its damaging consequences was the IPO process. The abuses of the process were not limited to who was allowed by the bankers to participate in the lucrative IPO process, and on what terms, though this aspect has been attracting the most attention in Washington. To better protect the interests of the retail investor, we propose a set of rules of the following nature:

1. A venture capital firm and its investors cannot sell an investment in an IPO except on a phased schedule, for example, up to one third of its stake after six months following IPO; another third after nine months, and the final third one full year after the IPO. And any such sales must be reported to the government as insider trading.

2. All insiders must sell on a program basis for the first two years after IPO. A program basis for insider sales is a preregistered plan of selling over a lengthy period of time from which there is no departing with a changing price for the stock.

3. Underwriters on an IPO have to certify that the business is real—especially with respect to revenues, if the company is being offered to the public without the traditional several quarters of profitability, and must forecast within a range the financials for the first year following the IPO—and can be sued if the company fails to meet the forecasts in the first year after IPO.

4. Investment banks should be required to engage an independent accounting firm to review the financial statements of firms which are candidates for IPOs.

5. In such a situation as mentioned in the point before, legal liability should go to the representations of the underwriters with no protection from the boilerplate of a prospectus accorded them.

6. An underwriter should not offer a company to the public without a minimum size float. During the bubble, many Internet stocks had very few shares in the public markets so that buying activity could much more easily drive prices up, and later, selling activity could much more easily drive prices down. In some instances during the bubble, multiples of the entire number of shares outstanding of a stock would trade in a single day.

Such regulations are not merely closing the barn door after the horses have escaped, because there are likely to be more bubbles. The modern hype machine makes this inevitable. But these reforms will limit damage of the bubbles to the investing public.

Some elements of the financial industry will cry wolf when new regulations are proposed. "Tampering with the securities houses' mix of banking and research," the head of research at one Wall Street giant claims, "could destroy the capital-raising machinery of this country..."[117] The answer, of course, is that there is no evidence that this is correct, and that not fixing the conflict of interest which helped create investors' losses in the bubble is certain to undercut the capital-raising machinery of the country. This is why more intelligent regulation is required.

In fact, having both research and capital raising for fees in the same firm creates a major conflict of interest. There is almost no way to preserve objectivity in research when the same firm is paid a fee for raising capital for the same company. We should at least rely on complete disclosure so that people are aware of and can assess conflicts of interest. It's often pointed out that conflicts of interest are common, and not necessarily bad. We do not, after all, prosecute a mother for having a second child, although her attention will now be necessarily divided between the two, and in some instances her loyalty as well. Perhaps disclosure and attempts by the banks to separate fee-based capital raising from analysis will be sufficient to protect the public. It should be tried.

The accounting profession plays a crucial role in the financial markets, yet its performance has been badly tarnished in recent years. The Enron scandal has brought much needed reforms to the public's attention. In general, accounting needs stronger regulation, an elimination of conflicts of interest, and a return to more rigorous accounting standards. Perhaps the modern business corporation is simply too different from the companies of the past, during which time accounting developed its current standards so that traditional interpretations can no longer be applied. Then what is required is creation of new standards that provide transparency to investors about what is going on financially in a firm. Something like a national blue-ribbon commission to visit the key issues, including off-balance sheet accounting, for example, and propose standards for them is much needed.

Finally, a much needed reform of the American regulatory process is for the Fed to take a broader view of its responsibility and attempt to protect the economy and investors from Wall Street, not—as it seems to do now—simply to protect Wall Street from the consequences of its own excesses.

Robert Glauber has long experience with financial markets as a government official, an academic, and as the CEO of NASD. In the following section, he points to the main characteristics of the bubble and how there have developed gaps in the regulatory safety nets which are intended to provide some protection to small investors.

Contribution: Robert R. Glauber

**Robert R. Glauber, Chairman and Chief Executive Officer
of the National Association of Securities Dealers, Inc.**

The Impact of the Internet Bubble on the Economy

After the fact you can recognize a financial bubble, but it's hard to see it when you're in it. Bubbles are usually caused by a shift in a technological paradigm, so that it's easy to make a story of fantastic opportunities for investors. Bubbles are funded by easy credit. The tulip mania was a futures market—no one took delivery, and purchases were financed on credit.

The bubble had a very real impact on the economy. It drove the business expansion in the United States in the late part of the cycle, and did it via (1) tremendous wealth creation that people borrowed against and spent; and (2) an investment-driven expansion. What drove the bubble in its early stages was the economy's rapid growth—corporate investment skyrocketed and then collapsed—it drove the expansion and then pulled the economy down. Especially important was the overinvestment in telecoms, due to easy credit. For dot-coms, some business models never had any profit in them, only revenue growth. These were ridiculous models for funding.

Another Bubble Is Likely

Another bubble is likely. But several things have to come together to make it possible: a story, a technology change, and monetary liquidity provided by the central bank.

Generally speaking, easy money is behind most bubbles—tulips, South Seas, all had a form of credit pyramiding.

Bubbles that originate in the securities market can affect the real economy.

Minimizing the Frequency and Intensity of Bubbles

There's some truth to the notion that a bubble is the price we pay for freedom in capital markets, and it is a part of our method of financing innovation. Bubbles come with free capital markets. It's easy to say they're a fact of life, but it isn't very helpful.

Instead, we can adopt policies to minimize the frequency and intensity of bubbles. The key questions are: Are there such policies, and can you recognize a bubble soon enough to limit its impact?

Sales Practices by Securities Dealers and Underpricing of IPOs

NASDAQ regulates sales practices by securities dealers. It's at the heart of what NASDAQ does, and NASDAQ has brought suits against companies for false representations in sales.

But during the bubble, something went wrong with the usual mechanisms that regulate the prices of shares brought to the IPO market. Many IPOs were massively underpriced. What happened here? What broke down? Why was it the companies going public didn't demand that IPOs be more fully priced? The kickback abuses by underwriters that are being alleged arose out of this. Only with underpricing do the investment banks have a product that is valuable to allocate. There are also allegations that investment banks chose not to allocate IPO shares to retail investors, but instead to institutions which could compensate the banks in some way. All this comes from systematic underpricing. Why was it there? This was a market solution that was wrong.

Qualification of Investors

NASDAQ requires that a broker must advise a customer to invest only in securities that are appropriate to the customer's financial objectives and situation. In this sense, there is qualification of investors in the United States.

This requirement is key to what NASDAQ does. This is not a fiduciary responsibility but is a regulatory requirement about sales practices. But the requirement doesn't necessarily apply with respect to pensions. America democratized the management of pension assets, and individuals can be victims of the latest fads. To the extent that pension holdings weren't in brokerage accounts and involved no broker, there was no accountability to the retail investor who was managing his or her 401(k) account—certainly the mutual fund firm didn't have it, and the person's employer didn't have it. A broker would have had some accountability, but often wasn't involved.

Nine Reforms to Restore Confidence and Rebuild the Economy

Restoring confidence in the credibility of financial markets so that the orderly growth of the economy can be resumed requires reforms.

Nine principal reforms would accomplish most that is currently needed. If the reforms are enacted, then the American economy can resume growth, and

Germany, and other developed economies, can safely import American methods for supporting economic innovation, including venture firms and other elements of the Financial Value Chain, which converts economic value created by entrepreneurs into financial value acquired by the average investor.

The key reforms needed in financial markets are as follows:

1. Each financial product should be placed in one of five risk classifications and be re-evaluated as to classification annually.

2. Every person who seeks to hold financial products should be made a "qualified investor" by income, net worth, and by previous investment experience, and financial professionals and institutions must rigorously advise clients about suitable investments. A positive step has been taken by the United States Department of Labor in permitting sponsors of 401(k) programs to engage investment advisors for program participants.

3. Fiduciary responsibilities should be imposed on buying-side financial market professionals, including especially mutual funds.

4. The conflicts of interest in investment banks and mutual funds that subordinated analysis to sales in the period of the bubble should be resolved by making analysis fully independent of sales and by prohibiting analysts from investing in stocks they cover. An extreme solution, if the banks do not reform themselves completely, is to deny banks any research function, and to depend upon the market to create specialized research organizations that sell their products on an open market.

5. Venture firms which desire to lessen or liquidate their positions or those of their investors in companies going public should be required to do so in a measured fashion over a significant period of time.

6. For firms taken public prior to three successive quarters of profitability, underwriters should be required to certify that the business is viable, and accept liability should the firm fail within a certain period of time, there should be a minimum float.

7. The SEC should reveal to the public what it learns in its investigations of wrongdoing in the securities industry even though a securities firm has settled a complaint. Ordinarily, when the SEC brings a complaint which is settled with a defendant, the settlement provides a firm but the defendant doesn't admit wrongdoing, and the record of the proceeding is closed to the public. So the public doesn't know what was being done and the wrongdoing is likely to continue. This is inadequate disclosure. The SEC ought to make public its findings, regardless of a settlement. In fact, today the public knows that something was going very wrong in the Internet IPO process, but hasn't heard what it was from the SEC.

CHAPTER 16: REFORMS TO PROTECT SMALL INVESTORS

8. A new regulatory regime is not needed each time there is another financial crisis. Much of the damage which is being done by the crises could be avoided with greater transparency. Why, for example, did the Fed not know that most of the major investment banks were deeply invested in Long-Term Capital Management? It discovered the fact immediately upon trying to mitigate the crisis caused by LTCM. America has the most transparent capital markets in the world, but the comparison is relative. Our markets are not yet transparent enough to avoid serious financial shocks of the type which are now occurring every two years or so.

9. Central banks—in America the Fed, and in Germany the Bundesbank—should be required to intervene at their discretion in financial markets to protect retail investors from excessive movements, both positive and negative, in the overall markets.

Talking Points

Avoiding another major bubble and its sad impact on small investors requires both more transparency about financial data and the transactions, and also greater regulatory protections for small investors.

Germany went through an Internet bubble just as did America, but with considerably less damage to the small investor. This is because in Germany the individual has far less control of her or his pension money than in America. Further, in Germany, there is a system that qualifies both investors and investments, and helps prevent individual savings from being invested in very speculative shares (whether in companies or mutual funds).

Ironically, the United States has a qualified investor system, but it has large gaps in it. In this chapter we have suggested nine principal reforms that would protect both small investors and the economy as a whole from the ravages of another large bubble.

More protection for small investors against losses will presumably mean that they have less opportunity for substantial gains. Some will object to this. If the financial markets functioned with less volatility than exhibited during the bubble, then further protection of small investors might not be required, and somewhat larger risks for somewhat larger gains might make sense. But with a system given to such speculative excesses as the bubble demonstrated, the risk, and even likelihood, of substantial losses is greatly disproportionate for small investors to the possibility of outsized gains.

VIII Less Damage Next Time

The Internet bubble was hard on many people and hard on the economy. It may seem surprising, therefore, to ask if we want another one. But many people believe the bubble to have been, on balance, good for us.

17 What Does the Future Hold?

Do We Want Another Bubble?

Many people think the bubble was a good thing. Among the venture capitalists and investment bankers who made money during the bubble, the view is common that the bubble was a great thing; what's bad is the postbubble. The party was great; what's bad is the hangover.

There are also people who believe that there was net value creation in the bubble, and they point to the continuing positive valuation of a few remaining Internet firms at more money than was invested in all the Internet firms by venture capitalists and angels. But of course the public invested also, in IPOs, and when total capital invested is counted, there is less certainty of any actual value creation.

Regardless of whether or not there was, by the measure of today's stock market prices, any net value creation in the mania of the past few years—and it appears there was not—there are thoughtful people who believe the bubble was probably constructive. In their view, it caused a quantum leap in people's perception that they had to embrace New Age technologies. Further, a mass market has been created, and the pace of innovation accelerated. Even, they conclude, if nothing can rectify the waste associated with the bubble, the outcome this time will be better than tulipmania because of the factors mentioned above.

But these judgments are subject to question. Was a financial mania really necessary to bring the Internet to people's attention, and in particular a mania of the unusual size that occurred? It seems unlikely. Companies to exploit the new technology might have been created without the bubble; new products and services might have impressed customers without the bubble; press attention might have attracted the interest of the public without the bubble; the better start-ups might have gotten funded and even been sold to the investing public without the bubble. And if all this had happened, the negative consequences of the bubble might have been avoided.

Contribution: Ted Dintersmith

**Highlights of an interview with Ted Dintersmith,
a General partner at Charles River Ventures**

Do you think that the bubble was necessary?

I can't imagine anybody could advance the point of view that a speculative boom like that is necessary. I don't how you'd even begin to make the case that it's necessary.

Let's start by why you determine it to be a speculative bubble. If you look back on other "speculative bubbles," the most famous being tulip bulbs, there were Japanese stocks, Taiwanese stocks, U.S. land like the Louisiana Purchase, the Gold Rush, you can go back and look where prices ultimately settled out relative to the peak. Then you can pick 100 Internet company stocks, and the downward correction is more severe for Internet stocks than was in a lot of other speculative bubbles. So the Internet speculative bubble was certainly real. It certainly happened. To say was it necessary seems inappropriate.

Why did it happen? It happened, I think, because of an interesting confluence of events. You had a long period of time where some visible technology stocks had generated lots of capital gains for those people who held. You had a fairly small number, Apple, Intel, Microsoft, Cisco, of very visible stocks.

I was just watching last night "You've Got Mail" and the woman says "I'm very rich, I bought Intel at 6." Forest Gump bought Apple Computer stock. You had a public that knew about the wealth potential of technology stocks, and then overlaying that was a lot of popular attention and hype around the Internet. Netscape went public with operating losses. Jeff Bezos on the cover of *Time* magazine. So suddenly you've got a public market that's highly receptive to holding technology stocks, who think those could be key to long-term wealth, with lots and lots of the press talking about how the "the Internet changes everything." The thing that was pivotal was that the public bought the Amazon.com business model, which was invest in a company and fund massive operation losses to generate rapid growth in the face of an unproven business model. That's the classic definition of venture capital, and that's exactly what the public market did. The public market became a price insensitive, massive source of late stage venture capital. And as opposed to traditional venture capital where nobody exits, the public markets allowed entrepreneurs, venture capital firms, and limited partners to exit.

Most curiously, the public market fascination with Internet stocks didn't happen for a month, it happened for 2.5 years. It slowly came up, then it got unbelievably frantic, and it stayed there for about a year. Which is bizarre.

The speculative bubble was constantly being filled with air by the investment banks of this country. They took the companies public, they organized the IPOs so that a limited amount of float was offered at low prices, and then after-market trading pushed prices sky high. The analysts of these banking firms then wrote glowing reports on the prospects for the stock, providing air cover for the key clients of the bank to sell their positions. It was a well-orchestrated transfer of wealth from the lay person to the Fidelities, T. Rowe Prices, and Januses of the world.

Was it destructive? The brutal beauty of the capitalist system is that prices determine resource allocation. The market sets prices, and it's a very powerful mechanism for directing resources within an economy: And the reason price controls are so inefficient is it's an artificial price instead of real price, so you get bad allocations of resources. We didn't have price controls, but we had out-of-whack prices. When some of these stocks went to infinity, it made no sense. It wasn't a market price, it was a hyped, artificial price, contributed to by the fact that these companies were taken public with a tiny percent of their float being offered, with the investment banks refusing to do any lockup release, so that modest swings in demand would drive stock prices up 10, 20 points in a day. Suddenly you've got, on paper, lots and lots of millionaires. So a lot of people did things with their careers and their money that they now look back on and regret.

Isn't there an argument that the market was incorporating option value, or the fact that the Internet permits such scalable businesses that the prices reflected an expected value of the possibility that any one of these companies could have become the market dominant player?

Yes, that was the argument. At the time it seemed like a pretty compelling argument. Yet today, even for the best companies, stock prices are 25 percent of what they were.

A company I was on the Board of went public. We had a $2 million revenue quarter, we had $10 million quarterly operating losses, and we had a market cap of $3 billion. Did that make sense? I was on the Board, and I didn't think it made any sense. But since I'm on the Board, I can't call people and tell them to sell. I had relatives who owned the stock, but I couldn't as a Director tell them to sell. From the inside you knew it was insane.

Was the regulatory regime inappropriate when the public markets found themselves acting as venture capitalists?

Do you really trust the government to know what the right price of a stock is? You had Greenspan talking about irrational exuberance, which at the time was a very laughed-at remark, but which looks pretty sensible in retrospect. You had the SEC pestering companies going public with so-called cheap stock charges—at incentive stock option prices that today seem grossly overpriced.

What is a "lock up release"?

Let's walk through a hypothetical example.

A company has 50 million shares and goes public. The investment bankers put enormous pressure on the company to keep the price low because they want the institutions who buy the IPO stock to make money. They price it at $8 a share, and it immediately goes to $50 per share. So now the company is trading at $50 per share with 50 million shares outstanding—meaning its market cap is $2.5 billion. But none of the insiders can sell or do anything with their stock, it's all "locked up," which is pretty standard. The SEC mandates that when you have a new issue, because they don't want "informed" insiders to transfer stock to naive outsiders until the stock is somewhat proven in terms of having a couple quarters of earnings releases. The investment banks insist on a lock up. What they really mean is they want to provide plenty of air cover so that Fidelity and Wellington and Putnam can sell all of their shares and not have their stock price crushed by insiders who get rid of it. So of 50 million shares, they may offer five million to the public. And so for a hot stock, everyone wants it, there are only five million shares outstanding, $40 million at the IPO price of basic stock being sold, so it gets bid up enormously. So if you had a more orderly release of shares out of lock up, so that if there's excess demand, it's met by a lot more shares being sold at $10 instead of a small number of shares being sold at $50, that seems to be a more efficient market transfer. But that's not how the investment banks like to do it, because at the end of the day they win their gold stars from Fidelity when Fidelity can buy at $8 and sell at $50.

The whole IPO process, especially the pricing and the share distribution, is very broken. But can we trust the SEC to fix it? I don't think so. If you look at the priorities that SEC and FASB have had, it's been on all the wrong things. Do I look for government solutions? It's hard to believe that the government understands what it is regulating. They focus on cheap stock issues, and pooling issues in mergers, and not letting companies reprice stock options when the stock is really down and management is struggling to keep the company intact—they've attacked all those things. They've ignored the fact that every single IPO for years and years has been priced with seven percent of gross proceeds going to the investment banking firms. This method of pricing IPOs, on the face of it, seems to be a pretty clear case of price collusion in an oligopolistic market. But that doesn't seem to matter to the SEC.

If you were the regulator, would there be a set of ideas that would make some sense?

Yes. Simple things to start. Anybody buying shares in an IPO of a company having some sort of a lock up should also have some sort of lock up. Why should I as a private investor have a six-month lock up, and a mutual fund as a public investor be free to use its clout to get 10 percent of the offering at $8 a share, then sell it all in three hours? That doesn't seem to make any sense.

Have the recent regulatory changes dealing with disclosure and the separation of the sell-side analysts from their investment banks been sufficient?

Some regulations govern what a company can say to any and all investors, trying to put all investors on a level playing field, which I think is probably a good idea. It doesn't say anything about how Joe the Analyst is issuing an aggressive buy while Joe the Analyst is selling his personal shares or Joe the Analyst's firm is dumping a ton of their shares. That seems like something that ought to be included under disclosure issues.

Was there a dedication among VCs during the bubble to creating sustainable businesses, or was the objective of the VCs to provide liquidity for their investors without judgment about the correctness of the markets?

It's almost a religious question. Different groups view it differently. At the end of the day, to be coldly honest about it, I think our limited partners care about what they do on a cash-on-cash basis, money out versus money in, for the venture firms they invest in. Some of them, a small number, tend to be pretty willing to hold the stock you give them. The longer their time horizons, the more inclined they are to hold the stock, the more they care about if you're involved in building a long-term company. Those that tend to sell early, which is probably the majority, care about cash-on-cash returns. They view our portfolio companies as properties or assets, and not your heart and soul. I think the LPs who got a ton of money out of eToys are just as happy as the guys who got a ton of money if they sold quickly out of Cisco. That's not all of them, but that's a lot of them.

Within our industry there are some guys who are market timers and financial engineers, and other people who are more focused on building companies. There's no right and wrong here. It depends on your values on whether you say one is better than another. One investor might be a shrewd market timer who can hype a company, get it out the door in a hot market, but consistently delivers 150 percent net annual IRR to his/her investors. Another investor might be more deliberate, build great companies, and deliver a 75 percent net annual IRR to his/her investors. Who is better? Well, the answer is, "it depends."

Is there still a speculative environment out there?

The exit values have crashed down. That's unambiguous.

What hasn't crashed down as much is the rate at which new companies get funded, and the valuations of those companies. So I think there's still some of the excess of the 1999–2000 period yet to be wrung out of the system.

Why hasn't the volume of investment crushed down more?

I think a lot of people are hoping for a big market rally. I am too.

But I just don't see how the math works. I think that's still the disconnect in our business. Everyone says, "Yeah, we understand and we're back to the old rules," but at the same time, we're still seeing large first-round financings. As that happens, in some ways it's sort of the same game over again.

Will There Be Another Bubble?

Whether or not there will be another bubble is a key issue, in part because we needn't take actions to avoid it if it isn't likely to happen. One school of thought is that there will not be. It won't happen again—at least there will be no bubble of this magnitude, doing the damage it did, in the foreseeable future.

The argument proceeds as follows: The dot-com and telecom bubbles required the confluence of a speculative mania with a technological discontinuity. The potential for mania resides in the human psyche and will be there always, but a technological discontinuity of the magnitude of the Internet is very unlikely. What was crucial about the Internet was that it promised to transform all of the economy. Every company's board was required to think through the possible impact of the Net on its business—whether consumer goods or capital goods, or services—and government and nonprofits as well. It was absolutely pervasive. So it was a technological discontinuity of enormous proportions, and gave rise to a speculative mania otherwise unlikely.

The argument continues that no such pervasive discontinuity is likely in the years immediately ahead. For example, biotechnology, including cloning, is a very exciting new technology which provides a major discontinuity, but one impacting primarily the health services. There could be a speculative mania there, and has been to some degree already, but it won't be of the size of the dot-com/telecom bubble because it is limited to a single sector.

The argument concludes that without a technological discontinuity on the scale of the Internet, there is not likely to be another bubble of the size of the one just past, so there is no reason for doing anything to try to avoid it.

But this view isn't convincing, so that the possibility of another bubble of the magnitude of the recent one is not ruled out. In fact, ironically, the notion that the Internet was a discontinuity of such great magnitude is itself merely an illusion fostered by the hype which accompanied the bubble. To see this, we should recall the Y2K scare. In the 18 months prior to January 1, 2000, the notion developed that computers would be disabled by the shift from the 1900s to the 2000s. A few people argued against this, but others insisted on it to the point that, concerned about possible disruptions of commerce and society generally, almost all firms, the government, and nonprofits, allocated time and money to trying to prepare for a Y2K crisis. It was believed likely to affect almost all organizations and functions in the world. Airline travel was supposed to be disrupted, communications impaired, computers of all sizes caused to malfunction. Corporations built backups, bunkers, hardened rooms. The federal government at one time suggested that it had spent over $100 billion preparing for Y2K.

The Fed inflated the money supply in the fall of 1999 to cushion an expected negative impact of Y2K on the nation's economy.[118]

And what happened? Nothing.

In retrospect it was all hysteria, in which many of the most sober officials of our society participated.

Something of a similar nature happened with respect to the Internet. That it is an important technology no one can deny. That its impact is so pervasive and substantial as the proponents of the view above assert is unlikely. But that people believed it was, and still do, and that this contributed to the bubbles, is undoubtedly true.

So what is needed to drive a bubble is not a technology of generally pervasive discontinuity, but rather one that can be made to seem of that significance. And there are likely to be many candidates for this role in the years ahead, some undoubtedly sons and daughters of the Internet. The media is continually advancing candidates for the next technological discontinuity, and as the memory of the dot-com/telecom bubble recedes, the likelihood of excitement about a new technology grows.

All the financial market players in the Internet bubble remain in place, most having prospered in the bubble just burst, even though entrepreneurs and retail investors did not. The players have the means and the incentives to repeat the bubble whenever another opportunity offers itself.

The supply and demand model of the bubble says that so much money poured into venture funds in the late 1990s that too much money chased too few good deals, causing valuations to rise enormously. Further, that when investment bankers were able to generate a public market for what had been companies at too early a stage, the venture funds hurried to supply the market with companies. One can almost hear the venture capitalists asking themselves, "If I can actually sell this thing, and I can get the capital to keep putting into other companies like this, then should I be doing it and not refusing to invest because the company looks like junk?" There seemed to be an endless supply of capital, and as long as the wheel kept spinning, everyone would be happy.

And none of this has changed. While the inflow of capital to venture funds has slackened a bit since the bubble burst, it still remains high by historical standards, and is high by the standards of what innovation now requires. So the money machine continues to spin, and the capital for another bubble is available.

The Hype Machine also remains active. The only question is, when will it again be listened to and drive share prices upward?

Here's an example. "Sometime in the next few years we will find ourselves surrounded by a pervasive, always-on network... The world is moving toward hyperconnectivity. Mobility and physical space will be the new drivers of innovation. And location awareness is the ingredient that will bind the physical world to the virtual."[119] It would follow that companies built to provide hyperconnectivity and location awareness would be prime candidates for investment, perhaps causing excitement, even mania, among investors about their prospects. This is how a bubble builds.

Finally, what is also needed is plenty of credit, and the Fed is supplying it. Presently, America's money supply is growing at what by key measures is the highest rate in more than 20 years, providing ample fuel for another bubble.

It follows that another bubble is a certainty. It's how financial markets today go after big opportunities. Every great move ahead is at the cost of too much money being thrown into an arena, a bubble being formed and bursting.

This is an enduring dynamic in capitalism. The scale of the recent bubble was bigger, but the dynamic is the same.

The thought has been that bubbles don't repeat. But the Internet bubble was in a real sense the second bubble for the personal computer. First there was speculation in the shares of companies that produced the machine; then there was a bubble in the technology of the Internet which connected the machines. And the second bubble was so much bigger than the first because it was really four bubbles in sequence building into one gigantic burst, as described in Chapter 2.

Smaller Bubbles and Less Damage

The Internet bubble did more damage to small investors and to the economy than it helped technology; in fact, it set technological advance back to a degree. In consequence, fewer bubbles—less excess in the capital markets—can be gained at little or no price in terms of innovation and progress in our economy.

The bubble was a result of financial institutions just doing their jobs. Venture firms took an unexpectedly large inflow of capital and spread it out to a large number of start-up firms, and quality of investments was lost in the process. Investment banks sensed the increasing public excitement about the Internet and packaged IPOs for sale. The media fanned the public mania; the government gave its blessing in variety of ways. As has happened so often in recent history, in many different settings, professionals were just doing their jobs, but the result was a disaster, especially for the most vulnerable.

Another bubble is likely, as said previously. The money is there and the financial markets have the same incentives as before. So the same unfortunate result is likely.

But small investors can be protected from the worst ravages of whatever size bubble might occur. Financial market institutions should be required to seriously qualify investors and investments in order to prevent a bubble from hurting small investors. Perhaps insulating small investors from the most severe consequences of a bubble is enough, and bubbles might then be allowed to occur. And in fact, keeping small investors out of bubbles will itself lessen the degree to which a bubble inflates.

It is useful to try to avoid further bubbles, not just to lessen their consequences, because bubbles threaten recessions in their wake and damage the process by which innovation finds its way into our economy.

The advantage of both protecting small investors from a bubble, and trying to limit a bubble itself, is that our economy will function better.

In the past, capitalist market economies suffered a long line of major depressions. In that period, many influential people argued that depressions were the necessary price of economic freedom and progress. They were not. We no longer have economic depressions in which 20–25 percent of our people lose their jobs, but nevertheless our economy grows successfully and people have a lot of economic freedom. We've been able to lessen the severity of depressions and still have economic growth and greatly improved living standards. Similarly, we don't need any longer to have speculative bubbles in which millions lose most of their savings and pension money. We can protect small investors and get rid of big bubbles without having the economy stagnate. Instead, if we better protect people, our economy is likely to perform better than it has in the past.

NEMAX (The German New Market) and NASDAQ

NEMAX ALL SHARE

10/3/97 - 12-13/01

NEMAX - All Share

Source: Datastream

Source: Datastream

Source: **Datastream**

B   Financial Value Chain Influencers

Financial Value Chain Participants/Relationships

Value created for	Value captured (getting paid)			Business involvement		Influence	Drivers of/ Importance of reputation	Risks
	How paid? Who pays?	Incentive/ dominant strategy	Time horizon	Scarce (limiting) resource	Mechanisms of influence over others	Key relationships		Legal exposures
Entrepreneurs/Management								
Founders	Self, customers, employees, investors, venture capital firms **Economy:** act on an idea	Capital appreciation	Build a large, lasting company.	Usually long term; it may be a life's ambition	Reputation, time, money, idea	Can choose who its investors are, can insist on a strategy	Customers, employees, investors	Success of enterprise drives reputation; reputation important to be able to attract future investors	Exists, although mitigated by corporate structure, directors' and officers' insurance
VC-installed management	Investors, self, customers, employees; although loyalty may be stronger to the VC that installed them **Economy:** represent liquid labor markets—bringing their expertise to a company	Options and salary	May be regularly used by the VC to turn around struggling companies, so may have a bias toward VC. If VC-suggested strategy fails, VC is likely to help manager find another position.	Shorter term than founder; once business is stabilized, or through IPO process, may move on to another venture the VC needs fixed	Time, reputation	Can try to influence strategy, but is not fully autonomous from VC	VC	Success of enterprise drives reputation; reputation not as important since VCs act as protectors, and will likely be in multiple companies during career	Exists, although mitigated by corporate structure and directors' and officers' insurance
Internal investor relations (CFO/CEO)	Management, investors, analysts, press, underwriters, customers **Economy:** communicates with investors and customers	Salary, maybe options	Be as positive as possible.	Shorter term— goal is to achieve free advertising through media and keep investors happy	Credibility	Information provided to investors, the press, analysts	Press, analysts	Known that investor relations is not objective so reputation largely unimportant	Liability if fraudulent

Financial Value Chain Participants/Relationships *(continued)*

	Value created for	Value captured (getting paid)		Time horizon	Business involvement		Influence	Drivers of/ Importance of reputation	Risks
		How paid? Who pays?	Incentive/ dominant strategy		Scarce (limiting) resource	Mechanisms of influence over others	Key relationships		Legal exposures
Accountants/ auditors	Management, investors, analysts, underwriters **Economy:** maintains quality of financial information for those analysts	Fixed fee paid by the company; with some controversy, partners at certain of the accounting firms also became investors in their clients.	Protective of reputation for objectivity while also maintaining relationships with the client company	Long term	Credibility	Giving a qualified opinion would be very embarrassing to management and would create big problems in raising capital.	Management, regulators	Consistent objectivity; reputation is absolutely key to their business.	Legal liability
Lawyers	All parties, regulators **Economy:** informs all parties of the requirements of the law and helps structure the relationships between key parties through contracting	Their client pays on an hourly basis.	To strongly advocate the position of their own client	Shorter term, transaction oriented, although with longer term reputation a concern	Time (better lawyers can choose which clients to take), reputation	Advice regarding previous transactions allows each party to be more sophisticated in dealing with the other. Lawyers often introduce entrepreneurs to investors and vice versa.	VC, management	Skill at advocacy and specific knowledge of relevant transactions drives reputation; reputation is important to securing clients.	NS*
Public relations firms	Management, press, investors, analysts, underwriters, customers **Economy:** communicates with investors and customers	Fixed fee paid by the company	Find creative ways to focus media attention on your company.	Shorter term— goal is to achieve free advertising through media	Reputation	Manipulation of information received by the press, analysts, investors	Press, management	Creativity and effectiveness in getting free press drives reputation. This is important to gaining clients.	NS*

239

Financial Value Chain Participants/Relationships *(continued)*

	Value created for	Value captured (getting paid)		Business involvement			Influence	Risks	
		How paid? Who pays?	Incentive/ dominant strategy	Time horizon	Scarce (limiting) resource	Mechanisms of influence over others	Key relationships	Drivers of/ Importance of reputation	Legal exposures
VC									
Venture investors	(LPs and selves)— identify markets, entre- preneurs, products or services to develop companies; self— option on external R&D, access to infor- mation flow, advan- taged opportunity to fully acquire, option control potential emer- gent competitors, capital appreciation; entrepreneurs—provide capital and maybe advice, contacts; I-banks—groom next generation of IPOs and M&A; corporate— groom next generation acquisitions **Economy:** screen and then provide risk capital and advice to unproven companies; allow established companies to exploit emerging technology; introduces companies to the public markets or acquirers.	LPs—manage- ment fee (2–3% of committed capital and 20–30% of gains); whoever acquires the portfolio com- pany (public if an IPO, corpo- rate if an acquisition)		Short as possible to maximize IRR (how funds are benchmarked against others); dictated by market conditions, sector popularity; typi- cally 3–5 years	VC time, pos- sibly capital (depending on investor type); access to good deals; capital, relationships with active VC	Entrepreneur— capital structure (subordinating execs' equity with VC's preferred stock, valuation and milestone ratchets, vesting, veto rights over sales and major changes in business, buy-back clauses, PIK dividends, liquida- tion preference with valuation multiples), operat- ing advice; I-banks—choose where to do their IPO/M&A busi- ness; influence projects pursued by company, help attract VC investment	Deal sourc- ing—entrepre- neur community, other VCs; Capital—LPs, other VCs; Liquidation— I-banks and corporate	Returns over time key source of reputation; affects all key relationships, especially capi- tal raising, also attracting entre- preneurs and investing with them on favor- able terms; returns impor- tant to attract LPs, credibility with I-banks	Nearly none. Sophisticated LPs and coin- vesting VCs, companies responsible for own legal coun- sel, acquiring corporates are sophisticated, I-banks are sophisticated.

Financial Value Chain Participants/Relationships *(continued)*

Value created for	Value captured (getting paid)		Business involvement			Influence	Risks	
	How paid? Who pays?	Incentive/ dominant strategy	Time horizon	Scarce (limiting) resource	Mechanisms of influence over others	Key relationships	Drivers of/ Importance of reputation	Legal exposures
Limited Partners (LPs) in VC funds — Their larger portfolio, of which VC is probably a small part **Economy:** provide capital to those with expertise in identifying opportunities	LPs receive their funds from various sources like pensions and often act as fiduciaries; LPs' objective is capital appreciation.	Spread investments into various quality VC funds, which allows diversification and gives option to invest in their next fund	Long term, the life of the fund into which they invest (7–10 years); they may receive distributions returning capital and appreciation as early as within a few years; typically are unable to sell their interests in VC funds	Percentage of their overall portfolio allowed to be allocated to this risky, illiquid asset class; administrative burden could be a minor constraint.	Threat not to reinvest in VC's next fund; once invested, legally an LP cannot take any role in influencing investment decisions lest he lose his LP status and thereby limited liability.	VC, the most popular of which can choose to exclude LPs from oversubscribed funds	Returns benchmarks for pension/ endowment administrator who makes the decision how to allocate among asset classes and which funds within asset classes	Fiduciary responsibility to those who have given them the funds to invest
Investment Banks								
Underwriters — Entrepreneur/ VC—raising capital on their behalf in the capital markets; money managers/public investors—with whom they place the equity **Economy:** introduces companies to the public capital markets	Company pays a percentage of proceeds at time of offering.	Make sure equity issued finds buyers on the day of the IPO; incentive to price stock as low as the company will accept without hurting underwriter's reputation; wants to hype (market) the deal, so they will not be required to support the price of the stock	Day of IPO and short period after when they will support the price; reputational concerns might suggest a longer term interest in the stock's success.	Reputation, sales force "bandwidth" to sell new equity to its institutional and other investors; receptivity of markets that can rapidly change and make an offering undoable	Terms of offering (lockup periods restricting VC and entrepreneur's ability to sell stock for a period after the offering), sense of market appetite for types of companies; influences what VCs will invest in or advise their portfolio companies; ability to affect equity analyst's compensation	VC, entrepreneurs, money managers, public reputation	Balance between conflicting reputations to get the best price for the company, and selling to money managers and investors stock that will appreciate after the offering	Various regulatory requirements, but generally offering documents are careful to minimize risks by maximizing disclosure

Financial Value Chain Participants/Relationships *(continued)*

Value created for	Value captured (getting paid)		Business involvement			Influence	Risks	
	How paid? Who pays?	Incentive/ dominant strategy	Time horizon	Scarce (limiting) resource	Mechanisms of influence over others	Key relationships	Drivers of/ Importance of reputation	Legal exposures
Sell-side equity research	Money manager/public investors—rely on equity research to evaluate public companies' business prospects; underwriters—help promote an IPO and then continue to cover it; entrepreneurs—a means to efficiently communicate their story to the wider public **Economy:** supposed to synthesize for investors the impact of changing industry and company conditions; has analytic expertise and access to best information	Paid from other, profit-generating parts of the bank, particularly the underwriters; sometimes based on the number of IPOs the analyst has helped market	Balancing reputation with investors against underwriter and company pressure to be positive	Follows companies long term, establishing a reputation	Reputation, access to management for information, time	Communicates to the public through the press, tries to persuade money managers and investors, companies try to please the analysts, can try to influence which companies the underwriters take public	Management, money managers, the press, underwriters	Reputation driven on ability to correctly predict stock price movements, also charisma; reputation is key to having influence over investors and being an asset to underwriters.	New regulations around their relationship with management; recent class action lawsuits have failed to assign liability for wrong predictions.

Financial Value Chain Participants/Relationships *(continued)*

Value created for	Value captured (getting paid)		Business involvement			Influence	Risks	
	How paid? Who pays?	Incentive/ dominant strategy	Time horizon	Scarce (limiting) resource	Mechanisms of influence over others	Key relationships	Drivers of/ Importance of reputation	Legal exposures
Mutual Funds								
Money managers (buy-side)	Percentage of money managed; their funds attract more money when they have performed better than the average within their risk category.	Better relative performance; may lead to imitative investing to be sure to not significantly underperform peers; may also encourage riskier investing so long as staying within the loose boundaries of the "risk category"	Quarterly reporting; ultimately, long-term performance is important, but also engage in short-term trading into and out of positions	Reputation, access to information	Decision to buy IPO stock, hold it, sell it	Underwriters to get IPO stock, equity analysts to get insight and information, trust of smaller investors	Returns over time; reputation is key to attracting capital to invest	Very little; investors invest at their own risk

Smaller investors; underwriters—place large blocks of IPO stock with them, who tend not to churn it as much as day traders

Economy: supposed to synthesize for investors the impact of changing industry and company conditions; has analytic expertise and access to best information

Financial Value Chain Participants/Relationships *(continued)*

	Value created for	Value captured (getting paid)		Business involvement			Influence	Risks	
		How paid? Who pays?	Incentive/ dominant strategy	Time horizon	Scarce (limiting) resource	Mechanisms of influence over others	Key relationships	Drivers of/ Importance of reputation	Legal exposures
External Factors									
The press	Public/its shareholders; investors, analysts **Economy:** collects and distributes generally nonfinancial information about companies to interested parties; not necessarily experts	Journalists are trying to build their own reputation; the media firm is trying to increase consumers of its media so as to increase the value of the firm.	Attract consumers of its stories, could lead to a bias toward sensationalism. Pressure to produce a great volume of stories may also lead to going with "easy" stories—reporting on fads (what others are reporting) and being uncritical of PR and management spin.	Very short term; the deadline for printing tomorrow's paper/ magazine/ television report	Story ideas, expertise	Can attract investor and customer attention to a company as well as publish stories on the successes and failures of all involved parties (investor gains, auditor mistakes, etc.)	PR firms, analysts, sometimes management	Depends on the media organization, but can be entertainment value of stories or depth of analysis. Importance of reputation also depends on the audience.	None—strong constitutional protection
Forecasting/ analysis firms (Gartner, Jupiter)	Management, investors, underwriters, analysts; press **Economy:** gains access to the best available market data and uses sophisticated analytic techniques to make forecasts	Paid semifixed fees for detailed reports on a subject	Balance between reputation for accurate forecasts and a need to market their own research in sensationalistic ways	Medium term; forecasts tend to change over time, and they are not necessarily held responsible for misforecasts, however, reputation will suffer if they are consistently wrong.	Reputation	Their predictions form the basis of business plans, investor decisions, analyst predictions, press accounts. These reports often are the starting point of investment fads.	Management, press, investors, analysts	Not necessarily held responsible for misforecasts, however, reputation will suffer if they are consistently wrong.	None

Financial Value Chain Participants/Relationships *(continued)*

	Value created for	Value captured (getting paid)			Business involvement			Influence	Risks	
		How paid? Who pays?	Incentive/ dominant strategy	Time horizon	Scarce (limiting) resource	Mechanisms of influence over others	Key relationships	Drivers of/ Importance of reputation	Legal exposures
Regulators										
SEC	The public; investors, analysts, underwriters who rely on the accuracy of financial information **Economy:** sets standards for the quality of financial information provided to the public and analysts	Not for profit	Accommodation between efficiency of markets and necessary regulation to created a trusted market environment	Long term	Time and financial resources	Jail, fines, ability to ban individuals from financial services jobs	Financial industry, politicians	Reputation for fairness and practical accommodation of market efficiency and adequate protections for investors; has monopoly on its function with the United States (financial activity could migrate elsewhere)	None
Federal Reserve	The public, everyone in the economy **Economy:** stimulates and restrains the economy as necessary to maintain orderly growth	Not for profit	Avoid damage to banking industry; avoid a recession, avoid inflation	Long term	Has all resources it needs	Interest rates, money supply, bank capitalization requirements	Financial industry, politicians	Reputation for fairness and practical accommodation of market efficiency and adequate protections for investors, but has monopoly on its function with the United States (financial activity could migrate elsewhere)	None

Financial Value Chain Participants/Relationships *(continued)*

	Value created for	Value captured (getting paid)		Business involvement			Influence		Risks	
		How paid? Who pays?	Incentive/ dominant strategy	Time horizon	Scarce (limiting) resource	Mechanisms of influence over others	Key relationships	Drivers of/ Importance of reputation	Legal exposures
FASB	Accountants, everyone who relies on the consistency of financial information **Economy:** sets standards for the quality of financial information provided to the public and analysts	Industry support	Provide transparency to financial reports	Long term	Time and personnel	Sets GAAP rules	Financial industry, accountant firms, companies	Reputation for fairness and practical accommodation of market efficiency and adequate protections for investors, but has monopoly on its function with the United States and increasingly GAAP is used internationally	None
Class-action lawyers	Investors, self; the SEC, whose enforcement is aided by lawyers' pursuit of wrongdoing **Economy:** bolsters regulators' enforcement of law and discourages law breaking by other players	Paid a percentage of the awards won for clients	Pursue the largest, most easily proven cases of law breaking by parties with deep financial resources	Short term	Time and personnel	Lawsuits require a lot of resources to defend against and when lost can result in very large financial penalties and reputational damage.	Relatively independent actors, not coordinating activities with other parties but opportunistically pursuing "deep pockets"	Frequently winning cases; credibility with the courts helps	None

Financial Value Chain Participants/Relationships *(continued)*

Value created for	Value captured (getting paid)		Business involvement			Influence	Risks	
	How paid? Who pays?	Incentive/ dominant strategy	Time horizon	Scarce (limiting) resource	Mechanisms of influence over others	Key relationships	Drivers of/ Importance of reputation	Legal exposures
The Public								
Pension/401(k) investors	Percentage of funds under management and perhaps a bonus based upon performance	Offer brand-name funds to plan participants, receive highest possible returns	Long-term retirement	Number of funds that can be offered and administered	Where it chooses to invest its funds (which money managers it offers to its participants, into which VC firms it becomes an LP)	Money managers, VC firms, management, employees	Competent administration of a reasonable number of choices for 401(k) plans, good returns for a defined benefit pension plan	ERISA obligations
Employees, benefits administrators; funds are aggregated for and often invested by money managers, VC funds often have Pension Fund LPs **Economy:** Exploits economies of scale to allow small investors less expensive access to financial expertise; is a vessel through which private savings are cycled back into the economy.								

247

Financial Value Chain Participants/Relationships *(continued)*

Value created for	Value captured (getting paid)			Business involvement				Influence		Risks	
	How paid? Who pays?	Incentive/ dominant strategy	Time horizon	Scarce (limiting) resource	Mechanisms of influence over others			Key relationships	Drivers of/ Importance of reputation		Legal exposures
Stock-holding investors	Self, consumers of press, provide liquidity to private investors (VCs) **Economy:** collectively provide capital and make judgments on the relative merits of companies	Capital gains and dividends	Depends on risk appetite of the investor; known for bouts of greed and fear	Depends on the investor	Capital, time and financial expertise	Chooses which stocks and funds to purchase and sell		Money managers, regulators, press	N/A	None	
Day traders	Self, consumers of press, fee-charging exchanges, provide liquidity to private investors (VCs) and other market participants **Economy:** arbitrage, quick incorporation of market information into stock price	Capital gains	Anticipate momentum and quickly buy and sell	Extremely short	Capital	Chooses which stock to buy and sell		None	N/A	None	

NS = not significant

248

Contributors

- **Beeck, Wilfried**—Intershop: Co-founder and COO; Mr. Beeck is responsible for Intershop's global business, including Sales & Marketing, Consulting, Customer Services, Human Resources, Operations, and Corporate Development. Previously, Mr. Beeck served as Intershop's CFO and managed a very successful IPO on the Frankfurt Stock Exchange in July 1998, as well as the NASDAQ listing in September 2000. Prior to that, Mr. Beeck was the president of Intershop's European operations, where his inside knowledge of the international software industry and his experience in developing a high-tech business have been instrumental to Intershop's success and rapid growth. Mr. Beeck founded his first software company in 1983 and has more than 15 years of executive experience in U.S. and European software industries. He studied mathematics and computer science at the University of Kiel, Germany.

- **Böhnlein, Dr. Barbara**—Buecher.de: Dr. Böhnlein is an Assistant Director at ABN AMRO Rothschild (AAR), the Equity Capital Markets Joint Venture of ABN AMRO Group and Rothschild and Sons. Before joining AAR, she held various positions at Credit Suisse Group and Deutsche Börse AG, where she helped build the Neuer Markt trading segment. Dr. Böhnlein studied economics at the University of Freiburg, Wayne State University of Detroit, and at the Institute of World Economics in Kiel. She holds a Ph.D. with distinction from the European University Institute in Florence, Italy.

- **Boos, Patrick**—Webmiles: Founder and former CEO of Webmiles.

- **Dintersmith, Ted**—Charles River Ventures: General Partner. Mr. Dintersmith has more than 13 years of experience in early-stage venture investing, focusing on software and information services companies. He is currently a director of Be Free, Bowstreet, Compete, Myteam.com, Netezza, NetGenesis (NASDAQ: NTGX), Revenio, Trellix, Wheelhouse, and Ximian. Prior to his career in venture investing, Mr. Dintersmith was general manager of the Digital Signal Processing Division of Analog Devices. He earned a Ph.D. in Engineering from Stanford University, concentrating on mathematical modeling and optimization theory. His undergraduate degree is from the College of William and Mary, where he graduated Phi Beta Kappa with High Honors in Physics and English.

- **Glauber, Robert R.**—Chairman and CEO of the National Association of Securities Dealers, Inc. (NASD) since November 2000. Since 1996, Mr. Glauber has been an active member of the NASD board. Mr. Glauber served as Under Secretary of the Treasury for Finance from 1989 to 1992. Prior to that, he was a professor of finance at the Harvard Business School. After leaving the Treasury, he was a lecturer at Harvard's Kennedy School of Government. In 1987, Mr. Glauber served as Executive Director of the Task Force on Market Mechanisms ("Brady Commission") appointed by President Reagan to study the October 1987 stock market crash. Mr. Glauber received his B.A. in Economics from Harvard College and his doctorate from the Harvard Business School.

- **Kohr, Dr. Juergen**—Datacom.net: Co-founder and ex-Managing Director of SIGS-Datcom. Prior to his work at SIGS-Datcom, he worked as a lobbyist for the consulting industry in Bonn and Brussels for five years. He is currently an independent consultant. He holds a B.A. in Economics, and an M.S. and Ph.D. in Business Administration.

- **Krizelman, Todd**—theglobe.com

- **Kurz, Julian**—FastResponse and Altimum: Co-founder, FastResponse and Altimum. Mr. Kurz received his education as an industrial engineer from the Technical University of Karlsruhe, Germany, and from Stanford University. Before co-founding FastResponse and Altimum, he worked for SAP, supporting the launch of the company's Internet initiative "mySAP.com." Also, he was a consultant at The Boston Consulting Group, serving companies in technology, communications, and the industrial sector.

- **Pech, Christoph**—Bank Credit vs. VC Financing Management Angels: Co-founder and Managing Director in charge of Key Accounting and Marketing at Management Angels GmbH. After obtaining his B.A. in Business Administration at Goethe University, Frankfurt, he continued his studies at the Universidad Pontificia Comillas in Madrid, Spain, and Leipzig Graduate School of Management. At the same time he obtained a diploma in Philosophy and Theology. Starting his career at Procter & Gamble, he switched to the B-to-B marketplace mondus.co.uk to help develop its international expansion strategy. In autumn 2000, with his friend Thorsten Becker, he founded the German interim management agency Management Angels GmbH, which focuses on rapid-growth business fields.

- **Sommer, Christiane**—Infomatec: Ms. Sommer is a journalist at Brand Eins (a German management and marketing journal).

Endnotes

1. Michael Lewis, *Next* (New York: W. W. Norton & Company, Inc., 2001), p. 65.

2. Linda M. Applegate, "Ventro: Builder of B2B Businesses," Harvard Business School Publishing, Case #9-801-042, June 28, 2001.

3. Charles Piller, "Fatal Flaw Dooms an Internet Venture Commerce: The Collapse of 'B2B' Trading Firm Ventro Illustrates the Folly of Getting Between Suppliers and Buyers," *Los Angeles Times*, June 24, 2001.

4. James Grant, "Sometimes the Economy Needs a Setback," *The New York Times*, September 9, 2001, op-ed page, online edition.

5. Mitchel Y. Abolafia, *Making Markets* (Cambridge, Mass: HUP, 1996), p. 82.

6. Charles P. Kindleberger, *Manias, Panics and Crashes: A History of Financial Crises* (New York: John Wiley & Sons, 1996). Kindleberger's study of financial crises was first published decades ago and was updated and reissued for the bull market of the 1990s. Kenneth Galbraith, *The Great Crash, 1929* (Boston: Houghton-Mifflin, 1979).

7. Amy S. Butte, "Day Trading and Beyond. A New Niche is Emerging," Bear Stearns Equity Research, April 2000.

8. Laura Cohn, "Day Traders' Power Grows," *BusinessWeek*, May 1, 2000; online edition.

9. Mike Dash, *TulipoMania* (New York: Three Rivers Press, 1999), pp. 187 and 193.

10. Ibid.

11. Anna Bernasek and Amy Kover, "Is This 1970 Again?" *Fortune,* February 21, 2000, online edition.

12. Brian Hall, Jonathan Lim, and Houston Lane, "Akamai's Underwater Options," Harvard Business School Publishing, Case #902-069, Spring 2002.

13. Steve Liesman, *The Wall Street Journal*, August 14, 2001, p. C1.

14. "A Global Game of Dominoes," *The Economist,* August 25, 2001, pp. 23-24.

15. Krishna Palepu, "The Role of Capital Market Intermediaries in the dot-com Crash of 2000," Harvard Business School Publishing, Case #9-191-110, June 7, 2001.

16. Paul Krugman, "Don't Count on It," *The New York Times*, September 5, 2001, p. A23.

17. Palepu, op. cit., casewriter interview.

18. *The Economist*, August 11, 2001, p. 55.

19. Andrew S. Fastow, quoted in "A Video Study of Enron Offers, a Picture of Life Before the Fall," by Shaila K. Dewan, *The New York Times*, January 31, 2002, p. C7.

20. Kurt Eichenwald and Diana B. Henriques, "Talk of Crime Gets Big Push," *The New York Times*, February 4, 2001, p. 1.

21. "The Ship That Sank Quietly," *The Economist*, February 16, 2002, p. 57. It should be noted that similar large, though not as large as Enron's, reductions were made by the PFC estimates in the total revenues of several other oil and gas trading companies. Enron was not alone in these activities.

22. Patrick McGeehan, "Wall Street Found Others Willing to Copy Enron's Deals," *The New York Times*, February 14, 2002, p. C1.

23. Floyd Norris, "Can Investors Believe Cash Flow Numbers?" *The New York Times*, February 15, 2002, p. C1.

24. Floyd Norris, "Enron's Doomed 'Triumph of Accounting,'" *The New York Times*, February 4, 2002, online edition.

25. Tim Carvell, Adam Horowitz, and Thomas Mucha, "The 101 Dumbest Moments in Business," *Business 2.0,* April 2002, p. 69.

26. Rich Karlgaard, "Enron End Notes," *Forbes*, March 4, 2002, p. 37.

27. Adam Lashinsky, "The Post-Enron Economy," *Wired*, February 2002, p. 47.

28. Kathy Chen, "State Street is Set to Oversee Enron Retirement Plans," *Wall Street Journal*, March 14, 2002, p. A4.

29. Floyd Norris, "An Old Case Is Returning to Haunt Auditors," *The New York Times*, February 4, 2002, p. 1.

30. Eichenwald and Henriques, op. cit.

31. "Briefing: Storage," *Red Herring Magazine*, September 15, 2001, p. 76.

32. Robert Reid, *Architects of the Web*, quoted in Robert Spector, Amazon.com, p. vii.

33. Jonathan Cohen, Merrill Lynch report, quoted in Robert Spector, Amazon.com, p. 197.

34. Thomas R. Eisenmann, editor, *Internet Business Models* (New York: McGraw-Hill/ Irwin, 2002), p. 365-366.

35. Eisenmann, op. cit., pp. 365-366.

36. Kaplan, David A., *The Silicon Boys* (New York: Harper-Collins, Perennial, 1999), p. 176.

37. Eisenmann, op. cit., p. 338.

38. Working without outside financial resources.

39. Kaplan, op. cit., p. 176.

40. Rob Norton, *The Decline of the American Venture Business 2.0* (October 2001), p. 84.

41. Shawn Neidorf, "Venture-Backed IPOs Make a Comeback," *Venture Capital Journal*, August 1, 1999.

42. buecher.de's name means "books.com" in German.

43. Not taking into account contingent payments in the future based on the achievement of sales targets.

44. BOL is Bertelsmann online, the online bookstore of Germany's largest media and print group.

45. Including acquisitions.

46. Schutzgemeinschaft der Kleinaktionäre (SdK) is a German organization that represents a number of small individual shareholders to bundle their interest.

47. The board's estimation at the general meeting was between EUR 1.3 and 1.5 per share.

48. Rachel Emma Silverman, "What Becomes an Industry Debacle Most? Perhaps a Dot.Com Monument," *The Wall Street Journal*, September 6, 2001, p. B1.

49. Sarah Lai Stirland, "Internet Bubble Popping American Business Ethics?" *Red Herring Magazine*, October 1, 1999, online edition.

50. "Wilted," *Texas Monthly*, February 1, 2001.

51. Ibid.

52. Ibid.

53. Ibid.

54. Andy Serwer, "Following the Money," *Fortune*, September 17, 2001, p. 103-112.

55. Peter Elstrom, "The Great Internet Money Game: How America's top financial firms reaped billions from the Net boom, while investors got burned," *BusinessWeek*, April 16, 2001, online edition.

56. Meera Tharmaratnam, "Police Called In as Tom.com IPO Hits Fever Pitch in HK," *Business Times*, Singapore, February 24, 2000 (Copyright 2000 STP).

57. There is research support for this proposition. See Elizabeth A. Demers and Katharina Lewellen, "The Marketing Role of IPOs: Evidence from Internet Stocks," University of Rochester, Paper ID: Simon School of Business Working Paper No. FR 01-15, August 2001.

58. Samuel Hayes, quoted in Susan Pulliam and Randall Smith, "At CSFB, Lush Profit Earned on IPOs Found Its Way Back to Firm—Favored Clients Did Trades That Gave Underwriter Very High Commissions—Scoring Big on VA Linux," *The Wall Street Journal*, November 30, 2001, p. 1.

59. Andrew Ross Sorkin, "Just Who Brought Those Duds to Market?" NYTimes.com (Copyright 2001, The New York Times Company).

60. Kaufmann, Henry, *On Money and Markets* (New York: McGraw Hill, 2000), p. 318.

61. Elstrom, *BusinessWeek*, April 16, 2001.

62. Elstrom, *BusinessWeek*, April 16, 2001.

63. Patrick McGeehan, "Henry Blodget to Leave Merrill Lynch," *The New York Times*, November 15, 2001.

64. Associated Press, December 10, 2001, online edition.

65. Elstrom, *BusinessWeek*, April 16, 2001.

66. Elstrom, *BusinessWeek*, April 16, 2001.

67. Allan Sloan, "When Big Guys Make Bad Moves: Dumb Telecom Deals," *Newsweek*, September 10, 2001, pp. 38-42.

68. Peter Elkind, "QUATTRONE: The Trouble With Frank," *Fortune*, September 3, 2001, online edition.

69. Cassell Bryan-Low, "Deals & Deal Makers: Latest IPO Boom: Number of Suits Alleging Abuses by Underwriters," *The Wall Street Journal*, November 29, 2001, p. C12.

70. Henry Kaufmann, op. cit., p. 305.

71. Elkind, op. cit., *Fortune*, September 3, 2001.

72. Henry Kaufmann, op. cit., p. 30.

73. Diana McCabe, *The Orange County Register*, Orange County, California, August 14, 2001, online edition.

74. Erika Gonzalez, "401(k) Plunge Long Overdue Wake-up Call for Investors," *Rocky Mountain News*, July 28, 2001, citing Cerulli Associates, Boston.

75. A report by Spectrum Group for the National Defined Contribution Council, reported on "Business Wire," April 26, 2001.

76. Palepu, op. cit.

77. Robert J. Shiller, *Irrational Exuberance* (Princeton, NJ: Princeton University Press, 2000), p. 203.

78. Elstrom, *BusinessWeek*, April 16, 2001, online edition.

79. Dan Briody, "Are Jilted Investors Legally Blind?" *Red Herring Magazine*, August 1, 2001, online edition.

80. James Grant, "Sometimes the Economy Needs a Setback," *The New York Times*, September 9, 2001, op-ed page, online edition. (James Grant is the editor of *Grant's Interest Rate Observer*.)

81. See, for example, Edward Chancellor, *Devil Take the Hindmost* (New York: Farrar, Straus, Giroux, 1999).

82. Scott Gordon, a managing director at Spencer Stuart, quoted by Ian Mount, "So What are You Doing on Your Unplanned Vacation?" *Business 2.0*, August/ September, 2001, p. 36.

83. Palepu, op. cit.

84. Mary Meeker and Chris DePuy, "U.S. Investment Research, Technology/New Media, The Internet Report (Excerpt from *Life After Television* by George Gilder, 1992)," Morgan Stanley, February 1996.

85. John Browning and Spencer Reiss, "For the New Economy, the End of the Beginning," *The Wall Street Journal*, April 17, 2000.

86. See the testimony of Fed Chairman Alan Greenspan about Long Term Capital Management at Testimony of Chairman Alan Greenspan, "Evolution of our equity markets," before the Committee on Banking, Housing, and Urban Affairs, U.S. Senate, April 13, 2000.

87. Henry Kaufmann, op. cit.

88. James Abolifia, op. cit., pp. 90-91.

89. Roger Lowenstein, *When Genius Failed* (London: Fourth Estate, 2001), p. xviii.

90. Rachel Emma Silverman, "What Becomes an Industry Debacle Most? Perhaps a Dot.Com Monument," *The Wall Street Journal*, September 6, 2001.

91. Ianthe Jeanne Dugan and Aaron Lucchetti, "After Soaring IPO And Fleeting Fame, What Comes Next?—theglobe.com's Founders Hit Midlife Crises at Age of 26," *The Wall Street Journal Europe*, May 3, 2001.

92. Ellen E. Schultz and Theo Francis, "Fair Shares? Why Company Stock Is a Burden for Many—And Less So for a Few—Workers Often Must Hold On To Stakes Held in 401(k)s; Top Brass Have Options—Hedging for the 'Upper Tier,'" *The Wall Street Journal*, November 27, 2001.

93. Danny Hakim, "Former Workers at Lucent See Nest Eggs Vanish, Too," *The New York Times*, August 20, 2001, pp. 1 and C13.

94. Sara Calian, "Poor Return: Merrill to Pay Unilever $105 Million," *The Wall Street Journal*, December 7, 2001, p. C1.

95. Kim Girard, "Crummy Job," *Business 2.0*, February 6, 2001.

96. Gail Kaplan, San Francisco management consultant, quoted in Ian Mount, "So What are You Doing on Your Unplanned Vacation?" *Business 2.0* (August/September, 2001), pp. 35-36.

97. Kaplan, op. cit., pp. 190-191.

98. Girard, op. cit. p. 77

99. Henry Kaufmann, op. cit., p. 307.

100. Geraldine Fabrikant and Simn Romero, "Chase's Early Alliances with global Crossings," *The Wall Street Journal*, March 18, 2002, pp. C1 and C4.

101. Elstrom, *BusinessWeek*, April 16, 2001, op. cit.

102. Christopher Palmeri and Arlene Weintraub, "As Global Crossing Sinks, Gary Winnick Stays Dry," *BusinessWeek*, October 22, 2001, p. 58.

103. Kim Kiser "Closed for Business: Two Year Ago, Learning Portals Popped Up Across the Internet's Landscape. Today, Many are Buried in the dot.com Rubble. What Happened?" *OnlineLearning Magazine*, September 1, 2001.

104. Mike Allen, "EduPoint Latest Victim of The High-Tech Downturn," *San Diego Business Journal*, May 2, 2001.

105. Greg Ip, "Banks are Limiting Lending Exposure to High Tech Firms," *The Wall Street Journal*, August 27, 2001, p. A2.

106. "Outlook," *The Wall Street Journal*, September 24, 2001, p. 1.

107. Testimony of Arthur Levitt, Chairman, Security and Exchange Commission, Before the Senate Permanent Subcommittee on Investigations, Committee on Governmental Affairs, Concerning Day Trading, September 16, 1999, p. 4.

108. James Grant, *The New York Times*, September 9, 2001, op. cit.

109. E. S. Browning, "Holding on: Once Again, Small Investors Stay Put When Stock Prices Decline," *The Wall Street Journal*, October 22, 2001.

110. Browning, *The Wall Street Journal*, October 22, 2001, Ibid.

111. Testimony of Chairman Alan Greenspan, "Evolution of our equity markets," before the Committee on Banking, Housing, and Urban Affairs, U.S. Senate, April 13, 2000.

112. Testimony of Chairman Alan Greenspan, Before the Senate Permanent Subcommittee on Investigations, Committee on Governmental Affairs, Concerning Day Trading, September 16, 1999.

113. Testimony of Chairman Alan Greenspan, "Evolution of our equity markets," before the Committee on Banking, Housing, and Urban Affairs, U.S. Senate, April 13, 2000.

114. Testimony of Chairman Alan Greenspan, "Over-the-counter derivatives," before the Committee on Agriculture, Nutrition and Forestry, United States Senate, February 10, 2000.

115. Dallas Salisbury, "The State of Private Pensions," in Sheldon Friedman and David C. Jacobs, *The Future of the Safety Net* (Champagne, IL: The Industrial Relations Research Association Series, 2001), p. 139-164, at p. 145.

116. Peter Loftus, "Secondary Sales of Private Equity Stakes Gain Ground as Venture Capital Dries Up," *The Wall Street Journal*, November 13, 2001; "Back-to-Back Losses Sting Venture Funds," Suzanne McGee, *The Wall Street Journal*, July 18, 2001.

117. "Bubble and squeak," *The Economist*, August 25, 2001, p. 59.

118. See comments of Fed Chairman Alan Greenspan in The Federal Reserve's semiannual report on monetary policy given before the Committee on Banking, Housing, and Urban Affairs, U.S. Senate, February 23, 1999; and Remarks by Chairman Alan Greenspan Before the President's Council on Year 2000 Conversion, Financial Sector Group, Year 2000 Summit, Washington, D.C., September 17, 1999.

119. David S. Bennahum, "Be Here Now," *Wired*, November, 2001, pp. 159-163, at p. 163.

Index

A

Abrams, Robin, 8
Accel Partners, 94
Accenture, 126
Accountants, 35–36
  at Enron, key role of,
    50–51
  and Financial Value
    Chain, 239
  and the Internet bubble,
    145–46
  key role of, 50–51
Aftermarket orders, 130
Akamai Technologies,
    24, 26–29
  burst bubble, 28
  operating costs, 27
  share price, 28
  and venture funding,
    27–28
Alliance Capital, 52
Alphamusic, 102

Altimum, 87–90
  angel, arrival of, 88
  company, 87
  funding, 88
  growing the company, 89
  outcome, 89–90
Amazon.com, 24, 39,
    60–62, 66, 82,
    100–101, 109,
    122–23, 226
  as first of the online
    retailers, 62
  flouting of the rules by,
    61–62
America OnLine (AOL),
    15, 81
American economy:
  economic success
    factors, 197
  entrepreneurial sector,
    197–98
  and Internet bubble, 197
  effect of collapse
    on U.S., 198

AMR Research, 8
Andersen Consulting, 126
Andrews, Edmund L., 197
Andriesson, Mark, 15
Angel investors, 47
Apple Computer, 20
Arthur Andersen account-
    ing firm, 50
Asian financial crisis, 174
Auditors, and Financial
    Value Chain, 239

B

B2B, 7, 21
B2C, 21
Bank Credit vs.
    Management Angels
    GmbH, 76–79
BankBoston, 8
Bay City Capital, 8

Beeck, Wilfried, 177
Benchmark Capital, 80
Berardino, Joe, 193–206
Bermudez, John, 8
Berners-Lee, Tim, 15, 27
Bertlesmann, 72–73
Bezos, Jeff, 60–62, 226
Blodget, Henry, 122–23
BNP Paribas, 10
Böhnlein, Barbara,
    100, 104
Boilerplate, use of
    term, 130
Bolt, Braneck and Newman
    (BBN), 14–15
Boo.com, 111–13, 115, 185
    customer frustration
        with, 112–13
    founders' strengths, 112
    inventory/shipping, 112
    log-on problems, 113
    Web site, 111–12
Boos, Patrick, 66
Breyer, James W., 94
Bubble curve, 38
Bubbles, *See also* Internet
    bubble
    cause of, 24
    economic losses caused
        by, 175–76
    future, 218, 225–33
    historical background,
        24–25
    minimizing
        frequency/intensity
        of, 218–19
    speculative, phases of, 23
    tulip mania, 24–25
buecher.de, 100–104
    life cycle, 100–103
    turning point, 103–4
Burn-rates, 69, 181
Burnes, Richard M. Jr., 108
Burnham, Bill, 132
Business Research,
    Inc., 107
"Buyer beware" principle,
    and investment banks,
    132–34

Buyers' side of the capital
    market, 135–36
Byers, Brook, 9

C

C2C, 21
Callaghan, Jon, 9
Capital markets, 42
    buyers' side of, 135–36
    current situation in, 211
    economic function of, 99
    as engine of progress, 12
    and innovation, 13–14,
        16, 189
    interaction between inno-
        vation process and, 16
    and the Internet, 13–14
    and internet bubble, 1–16
    purposes served by, 16
    social/economic utility
        of, 12–13
    western, 13
Capital, starving entrepre-
    neurs of, 176–77
Capitalist market
    economies, 233
Capitalist system,
    prices and resource
    allocation, 227
Central banks, 221
CERN, 15
Chambers, John, 181
Charles River Ventures, 80
Chase, 12
Chemdex/Ventro, 7
    corporate customers, 8
    current situation for,
        9–10
    flawed business plan, 8
    revenue, 8
    stock price, 8–9
    and venture capitalists,
        7–9
Chief executive officer
    (CEO), duties of, 107

Chinese wall, 132
Christenson, Michael, 122
Cisco Systems, 181, 229
CMGI, 8, 141
Coca-Cola, 167
Cohen, Jonathan, 62
College Marketing
    Group, 141
Commercial banks:
    credit, in Germany, 79
    and start-ups, 75–76
Compaq Computer, 20
Confidence, restoring,
    219–21
Conrad Elektronik, 67
Conrades, George, 27
Creative accounting, 146
Credit Suisse First Boston,
    36, 128–29
Creighton, Jeff, 182
Crosspoint Partners, 100
Customer Relationship
    Management (CRM)
    software market, 85

D

DARPANET, 14–15
DATACOM.net, 184–86
    and e-learning
        development, 187
    economic climate, 187
    existing brand/
        customer base, 184
    IT professionals/IT
        training, demand
        for, 185
    localized high-quality
        e-learning content,
        demand for, 185
    network training, 184
    offer, 185–86
    operational mistakes, 187
    outcome, 186
Day trading, 23–24

Defense Advanced Research Project Agency (DARPA), 14
Defense Department, and the early Internet, 14
Defined benefit plans, 168, 214
Defined contribution plans, 214
defined benefit plans vs., 168
Dell Computer, 19–20
Deutsche Bank, 12
Deutsche Bank Moran Grenfell, 128
DG Bank, 10
Dietz, Steven, 109
Dintersmith, Ted, 226–30
Disclosure, 229
improving at mutual funds, 212–13
Doerr, John, 170
DoubleClick, 24
Drucker, Peter, 181
Drugstore.com, 24
Duffield, David, 160, 164

E

e-learning, 180–83
development of, 187
Edupoint, 182–83
Learning Management Systems (LMS), 185
and venture capitalists, 182
Early investors, 125, 209
Early-stage financing of the Internet, 14–15
EarthLink, 24
Economic losses caused by bubbles, 175–76
Economic Supply Chain, 39
Economic utility of capital markets, 12–13

Economic value:
defined, 39
divergence of financial value and, 38–40
hype and, 39
Economic Value Chain, 39
Economy, rebuilding, 219–21
Edupoint, 182–83, 189
Efficient market hypothesis, 34
Egan, Michael, 160
Eichenwald, Kurt, 48
Eisenmann, Thomas, 81–82
Employee pensions, Enron, 53
Enktomi, 26
Enron, 44, 47–55, 198
accountants:
key role of, 50–51
objective of, 51
and equity analysts, 51–52
inflating the bubble, 49
as an Internet company, 48–49
investment bankers and, 49–50
legality of actions of, 53
making revenues/profits appear to grow, 49
market to market accounting, 50
methods for giving revenues/profits appearance of growth, 49
and off-balance-sheet accounting, 146
pension plan, 53
and politicians, 49, 52
preventing a repetition of, 215–16
and regulatory commissions, 52
retirement savings, 53, 167–68
significance of, 54
and Wall Street, 49–50

Entrepreneurs, 42, 198–99
blaming for the bubble, 59–60
and German banks, 76
and get-big-fast strategy, 83
and going public, 95–97
limited resources of, 75
mass hysteria, 126
playing bank against bank, 124
responsibility for Internet bubble, 125
and venture capitalists, 75–90
Equity analysts, and Enron, 51–52
ERISA, 213
eToys, 62–65, 122, 229
and bank analysts, 65–66
competition, 64
early investors, 65
profit, lack of, 64
stock market support, 64
vision for, 63
E*Trade, 24
Exodus, 28–29

F

Fastow, Andrew S., 47, 50–51
FastResponse, 84–87
company, 85
end of a dream, 87
funding, 85–86
funding meetings, 86
Federal Reserve System, 147–49, 174, 188, 231
FedEx, 87
Fiber optic communication cables, 175
Fidelity, 12, 136, 228
Fiduciary principal, essence of, 210

Fiduciary
     responsibility, 220
defined, 210
extending, 210–12
Financial instrument,
     price of, 34
Financial market
     Darwinism, 140–42
Financial press, 23, 162,
     165, 244
Financial products, risk
     classifications for, 220
Financial value:
     defined, 34
     divergence of economic
          value and, 38–40
Financial Value Chain, 5,
     33–45, 42–43, 49, 60,
     84, 97–98, 168, 180,
     198–99, 207, 215
     accountants/auditors, 239
     class-action lawyers, 246
     complexity of, 36
     day traders, 248
     defined, 33–35
     diagramming, 35–37
     FASB, 246
     Federal Reserve
          System, 245
     forecasting/analysis
          firms, 244
     formal functioning of,
          during Internet
          bubble, 37
     founders, 238
     how it should have
          worked, 42–43
     influencers, 237–48
     internal investor relations
          (CFO/CEO), 238
     lawyers, 239
     limited partners
          (LPs), 241
     money managers
          (buy-side), 243
     pension/401(k)
          investors, 247
     press, 244

public relations
     firms, 239
Securities and Exchange
     Commission
     (SEC), 245
sell-side equity
     research, 242
stock-holding
     investors, 248
underwriters, 241
VC-installed
     management, 238
and venture
     capitalists, 42
venture investors, 240
Financial value of a
     company, 34
First Call, 107
First mover advantage, 61
Florida State Pension
     Fund, 52
401(k) accounts,
     138–39, 175
     and equities, 139
     and Germany, 208
Fuentes, Baldemar, 85, 88
Future bubbles, 218,
     225–33

G

Garden.com, 108–11,
     115, 189
     and customer
          acquisition costs, 110
     early investors, 111
     going public, 109–10
     growth of, 109
     late investors, losses
          of, 111
     products, 109–10
     share price, 110
     Web site, 110
Gates, Bill, 19
German Securities Trading
     Act, 208

Germany, 4
Get-big-fast strategy, 61, 81
     and entrepreneurs, 83
     get-it-right instead of,
          83–84
     limitations of, 81–82
     and start-ups, 81–82
Gilder, George, 146
Gilette, 167
Glauber, Robert R.,
     218–19
Global Crossing,
     179–80, 189
Global Retail Partners, 109
globe.com, 157–66
     business press and,
          162, 165
     early investors, 164
     employee stock options,
          163–64
     going public, 161
     investment bankers and,
          161, 164–65
     investors in, 161
     origin of, 158–59
     risk, 163
     stock analysts'
          demands, 161
Goldman Sachs, 12, 36, 72
Governance, improving at
     mutual funds, 212–13
Greenspan, Alan, 4, 142,
     147–56, 196, 201, 228
     excerpts from speeches/
          congressional
          testimony, 150–55
Greylock Management
     Corp., 80
Gross, Bill, 141

H

Haefele, Alexander, 202–6
Halperin, Bob, 160
Harlos, Gerhard, 202–6
Hayes, Samuel, 121

Head, Howard, 110
Henriques, Diana B., 48
Hewitt Associates, 167
Hewlett Packard, 20
High valuations, 41–42
Highland Capital
   Partners, 80
Hiles, David R. H., 129
Horowitz, David, 160
Hype machine, 39,
   146–47, 232

I

IBM, 20
Idealab Capital Partners,
   114, 141
Incentives to save, and
   Internet bubble, 189
Individual Retirement
   Accounts, and
   Germany, 208
Inexperience leaders, 57–90
   Amazon.com, 60–61
   entrepreneur
      blaming, 59–60
   and the financial
      markets, 60
   learning failure, 62–73
   venture capitalists, 75–91
Influencing factors, 145–56
   accountants, 145–46
   Federal Reserve System,
      147–49
   hype machine, 146–47
Infomatec, 202–6
   bankruptcy filing, 205
   current situation at, 206
   failure to reach targets,
      203
   formation of, 202
   growth of, 202
   insider trading/price
      manipulation
      accusations, 204
   stock price, decline in,
      203–5

Innovation, 176
   and capital markets,
      13–14, 16, 189
   and mobility/space, 232
   technological, setback
      to, 179–80
Intel, 19–20
Internet:
   and capital markets,
      13–14
   early development of,
      16, 30
   early-stage financing of,
      14–15
   investors' flight from,
      98–99
Internet bubble:
   and capital markets, 1–16
   causes of, 19–31
      technology bull
         market, 19–20
   consequences of, 29–30
   and day trading, 23–24
   defined, 20–22
   economic consequences
      of, 188–89, 218
   exchanges, 25
   financial losses imposed
      by, 166–67
   Financial Value Chain,
      33–45
   formation of, reason
      for, 22–23
   how it happened, 17–56
   and incentives to
      save, 189
   inflating, 33–45
   players, 25
   source of, 23–24
   transfer of wealth, 29–31
Internet Capital Group
   (ICG), 114, 141
Internet companies:
   huge valuations
      defending, 43–45
      reasons for, 40–42
   new wave of, 188
Internet Index Fund
   (Munder), 137

Internet Strategy Fund
   (Merrill Lynch), 137
Intershop, 177–78
   corporate image, 177–78
   employees, 178
   and Internet bubble,
      178–79
Investment banks, 119–34,
   216, 225
   blame game, 125
   and "buyer beware"
      principle, 132–34
   changing of rules by,
      119–21
   competition among,
      123–24
   conflict of interests
      in, 220
   defense of, 131
   and duds brought to
      market, 121–23
   as gatekeepers, 124
   goal of, 124
   and gross underpricing,
      120–21
   and institutional
      investors, 121
   mass hysteria, 126–27
   partners in, 124, 131
   prospectus, 130, 133–34
   and regulatory system,
      132–33
   separation of sell-side
      analysts from, 229
   and start-ups, 75
Investor lawsuits, 129–31
Investors:
   and company
      prospects, 40
   qualifying, 219
IPOs, 23–24, 36–37, 41
   buyers of issues, 39
   ordinary allocation of
      shares in, 121
   regulations to protect
      investors in, 216–18
   underpricing of, 219
   valuation of, 43–45
   and venture
      capitalists, 127

J

Janus, 136
Junk bond mutual
    funds, 175

K

Kabel New Media (KNM),
    10–12, 15–16
    share price, decline in,
        10–11
    timeline for, 11
Kabel, Peter, 10
Kahn, Joseph, 197
Kapner, Suzanne, 129
Karlgaard, Rich, 52
Kaufmann, Henry, 122,
    132, 149, 175
Kenefick, James, 171
Kindleberger, Charles,
    22–23
Kinko's, 87
Kleiner Perkins Caufield
    and Byers, 7–9, 89
Kohr, Juergen, 184,
    187–88
Krizelman, Todd, 160–66
Kurz, Julian, 84

L

Laddering, 130
Lannon, Mike, 80
Lawsuits, 129–31
Lay, Kenneth, 48–49
Leander, Kajsa, 111–12
Leane, Jeff, 7
Learning Management
    Systems (LMS), 185
Lenk, Toby, 62–65
Lock up release, 228

Long Term Capital
    Management, 148–49,
    174, 221
Loss-making dot-coms,
    market valuations
    given to, 24
Lucent Technologies, 167
Lycos, 141

M

Macroregulation, 209
Malmsten, Ernst, 111–12
Market Darwinism, 140–42
Masie, Elliott, 181
McKinsey and
    Company, 48
Media hype machine,
    146–47
Mediantis AG, 102
Meeker, Mary, 8, 137
Merrill Lynch, 168
Mexican financial
    crisis, 174
Microregulation, 209
Microsoft, 19–20
Milkin, Michael, 179
Mills, Andy, 107–8
Minimum size float, 217
Morgan Bank, 179–80
Morgan Stanley, 8
Morgan Stanley Dean
    Witter, 36
Mortgage financing, 174
Mutual fund directors, as
    fiduciaries, 212–13
Mutual funds, 135–36
    American investors'
        interest in, 136–38
    fund managers, incen-
        tives of, 137
    improving
        disclosure/guidance
        at, 212–13
    and the Internet bubble,
        137–38

losses on, 30
and mimicking of the
    behavior of venture
    firms, 139
and the momentum
    game, 139–40
returns, 136–37

N

Nasdaq, 21, 23, 30, 209
    long-term growth trend
        vs., 38–39
    and Nemax (Germany),
        235–36
    qualifications of
        investors, 219
    sales practices by secu-
        rities dealers, 219
Nasdaq Composite Index,
    21–22
Nemax (Germany), 21,
    235–36
Net Fund (Munder), 137
Netscape, 15, 226
Neuer Markt (Germany),
    101–3, 202
New business cycle,
    creating, 173–74
New economy, 170–72
    old economy vs., 171
New economy companies,
    21–22
Newman, James, 130
Norton, Rob, 95

O

Off-balance-sheet account-
    ing, 146
Old economy companies,
    21–22
Old economy vs. new
    economy, 171

Old way vs. new way, 171
O'Neill, Jamie, 109
Option value, 227–28
Oxygen, 179

P

Paternot, Stephan, 160–61
Pech, Christoph, 76–79
Peck, Chuck, 167
Pension funds, 53, 166, 175
  defined benefit programs,
  211–12
Pension plans:
  as investors, 213
  putting into venture
  activities, 214
Perry, David, 7–9
Petroleum Finance
  Company, 49–50
Pets.com, 82, 122
Petstore.com, 82
Pigs, and investor
  behavior, 140–42
Polaroid, 25
Politicians, and Enron, 52
Portfolio managers, 42
Price of a financial
  instrument, 34
Priceline.com, 24
Private Securities
  Litigation Reform Act
  of 1995, 129
Procter & Gamble, 167
Productivity improve-
  ments, 40
Professional services
  firms, and young peo-
  ple, 169
Program basis for insider
  sales, 216
Promedix, 8
Prospectus, 130, 133–34
Prudent man rule, 213–15
Public confidence,
  insuring, 189–90

Public markets, acting as
  venture capitalists, 228
Putnam, 136, 228

Q

Qualified investor system,
  209–10, 220
Quattrone, Frank,
  128–29, 132
Qwest Communications
  International, Inc., 167

R

Reforms, 219–21
Regulatory system:
  and Enron, 52
  and investment banks,
  132–33
  needed changes in,
  200–201
Relative valuation, 45
Retail investors, 135–43
  blaming, 140–42
  buyers' side of the capital market, 135–36
  and dot-com stocks, 120
  and mutual funds,
  136–38
  pension money, specu-
  lating with, 138–39
  responsibility for
  Internet bubble, 125
  speculation, 142–43
Retirement savings:
  Enron, 53
  loss of, 30–31
Risk classifications, for
  financial products, 220
Road kill of capitalism,
  157–92
  globe.com, 157–66
  young people, 169–70

Roberston Stephens, 8
Rock, Arthur, 213
Rockefeller, David Jr., 179

S

Schiner, Helmut, 205
Schoch, Steven, 63
Schumpeter, Joseph, 13–14
Scientific Data Systems,
  sale of, 213
SdK, 103–4
Search engine, develop-
  ment of, 15
Securities and Exchange
  Commission, 129
Securities and Exchange
  Commission
  (SEC), 23
Securities Class Action
  Services LLC, 130
Securities dealers, sales
  practices of, 219
Sendwine.com, 80
Separtion of sell-side ana-
  lysts, from investment
  banks, 229
Sequoia Capital
  Partners, 114
Shaheen, George, 126
Sharples, Cliff, 109
Sharples, Lisa, 109
Shiller, Robert, 140
Skilling, Jeffrey K., 48
Small investors, 190
  fiduciary responsibility,
  extending, 210–12
  in Germany, 207–8
  qualifying, 209–10, 219
  reforms to protect,
  207–21
Social Security, privatiza-
  tion of, 199–200
Social utility of capital
  markets, 12–13
Software cycle, 25–29

Sommer, Christine, 202
Speculation, 24–25, 230
Speculative bubbles,
 phases of, 23
Stanton, John, 117
Start-ups:
 bubble contributors,
 145–46
 and commercial banks,
 75–76
 and get-big-fast strategy,
 81–82
 gross underpricing,
 120–21
 and investment banks,
 75, 119–34
 and large-scale
 marketing, 80
 retail investors, 135–43
 rising share prices of, 26
 taking public, 117–56
State Street Corporation, 53
Stevenson, Howard, 211
Streamline, 83–84
Sycamore, 21
System glitches, 15–16

T

Tagore, Suneil, 179
Technological innovation,
 setback to, 179–80
Technology and
 Communications Fund
 (PBHG), 137–38
Technology bull market,
 19–20
Technology Crossover
 Ventures, 94
Thomson Financial
 Services, 107
Thornton, John, 110
Tom.com, 120
Toys R Us, 64
Transfer of wealth, 29–31
Tulip mania, 24–25, 226

U

Underpricing, and invest-
 ment banks, 128
Underwriters, 216–17, 220
Underwriting standards,
 decline of, 132
Unilever, 168
United States:
 capital market, 196
 as world financial
 leader, 196–97
 effect of collapse
 on U.S., 198

V

Van Wagoner Capital
 Management, 176
Van Wagoner, Garrett, 176
Vanderbilt, Nicole, 63
Ventro/Chemdex, 8–10,
 15–16
 corporate customers, 8
 current situation for,
 9–10
 flawed business plan, 8
 losses faced by, 9–10
 revenue, 8
 shareholder lawsuit, 9
 stock price, 8–9
 and venture capitalists,
 7–9
Venture capital, 93–94
Venture capital firms, 220
Venture capitalists, 15, 42,
 47, 75–91, 91–115,
 216, 225
 Altimum, 87–90
 company, 87
 funding, 88
 growing the
 company, 89
 outcome, 89–90
 true angel,
 arrival of, 88

and Amazon.com, 61
Bank Credit vs.
 Management Angels
 GmbH, 76–79
building to flip, 93–105
business plans presented
 to, 43
and e-learning, 182
and entrepreneurs, 75–90
exiting an investment,
 95–99
FastResponse, 84–87
 company, 85
 end of a dream, 87
 funding, 85–86
 funding meetings,
 86
and the Financial Value
 Chain, 42–43
first-round funding
 (2001), 189
get-big-fast strategy
 limitations, 81–82
and the Internet bubble,
 113–14
investments in start-up
 companies, 22
and IPOs, 94–95, 127
mass hysteria, 126
pressure to spend, 79–80
public markets acting
 as, 228
role of, 107–8
success as, 93
wrong people, choosing,
 107–15
Venture investing via
 funds/specialized
 managers, 213
Venture investments,
 change in criteria
 for, 115
VerticalNet, 24
Vidyanand, Ramgopal
 "Anand," 85, 88
Volatility in stock price, 34
Volcker, Paul, 148–49
Volpe Brown Whelan &
 Company LLC, 8

Volume of investment, 230
Von Rheinbaben,
    Richard, 101
Von Ribbentropp,
    Dominik, 68, 73

W

Wage-cost-driven inflation,
    173
Wainwright, Julie L., 122
Wall Street:
    and Enron, 49–50
    and Internet stock, 128

Webmiles, 66–73
    decline of, 71–72
    funding, 67–68
    growth of, 69–70
    idea for, 66–67
    IPO, 70–71
    saving of, 73
    start-up, 68–69
    trade-sale, 72–73
Webvan, 66, 126, 189
Wellington, 228
Wetherell, David, 141
White Flower Farms, 110
Winnick, Gary, 179–80
World Wide Web
    (WWW), 15

X

Xerox, 25

Y

Yahoo! Finance, 23
Young people, and
    dot-coms, 169–70

8 reasons why you should read the Financial Times for 4 weeks RISK-FREE!

To help you stay current with significant
developments in the world economy ...
and to assist you to make informed business
decisions — the Financial Times brings you:

❶ Fast, meaningful overviews of international affairs ... plus daily briefings on major world news.

❷ Perceptive coverage of economic, business, financial and political developments with special focus on emerging markets.

❸ More international business news than any other publication.

❹ Sophisticated financial analysis and commentary on world market activity plus stock quotes from over 30 countries.

❺ Reports on international companies and a section on global investing.

❻ Specialized pages on management, marketing, advertising and technological innovations from all parts of the world.

❼ Highly valued single-topic special reports (over 200 annually) on countries, industries, investment opportunities, technology and more.

❽ The Saturday Weekend FT section — a globetrotter's guide to leisure-time activities around the world: the arts, fine dining, travel, sports and more.

FT FINANCIAL TIMES
World business newspaper

The *Financial Times* delivers
a world of business news.

Use the Risk-Free Trial Voucher below!

To stay ahead in today's business world you need to be well-informed on a daily basis. And not just on the national level. You need a news source that closely monitors the entire world of business, and then delivers it in a concise, quick-read format.

With the *Financial Times* you get the major stories from every region of the world. Reports found nowhere else. You get business, management, politics, economics, technology and more.

Now you can try the *Financial Times* for 4 weeks, absolutely risk free. And better yet, if you wish to continue receiving the *Financial Times* you'll get great savings off the regular subscription rate. Just use the voucher below.

4 Week Risk-Free Trial Voucher

Yes! Please send me the *Financial Times* for 4 weeks (Monday through Saturday) Risk-Free, and details of special subscription rates in my country.

Name_____

Company_____

Address _____ ❏ Business or ❏ Home Address

Apt./Suite/Floor _____City _____State/Province_____

Zip/Postal Code_____Country _____

Phone (optional) _____E-mail (optional)_____

Limited time offer good for new subscribers in FT delivery areas only.

To order contact Financial Times Customer Service in your area (mention offer SAB01A).

The Americas: Tel 800-628-8088 Fax 845-566-8220 E-mail: uscirculation@ft.com

Europe: Tel 44 20 7873 4200 Fax 44 20 7873 3428 E-mail: fte.subs@ft.com

Japan: Tel 0120 341-468 Fax 0120 593-146 E-mail: circulation.fttokyo@ft.com

Korea: E-mail: sungho.yang@ft.com

S.E. Asia: Tel 852 2905 5555 Fax 852 2905 5590 E-mail: subseasia@ft.com

FT FINANCIAL TIMES
World business newspaper

www.ft.com